You've Got the Look

The How To "Celebrity Look-a-like" Guide

With thought-provoking advice
to help anyone break into
the entertainment business

By
Denise Bella Vlasis

© Copyright 2003 Denise Bella Vlasis. All rights reserved.

No part of this publication may be reproduced, stored in a retrieval system, or transmitted, in any form or by any means, electronic, mechanical, photocopying, recording, or otherwise, without the written prior permission of the author.

Printed in Victoria, Canada

Cover Illustration and Design by Ed Parker, Jr.
Cover Concept by Bella
Edited by Linda Orlando
Book Layout and Design by Ed Parker, Jr.

National Library of Canada Cataloguing in Publication Data

National Library of Canada Cataloguing in Publication

Vlasis, Denise Bella
 You've got the look : the complete how to celebrity look-alike guide / Denise Bella Vlasis.

ISBN 1-55395-506-4

TRAFFORD

This book was published *on-demand* in cooperation with Trafford Publishing.
On-demand publishing is a unique process and service of making a book available for retail sale to the public taking advantage of on-demand manufacturing and Internet marketing. **On-demand publishing** includes promotions, retail sales, manufacturing, order fulfilment, accounting and collecting royalties on behalf of the author.

Suite 6E, 2333 Government St., Victoria, B.C. V8T 4P4, CANADA
Phone   250-383-6864   Toll-free 1-888-232-4444 (Canada & US)
Fax   250-383-6804   E-mail sales@trafford.com
Web site www.trafford.com   TRAFFORD PUBLISHING IS A DIVISION OF TRAFFORD HOLDINGS LTD.
Trafford Catalogue #02-1221   www.trafford.com/robots/02-1221.html

10   9   8   7   6   5   4   3   2   1

Table of Contents

Section One	Dedication	1
Section Two	Introduction	3
Section Three	The Categories: Finding Your Place	5
Section Four	Researching Your Celebrity	15
Section Five	Going Pro	21
Section Six	Ready To Work: The Possibilities Are Endless	27
Section Seven	Mix and Mingle: Breaking It Down	37
Section Eight	Putting Your Stage Show Together	51
Section Nine	The Variety of Work Available	65
	Acting	66
	Casinos	70
	Children's Events	72
	Charity Work	77
	Cruise Ships	81
	Drag Shows and Female Impersonation	83
	International Media	87
	Legend Type Shows	93
	Night Clubs	96
	Photo Doubles and Stand-Ins	98
	Print Work	102
	Telegrams	103
	Theme Parks	106
	Trade Shows and Conventions	108
	Voice-Overs	110
Section Ten	What Is a Union?	119
Section Eleven	Working Your Look	127

	Hair and Wigs	127
	Makeup: Giving Good Face	131
	Surgery and Skin Care	140
	Body and Fitness	146
	Costumes: Let's Go Shopping!	147
Section Twelve	Promotional Materials	151
	Photographs: *Strike a Pose*	151
	Your Cover Letter	161
	Your Resume	163
	Video/Audio Tapes and Promotional Reels	166
	Promotional Packages	168
Section Thirteen	Jobs and Networking	169
Section Fourteen	Agents and Agencies	175
Section Fifteen	Award Shows and Conventions	191
Section Sixteen	Web Networking	199
Section Seventeen	Job Checklists and Booking Sheets	211
Section Eighteen	Money and All That Goes With It	215
Section Nineteen	Traveling Abroad	225
Section Twenty	Contracts: Get It In Writing	235
Section Twenty-One	Standards and Copyrights	237
Section Twenty-Two	Moving On	249
Section Twenty-Three	In Closing	253
Section Twenty-Four	Reference	257
	Look-Alikes Contact and Booking Information	257
	Agencies	274
	Photographer Credits	295
	Resource	299

Dedicated to Connie and Ted Vlasis

My beautiful parents, Connie and Ted, you are my mentors of inspiration. I am grateful to your vision, hope, encouragement, and unconditional love. As unique and beautiful individuals and in your partnership, you inspire, teach, and give to people just by being who you are. Thank you for the life you have provided and blessed me with and the wisdom and support you continue to give!

Thank you to:

My family: My sweet sister Tina and her new hubby Frans; Max; my cherished big brother Ted Bo (Iry!) and my other adorable sister Kim; my gorgeous diva Victoria; my handsome godson Nick; my other brilliant and amazing Godson Teddy lll; Zack; my Auntie Maria; Grandma Lucia; and the rest of the Vlasis crew—I love you! Bumpa, thank you for your angel love!

My best friend Irby Gascon, life love, partner of truth, precious angel, and dream man! I love this life journey with you! You have opened my eyes for the first time to so many things. You are precious to me and I look forward to each new day of discovering you and our life together! Teedy and Cooney and the Gascon family, thank you for your wonderful warm love. Frankie Shammas, my life friend and someone whom I love so deeply. You make me laugh and feel, and I cherish you completely! Heidi Anderson Jarrett, my soul sister angel girl, whom I honor in endless ways, my love for you is beyond a lifetime; thank you for the incredible choreography. Tatiana Turan, beautiful soul sister, I am so proud of you—your wings are golden and incredibly beautiful! Thank you for sharing this journey with me! Johnny G, your exquisite photography, patience, words, fire, artistic brilliance, and friendship, and especially all the gorgeous photographs! Kiki Lee and Bobby Herr, I love and miss you both; Nettie, a magical child with gifts that heal, always surrounded with special angels; Leslie Sloane, healer, angel, and precious friend who always makes me laugh—thank you for your beautiful visions! Michael Dorian, we have made it to over a decade of love and friendship, doll. Forever we will be friends. Thank you for being my makeup artist and stylist! My other family: Thierry and family (especially my beautiful godchild Annachrista); Lamoure, you bless us with divine intervention—thank you for bringing music into my life; David Comfort, I am blessed with your friendship and wisdom that has forever enriched my life; Maria Comfort, I love you; Tapia Corel, for your support and work on MYL; my girls at US Postal (Cherylyn Stewart and Emma); Father Paul and June, thank you for the encouragement and appearing just when we needed the guidance; Joe and Kathy Dimmick; Jack and Dee Dee; John and Linda; Leslie and Tom Beers, you rock! Thank you for the amazing video! Allen Sowelle (my favorite editor of all time-you have many gifts and I can't wait to see you reveal them to the world!); Brian Kramer, thank you for the gorgeous photos; Debby Reynolds Dance and Rehearsal Studios, Burbank CA, My favorite place to dance!
All the agents listed in this book: thank you for all your hard work. I really appreciate what you do!

All the look-alike talent, from years past and present: thank you for doing what you do! Without you, this would not be possible. Linda Orlando, thank you for your incredible gift of EDITING!!!

Ed Parker, your beautiful eye for art, your beautiful heart and soul, and your ability to create magic for me! You are so deeply appreciated! And this time around I did it MY WAY!

Thank you also to Stevie Wonder, Seal, Luther, Ted Neely, Carl Anderson, and Maxwell for creating beautiful music that inspires me to write! Finally a huge thank you to Madonna, for providing a doorway of endless possibilities...

"You know you have made it in Hollywood when you have your very own celebrity look-alike, or when someone is impersonating YOU"...

Introduction

So you look like, sound like, or can act like someone famous? Have perfect strangers stopped you and asked you for an autograph? Have you been asked questions such as "Are you…" or "Has anyone ever told you that *you look just like…*?"

All over the world, celebrity look-alikes with little or no showbiz experience are being discovered and hired to entertain and perform, and they are either making it a full-time career or allowing it to be a lucrative second income. Of course, if you can sing, dance, or act, the opportunities to find work can be extraordinary! Put your creative talents to the test. There is no other form of entertainment like this. You can get work simply by looking like someone famous. If you happen to resemble a famous celebrity, politician, musician, spokesperson, comedian, or anyone *hot* in society, entertainment, or the media, then you should consider the idea of working as a celebrity look-alike. The look-alike market is so large that there is enough work for anyone interested in working, no matter who you are or where you live.

Looking like, resembling, or sounding like someone recognizable can have its rewards. I am living proof of this and with over 17 years of working professionally in this field, I can now help anyone begin their own career as a celebrity look-alike and turn dreams into reality. After publishing my first book, **Made You Look** (Thrillennium books), I found myself answering daily e-mails and phone calls from people around the world, asking me to further explain how to get started as a look-alike. I decided to dedicate myself to documenting a precise step-by-step instruction manual and include every element needed to teach anyone how to get work as a professional celebrity look-alike. I use my own personal experiences as examples to demonstrate the valuable lessons and information needed to begin to work professionally.

I have included quotes from some of the industry's best look-alikes and agents to share their personal advice; who better to learn from than people who actually work professionally in this field? I have also included contact and booking information for over 100 companies that can book you as a celebrity look-alike, once you are ready to go. This guide reveals trade secrets to finding and securing exciting and profitable work as a celebrity look-alike. Learn first hand about contracts, what agents look for, what to charge and how to get paid, show ideas, costumes, makeup, photography, and so much more.

This guide will take you through a series of steps to guide you into a wonderful part-time job or maybe even a new full-time career. Now you can stop dreaming about being in show business and get your feet wet with hands-on, real life experience. Who knows what possibilities may be in store for you as a celebrity look-alike? You may just find yourself starring in a feature film or commercial, performing on stage with a live band, mingling at a corporate event, or just having fun entertaining your friends at parties.

With a strong dedication, a passion to follow your dreams, and reference to this guide, you too can be among Hollywood's finest entertainers!

Break a leg!

The Categories

Finding Your Place

Before you begin to consider the possibilities of working as a celebrity look-alike, remember: To have the greatest success, you should impersonate someone who is recognized as a "star" and considered famous in the eyes of Hollywood. Agents, future clients, directors, and party and event planners request certain celebrities more frequently than others, and for many events, the celebrity who is most famous or most recognizable may be the most requested character for bookings. The exception to this theory is a look-alike talent that is a *dead-ringer*. A dead-ringer look-alike is close to identical in their appearance to the celebrity they are impersonating, and may be hired or requested by agents solely for their strong resemblance and not necessarily for having a talent. On the opposite side of the spectrum, an exceptionally talented performer who may not look like someone "Hollywood famous" or even have a dead-on look to a celebrity, but has an entertaining and impressive impersonation of a celebrity may get hired and requested over and over for their great performing abilities. So you see, there are several kinds of possibilities and certainly avenues for all people, after they figure out which category best suits their looks and/or talents.

To begin your work as a look-alike, you must decide which category is going to best suit you.

Marv Cline as Alan Alda; Photography by Carol Morris

The Dead Ringer:

Dead ringer means you are the spitting image of a celebrity. This means that people constantly mistake you for that celebrity. You need to be objective and really know if your looks are exact. Your height, weight, hair, eye color, body type, measurements, and style should be so close to the celebrity that people actually believe you are the star. If you are, in fact, a dead ringer for a celebrity, you will most likely get hired for your uncanny resemblance. This must mean that you are mistaken for the celebrity daily, and not just once, twice, or three times. Many great look-alikes fit into this category. They may not have had any performing experience before becoming a celebrity look-alike, but their appearance was so similar to a famous person that, after hearing comments from strangers over and over, they decided to try out the world of look-alike work. Many agents are interested in hiring dead ringer look-alikes, because most people like to hire someone who can pass as the real star. However, looking exactly like a celebrity doesn't mean that you won't have to catch up on your performing abilities—you will still need some talent (or at least be willing to work on it) to be hired.

A Character of a Star:

Character of a star means that you have created a "character" that mimics a character portrayed by a celebrity in a film, a television show, or the media. If you do not resemble someone famous, there is no need to abandon the idea of being a celebrity impersonator. You can do what many other successful look-alikes have done—recreate a recognizable *character*. Bring to life a favorite character that a celebrity is well known for. This is an excellent way to make a place for yourself in the celebrity look-alike world. Using the magic of hairstyles, make-up, and costumes, the performer who may be looking for another outlet for his or her creative talents can find work this way. If you think you can recreate the appearance of a fun and entertaining character, then your abilities as a performer can carry you through even if you don't look exactly like the celebrity who portrayed that character. **For example**, you may not be the spitting image of Jim Carrey, but if you can do a terrific impersonation of his colorful character from the film *Ace Ventura*, then with the right hair and makeup you can be an "ace" celebrity look-alike! Other examples include Austin Powers, Charlie Chaplin's "Little Hobo, Elvira, and Indiana Jones. There are also stars who can be mimicked because of particular costumes, features, or mannerisms they are known for, such as Groucho Marx, Carmen Miranda, W. C. Fields, and Mae West. Another idea for you to consider is dressing as an **animated character**. Costume rental shops supply costumes of animated characters from film and television, children's stories or animation. Be creative and have fun finding a star or character that you can identify with or impersonate well.

Richard Halpern as Austin Powers;
Photography by Mark David Studner

7

Irby Gascon as Elvis Presley; Photography by Brian Kramer

The Sound-alike:

A performer who may not necessarily look exactly like a famous celebrity, but can sound just like a recognizable voice, can certainly find work using his or her voice. This means voice-over work for film, television, commercials, songs, radio spots, announcements, live tribute performances, stand-up comedy, and specialty work for voice talent.

Kurt Meyer as Indiana Jones; Photography by Rick Bultay Photography

Actor, singer, musician, dancer, or model turned look-alike:

If you are already a professional performer and you are looking for extra work in between your other performing jobs, look-alike work is a perfect kind of job to allow you the freedom to do what you love to do, without having to interrupt your other performing work. Since each look-alike job is contracted individually, you can easily negotiate each job as it comes through. Since you are already a polished performer, stepping into the role of a look-alike should come quite naturally. Many great look-alikes are seasoned actors, singers, and dancers first, so when they begin to work as a look-alike performer, with the right costumes and makeup, an instant impersonator is born. After working as a look-alike, most actors and musicians find it to be the perfect job to supplement other work and provide extra income.

Not all look-alikes can fit the bill of each kind of look-alike job available.

Decide for yourself honestly where you fit...

As you begin to consider the possibilities of working as a celebrity look-alike, you need to determine what your natural strengths are, and what kinds of jobs will come most naturally for you.
Not all dead-ringer look-alikes have stage performing abilities. Just because you resemble a star does not mean you have the skills to be a strong stage performer. Are you better at utilizing your look to carry you over as a more convincing celebrity? If you are not comfortable being on stage, then you may want to perfect your people skills and become a great ***mix and mingle*** look-alike (more on mix and mingle later). Mix and mingle requires a talent, and not all stage performing look-alikes have the ability to carry on entertaining conversations with perfect strangers. Some look-alikes perform solely in Legend type shows or exclusively on big stages and never work on the corporate circuit as a mix and mingle talent. They may have to wear heavy make up to play the role of their star, and this is not going to carry over when a mix and mingle job requires you to be close and personal with people. Most look-alikes know their strong points and stick to the kinds of jobs that best feature their natural abilities. It is very important to know how to be realistic with your look. If you are a "fan" of a celebrity, it is best to not to become an impersonator. Fans tend to be unrealistic about their own look, the opinion(s) of the celebrity they hope to look like, and in most cases, they are not able to present themselves as professional entertainers.

Once you know who you look like or sound like, or when you have decided what character you can successfully impersonate, it's time to learn all about your celebrity choice.
This means you must study, study, study! Before you attempt to begin working as a look-alike, you must spend however much time it takes studying your celebrity for you to "become" that person. As a professional performer, your study should be a process that never ends. Begin your research by finding movies, videos, documentaries, magazines, books, newspapers, posters—anything that can provide you with valuable information about your star. Look at the face, eyes, mouth, hair, and body. Listen to the voice, speech, accent, laugh, or cry. Search out every identifiable trait associated with that person. What makes you notice and recognize your star immediately when you see him or her? These features are the ones you will need to re-create so that people will immediately recognize you as that star. Find out what you both have in common. Is it a look in your eyes? Your smile? Your body type? The way you move? Whatever it is, you must learn how to exaggerate and emphasize that quality and make it your strength. Determine which quirks and characteristics are most successful in bringing your star to life, and then be rehearsed enough so that you can turn yourself into that person at a moment's notice.

All celebrities have something about them that helps the public recognize them immediately. Find these trademark features and try them out in front of a mirror, or for a friend, in an acting class, at a costume party, or with other look-alikes. Keep practicing until you feel completely confident that you can recreate that celebrity without even having to think about it. You will know when you find those one or two trademark features, because of the immediate reaction from your audiences.

It's in the eyes………..

Our eyes ARE the windows to our soul, so we must remember how very important our eyes are to our overall presentation as an impersonator. Pay attention to your eyes, and begin to study and learn how your celebrity communicates with his or her eyes. As an impersonator, the eyes are one of the most important qualities needed to match your celebrity. When the eyes are off, the whole presentation is off. An audience may not be able to put their finger on what is wrong with an impersonator's look when it seems "off"—but chances are that it is THE EYES!

Learn more about your celebrity by carefully observing his or her eyes. You can discover many elements of a person by looking into their eyes. We all hold a distinct energy in our eyes, and who we are will be prominent there. When learning about becoming a professional look-alike, an important detail to try and match is a similar type of energy and essence to your celebrity. When the energy/essence of one person is similar to another, it is this element that makes people feel like "those two people look the same." Most look-alikes match the celebrity they look like in several ways, and the greatest success stories come from look-alikes who share a similar look to the eyes, along with the correct overall look, talent, and essence.

Begin to pay attention to what type of aura your celebrity conveys, and then try to analyze how you can re-create the very same feeling. The places to practice these expressions are in your eyes, and then in your stance, walk, voice, and overall presence.

Practice in front of a mirror, finding the most accurate expressions with your eyes. Find several ways to hold your face, eyelids, eyelashes, looks, and expressions. Play with different looks, and try holding your eyes in several different expressions to match your celebrity. Learn what you need to do to your eyes to make them match your celebrity. If you do not have the same color eyes, you might want to consider using color contacts. If you need to re-shape your eyes, look into makeup application techniques to create new ways to reshape your eye area. When you speak to people as your character, catch their attention with your eyes. Making eye contact with people and holding their attention with the impact of your eyes will make an impression that most people will not forget.

The 15 minutes of FAME look-alike…

Many people working in the celebrity impersonator field have over the years had varying amounts of success. There are several professional look-alikes who have experienced over a decade of bookings and still continue to work. Then there are others who have jumped head first into working as a celebrity look-alike simply because of an uncanny resemblance to someone who is temporarily in the public eye or in the headline news, such as Monica Lewinsky, Anna Nicole Smith, Ozzy and family or Ross Perot. These faces that are known for having 15 minutes of fame have allowed for the look-alike to also cash in on that 15-minute ride by being a recognizable face to cash in on.
There have been ongoing 15-minute look-alikes who were able to jump into the market at just the right moment to create non-stop work for themselves with some amazing results.
Feature films, television shows, and news programs have all employed 15-minute look-alikes as well as corporate functions and personal appearances, so if you happen to look like the NEXT 15-minute celebrity, then read on and get ready for the ride of your life (well, at least a 15-minute ride!).

Look-Alike Trivia Question:

Q. Who are (generally) the "most requested" celebrities?

A. Marilyn Monroe and Elvis Presley. Both are legendary superstars that symbolize Hollywood, glamour, and celebrity. Both celebrities are corporate-friendly, and easily recognized by most people of all ages and races.
| Every agency has numerous look-alikes of each character.
There are distinctively different professional levels of Elvis and Marilyn impersonators, but here in L.A. the following two look-alikes have become the most sought after and have brought their impersonation to a new level of professionalism…

Susan Griffith as Marilyn Monroe Susan Griffith Photography

Q. What is it like impersonating Marilyn?

A. **Susan Griffith as Marilyn Monroe:** "My resemblance to Marilyn Monroe has certainly opened the doors for me to work as a professional look-alike, but I truly feel that it is my business skills and professionalism that have allowed me to continue to work for as long as I have. Look-alike work requires more than just looking like a celebrity. To be able to continue to make it a full time career, you must have sharp people skills, business skills, and performing skills. Since I am an actress first, I have been able to be cast in films like Pulp Fiction and Marilyn and Me. Working in film, television, and stage (even as a look-alike) you will get work because of your skills FIRST and your look second."

Scot Bruce as Elvis Presley Photography by Jack McDonald

Q. What about impersonating Elvis?

A. **Scot Bruce as Elvis Presley:** "What I want to mention as advice would be a short ramble on the idea of "not losing one's identity." Making the distinction between the gig and everyday life. We all want to do our characters the best we possibly can, and that means embracing every aspect of that character's persona (like a good method actor should). So often we've seen people forget who they are (I probably don't need to mention that it's most prevalent with Elvis and Michael Jackson impersonators). Perhaps that topic has been flogged enough, but it's one that I feel is extremely important."

Research

Research is a very important part of your job as an impersonator. Here are some tips for how to get started studying your celebrity.

1. **Collect photographs** of your celebrity. Search through periodicals, newspapers, gossip magazines, biographies, posters, and the Internet. By starting a collection of photographs, you will equip yourself for times when you need to reproduce facial expressions, makeup, hair, costumes, and specific looks. They will be helpful when you need to capture and re-create certain details of your star. Keep the photos of your star handy, as you may need refer back to a particular costume, hairstyle, etc.

2. **Read and memorize basic details about your celebrity.** The more informed you are about your star's life, the more confident you will be when answering questions in character as that star. Take notes on repeated expressions, angles they use for photographs, body language, and postures. What makes you notice and recognize them immediately? These will be the elements you will need to re-create so that people will recognize you instantly as that person. Memorize some background on their life as well. It is important to study your star's voice, laugh, and mannerisms, but it is just as critical to learn basic details about who they are, such as where they came from, what kinds of stories they tell, successes and failures they have had, and the films, television shows, or songs they have been featured in. Develop an intimate knowledge of the person you are portraying. This will help in your impersonation.

3. **Find what it is about you that is similar** to your star. Most successful look-alikes know exactly what their strengths are and they use those qualities to make their act believable and entertaining. One example of what your strong point can be is the quality people point out to you all the time that reminds them of your star. For example, if perfect strangers say, "Hey, your laugh sounds just like…" then your laugh should be the center of your por-

trayal. Whatever your strong point is, you should emphasize that point and build your characterization around it.

4. **Learn which techniques are the strongest** for quickly bringing your star to life, then be rehearsed enough so that you can call upon those techniques at a moment's notice.

5. **Listen to your star's voice.** Make a cassette of your celebrity's speaking voice and speak along with it, to match the sound. Get your voice in shape and know what to do to create the famous diction, pronunciations, and tones that make your star's voice recognizable. **Tip:** Keep a tape of your celebrity's voice in your car, to listen to on the way to your jobs.

6. **Collect videos**, movies, award show recordings, or any footage where your star has been featured. Learn famous lines ("you like me, you really like me" or "thank you, thank you very much"), dialogues, acceptance speeches, etc. Watch them over and over. Watching footage of your star should be something that you do regularly.

7. **Keep yourself updated** on your celebrity. Check fan Internet sites, magazines, or television shows on a regular basis to keep up with current hairstyles, clothing, and looks, as well as information about your star's current projects, activities, and relationships.

8. **If your celebrity has a famous sidekick**, look for a performer who can portray that famous partner. You will most likely get a request now and then for the famous sidekick. This will allow you to get potentially more work offers, and make your act more entertaining.

9. **Take a class** in dance, voice, makeup, or acting, if you need a little extra confidence or just some practice before you jump into the look-alike world. Sometimes a creative class will inspire you, or give you confidence if you're not used to performing for an audience.

10. **Network:** Learn how to start promoting yourself. Come up with regular ideas for yourself on how to book yourself, with an original theme or idea you thought up. Keep a journal of fun ideas that would incorporate your celebrity into an event.

11. **Find what elements make you FEEL most like your celebrity.** It may be a style, fabric or color. What you wear will effect how you feel and your mood, so if there is a particular color or style that gets you in the right mood, make sure your costumes will combine these elements. Any little bits help when you need to play the part.

12. **Know what angle is your best angle**, the one that helps you look the most like your celebrity, so that when you are ready to do any kind of filming or photo shoot, you can advise the camera person at which angle to shoot you from.

Remember, your research should be fun. Like embarking upon any new adventure, your search should add a creative outlet to your life without contributing too much stress. Take your time, and have some fun along the way.

Tips for learning how to practice...

Try putting a mirror beside or just in front of the television so you can see your reflection next to the television screen as you watch footage of your star. Now you can see yourself and the celebrity on the television screen simultaneously. This is a great way to practice your walk, voice, body language, dance moves, facial expressions, or any other trademark characteristics so that you can perform them exactly as your star does.

Learning choreography or precise movement from a video.

As you watch the videotaped performance of your celebrity, or need to study movement, have scratch paper handy and take notes on each step by freeze-framing each step (by hitting the pause button on your VCR machine). As each frame is frozen, draw a stick figure of the movement on your note pad. If you can draw each movement, step by step, it will allow you to understand each transition of movement, and help teach you the choreography completely step by step. Review your stick figure drawing, one movement at a time, and go over them slowly without music or the video playing. When you have marked each movement slowly, you can then pick up the pace and begin to move along to the video with the tape playing at regular speed.

Practice diction.

For your voice or matching pitch to your celebrity, try prerecording your celebrity's voice onto a cassette tape, using famous lines from movies, recordings, award show acceptance speeches, and television show performances. Record as many different clips as you can, leaving a blank spot in between each clip for you to speak the same line after your celebrity speaks it. You will be able to listen carefully to your celebrity's voice, wait for a moment, then speak it yourself to see how closely you can match the voice. This tape can also be played as you get into makeup and wardrobe, or even in your car on the way to your job.

Find your own space to practice.

As you begin to learn how to be more like your celebrity, find a quiet, comfortable space where you feel uninhibited to try out new steps, sing, dance, and begin practicing dialogue. You will want to find an area that will allow you to **let loose** without an audience. You may wish to create a space where you can lay out photos of your star and have a mirror for your rehearsing, and a television/VCR handy. You will more than likely practice more often when you have a nice place to be free to create.

Do your own research to identify your impersonation—don't copy a copy.

In all of my years as an impersonator, I find it funny, bizarre, and ironic how many look-alikes actually seem to impersonate another impersonator. Most commonly when an impersonator doesn't have a lot of self-confidence, they look to "the best" and copy that person's impression of a celebrity. Sure, it is flattering to the talent who is being imitated to have others assume they know the best way to be the star they're portraying, but it can also be quite frustrating. A look-alike who is considered "the best" imitator of a certain celebrity has put time, energy, and thought into creating an expert impersonation of that celebrity. So rather than looking to the impersonator for ideas, look to the celebrity and begin to see how YOU wish to portray the celebrity. It is *your job* to invest time, energy and creative thinking as you put your act together. Each person has their own special, unique way of presenting an impersonation of a celebrity, so be creative and watch *the star you are impersonating* and not the other impersonators. Find your own personal signature that people can remember *you* by.

Q. What is your advice before someone begins?

A. **Cheri as Xena Warrior Princess:** "My advice to anyone in becoming a look-alike: When you realize you have the look, go for it! Research it! And get your name out there. Be the best you can be and remember there is a lot of competition out there and sometimes you need to work hard and keep persistent in the job you love to do. Nothing ever comes easy in life; you have to work hard to achieve your goals and to make a good income in this business."

Anne Kissel as Roseanne;
Photography by Devon Cass

Q. What is your funniest look-alike story?

A. **Anne Kissel as Roseanne:** "The new employees in my husband's company saw my look-alike pictures in his office. They all assumed they were actual photos of Roseanne. None of them knew I worked as a professional look-alike, so they thought my husband had the hots for Roseanne—until they found out the truth! About being a look-alike: Be professional at all times. I saw Roseanne again for the fifth time in NYC last month, and having seen me on TV, she said to me, "I like the way you *do* me!" I said to her, "Thank you, and I would never portray you in a negative manner." I think this is key as a look-alike: Respect the star you portray, no matter what! I was approached to act as her in a movie, but did NOT like the way the script portrayed her in a negative light, so I declined the role. Did the movie ever get made? Not that I'm aware of, and I'm glad. I wouldn't want someone to make fun of ME, so I think we owe at least that much to our stars."

Q. Can you share a look-alike moment?

A. **Robert S. Ensler as Dean Martin:** "Last year, I had someone who was surfing the Internet go to my web site. He had seen a promo video on our site that featured 'A Concert of Martin & Lewis' at Paladino's Club in Reseda, CA. He wrote to me begging for a copy of this 'unheard-off' performance to add to his Martin & Lewis collection. I think he thought the video was an actual bootleg of an old Martin & Lewis act. (The video wasn't crystal clear visually, but perfect Martin & Lewis sound and shtick.) Needless to say, that e-mail made my day, with him thinking my video was the real thing."

Gary Smith as Robert Redford Photography by Robert Peters

Q. Do you have any tips for someone just starting out in entertainment?

A. **Gary Smith as Robert Redford:** "When starting out, be sure to take constructive advice only from friends you trust and respect. When working in entertainment, you are subject to comments from just about everybody (and believe me, you will hear them), so the importance of supportive, positive people around you is absolutely necessary. You want the energy of encouragement around you, and this support will help you develop confidence in yourself."

Yes you CAN!

Going Pro

The interesting thing about show business is that there is no one exact "method" of getting a break in Hollywood. There are many different success stories of working actors and look-alikes that share in the experiences of getting work, whether they have had years of training or no experience as a performer at all. Some of these performers were told "NO" time and time again. The bottom line is that there is NOT "one way to make it." I am not implying that a performer will not have to work hard and study his or her craft, but no one person can predict the success of anyone's future as an entertainer. There are hundreds of stories of performers who may not have had training yet somehow landed a role in a feature film. There are also stories of studied performers who were told that they "didn't have what it takes," and still ended up becoming a celebrity. Even incredible well-known singers were once booed off stages like The Apollo Theater.

Television shows Like American Idol try to give an example of how ruthless the entertainment industry can be. This show features young singers who have huge hopes and dreams to make it as a pop star. After performers are put through a rigorous audition, they are critiqued by a panel of judges who (supposedly) know "what it takes to make it."
The truth is, this business is and can be cold-hearted, but *one person* cannot predict the future of anyone who has focus, a love for what they do, and a determination to succeed.

If you ever find yourself in a situation where someone tells you that you *can't/won't or don't HAVE WHAT IT TAKES*, hear MY words in the back of your mind: "Yes you CAN! NOTHING is impossible. Believe in yourself, your hopes, and your dreams." Visualize yourself living your dream, and don't even allow the word *can't* to be a part of your life.

Becoming a Professional

In order to begin working for bigger agencies for large scale events (and budgets) you will need to work your way into the same league as the top professionals. In order to be considered for these kinds of events, you will need to understand the following guidelines. To start working as a professional look-alike talent, you will need to be dependable, professional, reliable, and entertaining.

So what does it take to become a pro?

• Showing up on time (at least 30 minutes in advance) to every job. Agents count on their performers to be on time and ready to go. Many agents would readily call upon someone they know they can rely on rather than a "dead-ringer" look-alike who is undependable. It's a major plus if you happen to be both reliable and a dead-ringer.

• Take the time to learn dialogue—famous lines from movies or songs to say while on the job—and make your impersonation believable while mingling with people. Be prepared with some kind of short skit to perform on a moment's notice if you are asked to. Study your celebrity, and know which angle and pose to hit for photographs. You should comfortably and confidently be able to speak, sing, or move in a way very similar to your celebrity.

• Invest in a great costume and always present yourself in believable wardrobes, costumes, hairstyles, and makeup that make you look exactly like your celebrity.

• Promote the agent you are working for. Do not give out your own phone numbers, and always represent yourself, your agent, and your client in a professional manner.

• Have professional promotional materials. Agents rely on having professional photographs, videotapes, and resumes or bios of their performers.

• Make sure that you can be reached by a pager or cell phone, and return calls immediately, since many jobs must be booked quickly on a moment's notice.

• Become reliable. Make sure you are known for your consistency and reliability.

After accepting a job from an agent, be sure to follow through and show up for the job on time and prepared.

- Find a way to give back your gifts. Consider an appearance or performance for charity events.

- Know how to separate yourself from the star you impersonate and realize that the impersonation is simply an act to be used for work purposes only. Exhibit a sense of respect for your celebrity at all times.

- Maintain a professional appearance and attitude under any work condition. Working conditions vary wildly, so the ability to remain neutral and composed, regardless of the work environment, is a sure sign of a professional.

- Develop people skills with all kinds of people in all walks of life. Most look-alike work requires interaction with the public and being entertaining, just having conversations with perfect strangers. Just talking as though you were your celebrity means that "you're on" as a look-alike.

- Create a star quality to be able to carry off a stature of celebrity. Your portrayal of a famous person is believable because of your poise. A true professional can liven up any atmosphere just by their presence and an upbeat, appealing, or interesting personality.

- Maintain a humble and grounded attitude in any situation. Celebrity look-alikes often find themselves in some very impressive places, and sometimes among very impressive faces. Those who can understand that it is only a job, and not get carried away with a fantasy, (or read their own press, so to speak) will continue to be in the league with the pros. Remember, just because one job seems fabulous, that doesn't mean that the next job will be.

- Help (not compete with) fellow performers. Those who assist others will always receive the same in return. Performers who take the time to be helpful, offer advice, or refer others help create a positive energy for others to follow. Gossip, criticism, or competitive attitudes only breed negativity. Top performers understand that there is room for all of us. Decide to contribute to the ideas of abundance and wish well for your peers. There is enough work for every person who puts their heart into what they do. Have integrity in all you pursue and then watch it come back 100 fold.

- Follow up with an agent after he or she gets you work. Check in with them after the job is done (but don't drive them crazy - one call is sufficient), thank them for their hard work, and let them know that you appreciate being hired for the job. Many agents like to know their hard work is appreciated.

Q. Your look as Cher is astonishing! Does having a dead-on look make your work easier for you?

A. **Sandra Wood as Cher:** "It is not easy work, no matter what. I think most people outside the business think it is nothing but fun, excitement, and glamour. To show up at an event looking like a movie star, walk around, take a few pictures, make money and go home. Most of us have put a great deal of time, energy, and money into studying and developing our characters and we do so on an ongoing basis. It takes not only a strong resemblance to the character, but also it takes someone with the ability to do good makeup, invest in great costumes, and/or someone who can perform (dancer, singer, or musician). It takes someone with the ability to be in front of an audience and display good ad-lib skills, good negotiating skills, and good people skills, in addition to comedic skills and acting ability. As a final thought, I feel that no matter which path you choose to take as an impersonator - sound-alike, dead-ringer look-alike, or character - one should strive to do their very best to keep the standards high because it strengthens the profession overall."

Sandra Wood as Cher Sandra Wood Photography

You're ON...

Jade Roberts as Sylvester Stallone: "Working as a professional look-alike, you must always be prepared to be "on" at a moment's notice. For many look-alikes, you may be in a position where someone puts a camera in your face and tells you to "GO." Once, at a corporate function, a man shoved a microphone in my hand and said, "Interview everyone for the big video screens inside," and I thought, "About what?" Right there I learned I needed to be ready to improvise! The crowd was full of media types, and interviewing was not mentioned in the rehearsal. If you can prepare one-liners or well-recognized dialogue that your character would say BEFORE your gigs, then you will always be able to handle situations like this."

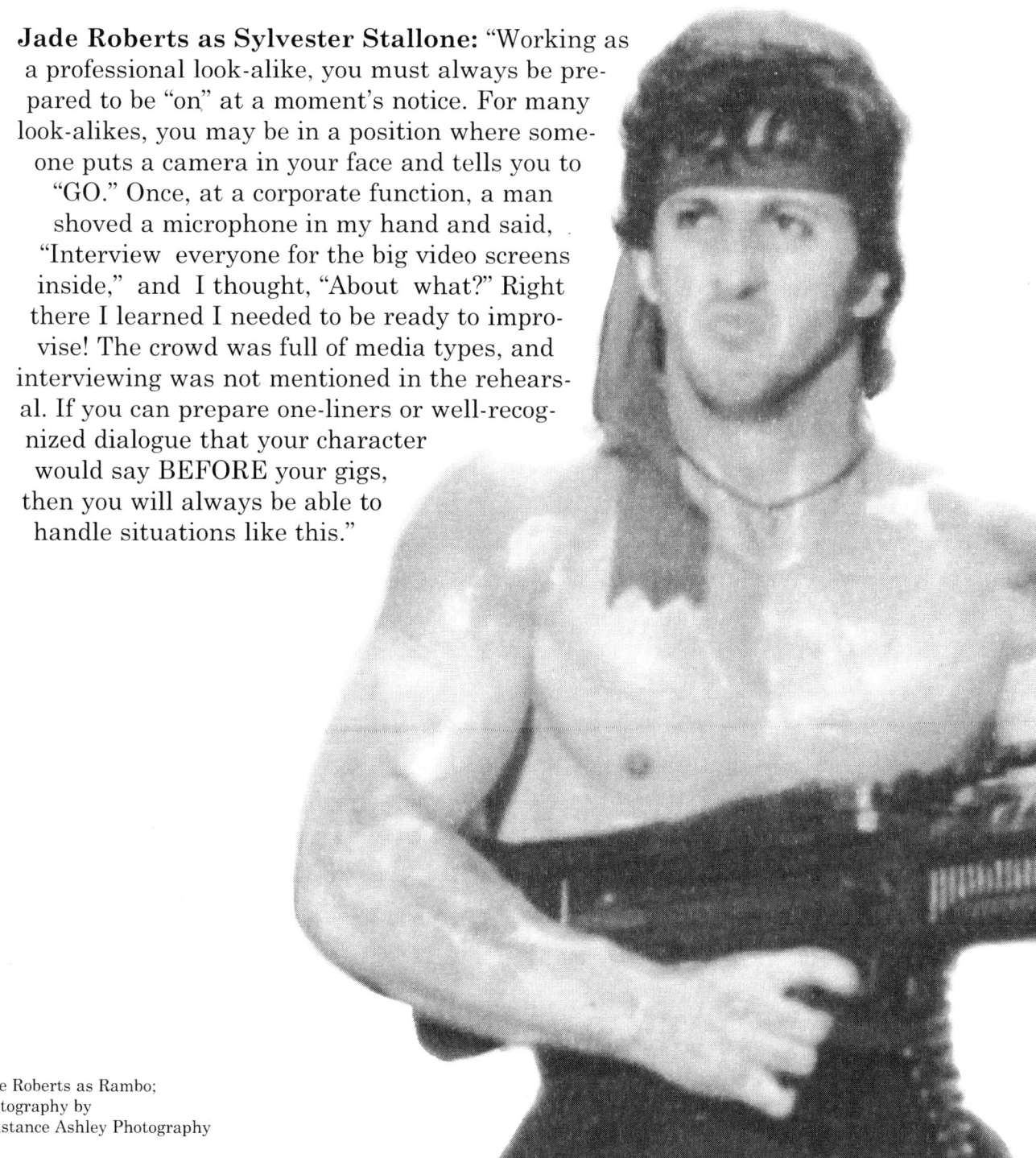

Jade Roberts as Rambo;
Photography by
Constance Ashley Photography

Ready to work:

The Possibilities Are Endless

What can you do as a look-alike?
The possibilities are endless...

The truth is, the possibilities are endless. If I wasn't living proof, I might not believe it myself.

Your bread and butter will most likely come from being hired to perform or appear at corporate events. These are very common job opportunities for look-alikes all over the world. Major hotels, clubs, restaurants, resorts, country clubs, and Hollywood-themed venues regularly hire look-alike talent to entertain at their events.

As a look-alike, you need to understand what is meant by the phrase "**mix and mingle**." When an agent calls you for a job, he or she will explain the job and let you know whether you will be hired to mix and mingle (also known as meet and greet) or perform a live show of some type. Mix and mingle means just that—you are required to interact with guests at the event or party, in character as your celebrity. Basically, you are there to entertain by adding a star element to the event and making the guests feel as if they are among celebrities. Mix and mingle requires a natural talent to think quickly and be spontaneous with people. You will need to be comfortable walking up to strangers and immediately be able to make entertaining conversation. Even if your "celebrity" is not known to be "people friendly," as a look-alike talent, you must be able to create the character you portray to be approachable, talkative, and easy to be around. You are paid to entertain, so remember that just talking with people needs to seem like entertainment to the guests. It does not matter if you are the splitting image of the biggest star in Hollywood, if you do not know how to be entertaining through actions and conversations, then agents will not want to hire you to mix and mingle. From the minute you arrive at any event, you should consider that you are "on" (stage) and people will watch you from the moment you arrive until the moment you leave the event. You need to understand that even when you are in the restroom getting ready, you are still somehow part of the illusion. You are not expected to perform until you are "on the clock" so to speak, but keep the awareness that if you look like a celebrity, people will be watching you as if you are that celebrity. Be cautious and aware of what you say at all times.

When working as a mix and mingle talent, you may be booked to entertain all kinds of people from all over the world, so it is vital for you to know how to communicate with all people of all ages. Each event or party can range from 10 people to 10,000 people, so when you are mixing and mingling, you will need to gear your performance accordingly.

With a small group of guests, you can actually make conversation with them, and interact much more personally. When working in a ballroom with hundreds of guests, you will need to move quickly, making your impersonation larger by exaggerating it, so that you can be more recognized in a crowd. Instead of having personal one-on-one conversations, you will need to entertain several guests at a time and entertain bigger groups of people by being a bit "bigger" than usual. Be ready to adjust your character to each situation. Posing for photos is also part of a mix and mingle assignment. When you are working with the public, you will often find yourself inundated with a lot of questions about your character. Be prepared. People might quiz you about the latest updates of your star. They may talk to you and ask you a question as if you are the real star. By preparing yourself and knowing the basic answers, not only will you keep the audience happy, you will also impress the people for whom you are working.

Knowing detailed information about your celebrity as though you were that person is one of the requirements of your job and performance, and success in this area will set you apart from the amateurs.

Photography by Johnny G Photography •
Action shots by Brian Kramer Photography
Glamour shot by Glamour Shots Photography •
Vintage Madonna by David Comfort Photography

Mix and Mingle conversations

Q. Do I act like the "celebrity" I'm impersonating? Or do I act like the "role" they play from the film they star in?

The answer is that it is completely up to you how you wish to portray your celebrity. You may wish to be the "role" of the character your celebrity played on film. When you are mixing and mingling, you can carry on your conversations as the character from the film your celebrity has starred in rather than as the celebrity you are impersonating. Or, if you wish, you can combine the celebrity and the famous role.

Example: You can look exactly like actor Clint Eastwood and decide to mix and mingle in the look and costume of a famous role from a Clint Eastwood film like Dirty Harry, and still make conversations as yourself or Clint or the Dirty Harry character.

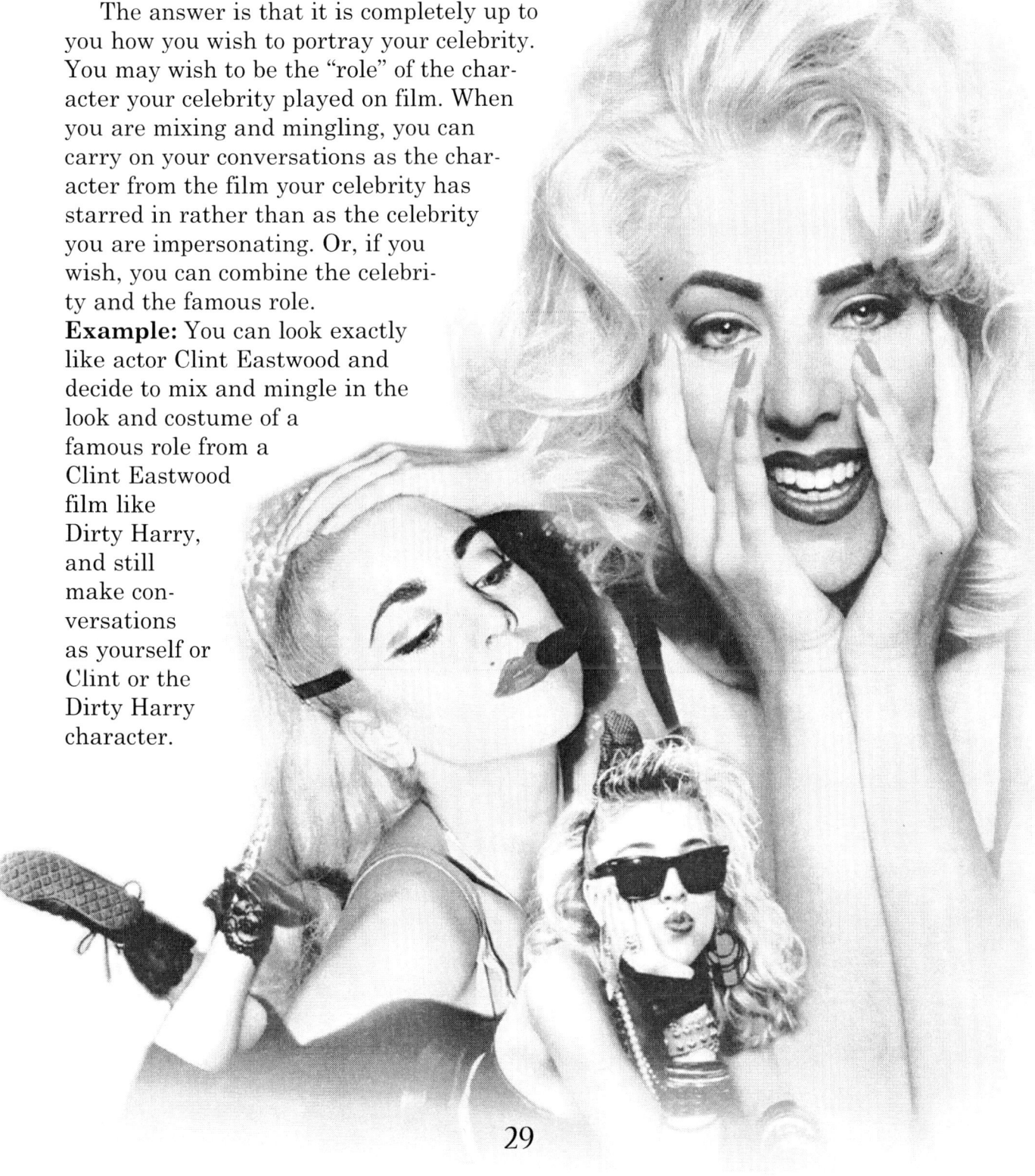

Joe Dimmick as Clint Eastwood
Joe Dimmick Photography

Q. Will people talk to me as ME (the performer) or will they expect me to answer as if I am the real celebrity?

The answer is both. You will find that when you mix and mingle, you will get all kinds of reactions from your audiences. This is why you should educate yourself on what your celebrity is currently doing in their life. Some people will (with a straight face!) ask you about your life (meaning your celebrity's life), and they are hoping for a straight answer, preferably a correct answer. It is almost a "test" for some people to make sure you know what you're doing. You will experience a fan of the celebrity asking you for an autograph, a photograph, or an answer to a question regarding the celebrity's life. Other times, guests will speak to you as a regular person and not expect you to BE your celebrity. They may ask, "How long have you been impersonating?" or "What else do you do?" How you wish to answer and interact with people is your choice.

Note: Most events involve big budgets and lots of hard work and planning by your agent and event planners. So you will need to conduct yourself accordingly.

Remember, you are working for a group of executives or corporations, and many of these jobs may be conservative or black-tie events. When you are working, keep this in mind and make your conversations and behavior suitable. If you're portraying an "over the top" type of personality, it is not necessary for you to act outrageous. Find a way to give just a hint of being over the top, without overacting it.

For example: Working as Madonna, I have performed and appeared at many incredibly conservative black tie events, industry parties and corporate functions where most of the time I am requested to be more "conservative." Portraying a character that is known to be more free spirited, one may think it would be impossible to tone down and still carry off the personality of Madonna. It is my job to have the ability to portray an entertaining, approachable impersonation of her. Finding a balance of professional interaction - without being too corny or out of character - is how to have a satisfied client, who may otherwise not book a character like Madonna for their exclusive evening. Event planners and agents will come to recognize you by your reputation as to how you work with corporate crowds, so whether or not you make the top list of talent to book (by the agents) will depend on how you conduct yourself for grand affairs and events.

Maintain respect, every time you work: You are borrowing another person's image, so be respectful of your star, the group you are performing for, and the agent you are representing. Make your actions and conversations "corporate friendly," unless your agent and/or clients direct you otherwise.

The look-alikes who know how to entertain as their character and add some elegance or laughter to an event are the look-alikes who will consistently get calls from agents. You may be surprised to know how many agents actually hire talent because of a "great, professional, and creative personality." How can you make a mark as a mix and mingle talent? Preparing material that incorporates dialogue about the particular company you're working for is a great touch and is always remembered by clients and guests. Think of ways in which you will stand out in a clever and professional way. Remember, your client is watching you as you work and evaluating how good your performance is going over with the guests. Did they get their money's worth? They will generally give a report of some kind to your agent afterward.

Your reviews for the evening can make or break your next job possibilities. How hard you work is entirely up to you. Critique yourself: "How much did I add to the event?" "How memorable was I?" "Were the guests entertained by my performance?" The word gets out fast, so if you're a new kid on the block, you should work hard to accumulate great reviews right off the bat. Hopefully if you are interested in becoming a working look-alike, you attitude is enthusiastic, and this will show in how you approach your jobs. Be careful not to become a jaded performer who constantly looks at his or her watch with boredom while hired to perform at an event. There are always hundreds of eager performers who would love to work and make the money, so remember that when you choose to do a gig, your appreciation for the job you are doing may just be the reason why you get your next booking.

Most agents will hire a performer with a positive, easy-to-work-with personality over any other kind of performer. As an agent myself, I always book the look-alikes who are happy to be working and show their gratitude.

Q. What if I look like someone who is harder to recognize in a crowd? How can I mix and mingle when people may not know who I am supposed to be?

The answer is that it is always a good idea to discuss this with the agent who is hiring you for a job. Clients may not think about how it may be harder to spot a more "normal" looking celebrity impersonator in a large ball room, and you will want to go over this with the agent when they are submitting you for a job. If you are not as quickly recognizable as Marilyn Monroe, then you can ask the agent to ask the client to better prepare the event for your appearance. A possibility can be having the deejay (upon your arrival) make a loud announcement… "Ladies and gentlemen, Ricky Martin has just arrived!" The client may wish to post a sign, movie marquee, or movie poster stating which impersonator celebrities will attend the event. Preparing the guests will help them to recognize you once you arrive. It is up to you to make your impersonation as easy as possible for people to "get" who you are supposed to be. You are hired to be a celebrity, so when mixing with guests, you will need to make your appearance instantly identifiable. Be creative and go the extra mile to paint the picture for people. Remind your agent (since most agents do not think about things like this) that the better the set up is for the look-alike, the more successful the overall performance will be for everyone. If you need to put a little extra time into thinking about how you can stage your arrival, or improve your meet and greet (so that the guests understand you are a hired look-alike).
Again, it is up to you to tell your agent to talk to the client and come up with fun ways to make it special.

Q. What if someone asks who am I supposed to be while I am mixing and mingling? Should I take this personally?

The answer is no, no, no! Almost every single look-alike at some point in their career has heard this question. Even incredibly obvious characters have heard, "Hey, who are you supposed to be?" This is not an insult, and should not be taken as one. I've seen too many look-alikes take this kind of comment to heart. Not everyone will know the celebrity you impersonate?it's just that simple. **Amazingly, the real Charlie Chaplin once lost a Charlie Chaplin look-alike contest!**

Note: It is not just look-alikes that have a hard time keeping their own identity separate from the celebrity they impersonate. Once in awhile you may experience (as you mix and mingle) a guest interacting with you as if you are the celebrity, and continue to hold conversations with you as if you are the star. This can be all in fun, if there is a clear idea that the conversation is for entertainment, and it is clear that you are an impersonator. Often, this can be an odd moment for the look-alike talent. There is a very fine line in keeping reality separate from what is meant to be entertainment (especially in the world of impersonators).

My personal experiences in dealing with the general public as a Madonna impersonator have gone to every kind of extreme. Many times people may feel like meeting me will be "their closest experience to meeting the real Madonna" and somehow that is good enough. In other situations some people hope that I am some kind of personal messenger to Madonna and I will somehow deliver a personal opinion to her.

On a more extreme note: Once while I was mixing and mingling at a very upscale event in Palm Springs, CA., I decided to add some humor to my meet and greet. I thought I would have some fun by portraying the recent "Mother Madonna" by adding a baby stroller with a toy doll to my act. During my meet and greet work, I walked up to a table and said my "hellos" to everyone dining at the table. As a guest came up to ask for a photo with me, one of the other guests at the table (who worked in child care) took my plastic Lola doll and hid her from me. This woman could not separate me from Madonna, or a *toy doll* from Madonna's real daughter. The woman proceeded to yell at me about how irresponsible I was for leaving my child. She was NOT a fan of Madonna, and could not make the distinction between reality and my "act." After about twenty minutes of gently talking with her, I explained, "I am an impersonator with a toy doll." It took extra time and patience, but I was able to appease the situation and walk away. This was a huge lesson in walking "the fine line."

Mix and mingle requires you to entertain everyone at an event or party, but not everyone will be a fan or admirer of the celebrity you impersonate, and this may make your mix and mingle a bit more of a challenge. If you find yourself in a situation where the guests become uneasy with your presence, you can still remain professional and show them a kinder, friendlier version of your celebrity by making conversation, taking a photo, or signing an autograph, or you can choose to walk away from the guests. You don't have to deal with rude comments, either, so it is best to remove yourself from any situation where your instincts tell you to move on. But most of the time you can open a closed mind by allowing the guest to feel that you are *approachable*.

Rosalinde Trooper as Pamela Anderson; Photography by Vincent B Nixon Photography

Q. Does being a look-alike lead to more work?

A. **Rosalinde Trooper as Pam Anderson:** "When discovering your own place in the look-alike world, don't be surprised if you happen to stumble upon your very own career as an actor." Bearing an uncanny resemblance to bombshell actress **Pamela Anderson** has paved the way for actress Rosalinde to land roles on hit television series. According to Rosalinde, "Our similarities have helped me get more work as an actress, and have allowed me to pursue more film and television work," she says. Since beginning her look-like work over five years ago, Rosalinde is having a ball with the "is that HER?" effect she has on people, and she is working *double* now!

More about Mix and Mingle

When you begin to work as a mix and mingle talent, be aware that sometimes you may be bombarded with people grabbing you, pulling at you, or demanding you to take a photo with them. It can get crazy, hectic, and even scary at times, so you need to keep clear-minded when you start working at any event. People may approach you and ask you to do something as your celebrity. Ask questions and make sure they are the person with the authority to demand the request. Be aware of the pictures you are taking, and don't be afraid to speak up if something does not feel right to you. Just because you are the hired entertainment does NOT mean you must be subjected to anything that makes you feel uncomfortable. Whether it is a person grabbing you inappropriately, a rude comment, someone requesting you to pose for a photo, or dealing with someone who may have had "one too many," you have the right to remove yourself from any kind of uncomfortable situation. You will want to find the agent or event coordinator and explain the situation.

When you are at your event location, remember that anyone you meet just may be a guest, agent, or client of the job you are hired for. Take discretion when making small talk in the restrooms, lobby area, or parking lots, as you just don't know if the person you're chatting with is the person responsible for hiring you. Keep this in mind every time you go anywhere to work.

Helping the conversation get started:

If you need help developing your people skills and learning to initiate conversation with people, there are always some basic mix and mingle conversation starters. It is not always easy to know what to say to strangers, but the more you work as a look-alike the easier it will become to get the hang of it. If you're just starting out, and need some ideas of what to talk about, here are some suggestions that can work for any job:

YOU: Hi, welcome to _____...... ("Hollywood" or where ever your scene is supposed to be set)

YOU: Where are you from? Is this your first visit to _____? (Many events fly the guests in from elsewhere).

YOU: (Combine some dialogue about your celebrity, speaking as if you are really the celebrity- with a sense of humor of course) Example: " We'll I've been so busy with my new baby Rocco, and now that I moved to London and am starring in my husbands next film, shooting videos, touring, or (current latest project), I barely have time to make it to these functions...How about you?" (Usually gets a laugh)

YOU: In a humorous tone, speak as your celebrity with reference to their company/event personal information. You can even combine what they do for the company into this dialogue, using key phrases, employee names, and the name of their company or product.

YOU: Open the conversation with a famous line that your character would say. Example: " Oh- can we talk, oh darling what designer are you wearing? Would you mind posing for a photo for PEOPLE magazine? (Many of the meet & greet jobs will have hired photographers to photograph you with the guests, so it can be fun to incorporate the photographs being taken of you, with "the media" photographing "the celebrities").

YOU: Sometimes it is a nice touch to ask people questions about THEM. This way you switch the importance off the talent and make the guests feel like they are the important people (which in this case, they are). You can ask general questions about their life, work, family, hobbies and personal interests

Mix and Mingle

Breaking It Down:

- **Situation 1:** **Large ballroom; 1600 guests from all over the world. Loud music is playing; people are eating and drinking.**

What do you do: First, you need to express to your agent and event person that an announcement would help make your entrance easier on you and the guests (if you are a hard-to-recognize character). The DJ (if there is one) or emcee of the evening can announce your entrance as you arrive into the ballroom. This is a great time for the DJ to include that "the celebrity" is available to pose for photos. As you move into the ballroom, you will want to keep conversation to a short minimum, and move through the crowd quickly and in a slightly exaggerated manner so that people can spot your impersonation even if they cannot hear you. Pose for photos, smile, have a good time, and make your way through the entire event so that no one misses your appearance. Interaction with other look-alikes is always fun for people to watch, and if you can, make sure to acknowledge the company President, client, or any other extra special person attending the event.

- **Situation 2:** **Small room at a hotel with 40 guests from "corporation ultra-conservative." You are hired to meet and greet, but the guests are not responding to your efforts to entertain.**

What do you do: You can start by giving your absolute all, and go the extra mile to be warm, approachable, and friendly, and try being the initiator of all conversations with the guests. Since this is a smaller-than-typical job, it can be more of a challenge to know what to do to make the guests enjoy the show, but this is where you need to keep your chin up and do your job. If you feel like the guests would rather not have conversations with you, you may think of a way to do your "shtick" from a distance, and they can appreciate you from afar. Sometimes you will find that guests (for whatever reason) act uncomfortable, awkward, or even rude to a look-alike, and when you are in a situation where there is not a big room or group to allow you to move on, then you must make the best of an uncomfortable moment. Don't break character or let anyone get you down; just keep your energy positive and hope that these kinds of jobs are few and far between.

- **Situation 3:** **At the front door of the event, you are hired to greet the guests as they arrive and walk in to the party.**

What do you do: You smile, look your best and understand you have about 10 seconds to make your mark on people as they walk past you. This is another typical look-alike mix and mingle situation. Many times the red carpet is rolled out for the guests, and the look-alike's job is to stand off to the side of the carpet and greet the guests, or actually grab a guest and walk down the carpet (over and over) until all the guests are in the event. Think fast, and have one-liners ready to go, as this type of job goes by fast and you will want to be entertaining as quickly as possible. You may also pose for photos in between all the chaos.

- **Situation 4:** **You are hired to mix and mingle for three (or more) hours, but you need to go to the bathroom.**

What do you do: It is always a good idea, when you will be working for over two hours, to put in a 10- to 15- minute break. Tell the agent when they book you for the job that you will need a small break to freshen up, go to the bathroom, get some water, etc.

- **Situation 5:** **At your meet and greet job, the client asks you to perform one number or asks you to perform more than your contracts states. You may be asked to perform another song, or memorize dialogue to perform during the event, etc.**

What do you do: You politely tell the client that you must okay the extra performance with your agent. You will need to negotiate extra money for yourself as well as for the agent. Let your agent handle all the details. If you are not able to get hold of the agent, then you must decide if you are willing to do the extra request, and let the client know the additional costs. This goes the same for staying past your booked times. There may be times when you will choose to do an extra performance without additional money, just to add to the event, but this is entirely up to you.

- **Situation 6:** **You are meeting and greeting at an event where people have been drinking too much. The guests become aggressive, obnoxious, or grabby.**

What do you do: You remove yourself from this location immediately. Just because you are the entertainment does not mean anyone has the right to treat you without respect. You can remove yourself from any situation like this, find the agent, and explain what is happening. You may be on stage and have this happen, or in the middle of the dance floor. Look-alikes have had wigs, hats, and body parts grabbed at inappropriately. They have been tossed in the air, thrown around on the dance floor, and picked up by "the big guy" to pose for a photo (my personal pet peeve). Some people may get it in their head that just because you are "hired" that you have to do whatever they say. You need to take direction ONLY from your agent, the event manager, or the client, and most certainly NOT from a drunken partygoer. If you find yourself in the middle of a crowd and it gets dangerous, you will want to leave this area and try your meet and greet from another part of the party. You need to set yourself in areas that make sense for your character as well. For example, it certainly takes away from the mystery and illusion to see Prince Charles on the dance floor with a bunch of rowdy drunk guests doing the Macarena.

- **Situation 7:** **As you are mixing and mingling, someone asks you for your business card.**

What do you do: Hand them one of your agent's cards, but check with your agent first, as many events are booked by a destination resource company, event producer, or planner, and you may need to give out the cards of these companies and not the look-alike agency. It is not uncommon to have several agencies or event planners working for the same one event. You will need to double check BEFORE you start working as to which company you are to represent. The agent who hired you for the job may be hired by another agency, so find out all of those details before going to your job.

- **Situation 8:** **An agency hires you to meet and greet but does not give all (or any) of the details of the job. You accept the job offer, assuming it will be okay. You arrive at the event, and are not comfort-**

able with the atmosphere of the party, or the conduct of the people who are hiring you.

What do you do: It is your job to ASK QUESTIONS when an agency calls you for a job. Many look-alikes have had to learn this the hard way and have ended up in some really uncomfortable, even dangerous situations (myself included!). Some agencies just want to get a job booked, so they may not ask the client the important questions to screen the situation for the talent. You never know who the people are that are hiring you, and in some cases, if you choose to perform private parties in private homes, or any other kind of booking where you do not have the safety of a public location or hotel, you need to know exactly where you are going and exactly who you are working for. Get the details from the agent.
So, with all of this said, what do you do now that you have arrived at the uncomfortable booking? You politely talk with the person who has hired you, and ask what is expected of you at this event. You can explain that you may not be comfortable with the situation, and then decide if there is a solution that can be found. If you can agree to what they have requested, then you can have the understanding from the client, and continue your job. If you do not agree, then you will want to explain the situation to the client, and explain that you are not comfortable with the circumstance, and that the agency did not explain the job details clearly to you. If you find yourself booked at a party where you feel this uneasy after you arrive, you do not have to go through with performing. However, if you have been told the circumstances of the job and you do not want to accept it, you can communicate all of this BEFORE you accept the job and save everyone all the headaches of a booking gone bad.

• **Situation 9:** **You have been hired to meet and greet for one hour and you accept the booking. When the agent asks you your price, you give your general 1-hour meet and greet price, but after you arrive at the event, you realize the event is a multi-million dollar affair and there may even be other look-alikes who are hired, but making twice as much money as what you asked for.**

What do you do: First off, it is your responsibility to ask for the fee that you believe is fair, no matter where you are booked. Second, it is not your business what the agent is making for commission, or what any of the other talent is making. When you are booked for a job, you need to quote your price by what you need to make, not how much money the client has or how much commission the agent will be receiving. Most look-alikes have no idea of the hours and work that agents put in for booking an event, so what they make is their business and should not change what you are asking for. If other look-alikes are making more money than you, there is probably a good reason that their price is higher and they are able to charge what they did. If you feel like you should be making more money, then base the fee you charge on your reputation, skills, and abilities, and not on the appearance of an event or client.

• **Situation 10:** **You are booked on a job where they say meet and greet, but the meet and greet is not the typical set-up. (Maybe it is riding in a limo with the guests, or dealing with ONE person of a company, or making a phone call as your celebrity, or hand-delivering concert tickets.)**

What do you do: Meet and greet comes in many different packages, and you will want to be able to go with the flow of the booking type. Can you entertain a group of people just riding in a car with them? This is a job that does come up for look-alikes, and if you should get a booking on a job as such, think about ways you can make a "driving" meet and greet a form of entertainment. Can you hold the attention of one person for 15 or 30 minutes? Whatever form your meet and greet booking takes, you will need to be prepared to adjust to any circumstance, so have your head ready for enthusiastic conversations, have your one-liners ready to go, get your voice tuned up to sound like your celebrity, and most of all, center yourself before you begin your job, and physically prepare for your one, two, or three hour performance.

Louise Gallagher as Elizabeth Taylor; Photography by Seth Mayer Photography

Q. What was your scariest moment while mix and mingling?

A. **Louise Gallagher as Monica Lewinsky:** "While performing a job as Monica Lewinsky in Las Vegas a few years ago (it was shortly after the huge Bill and Monica scandal had dominated the news and before the whole impeachment thing), I was working with a Clinton look-alike at this large private party at the Hart Mansion for a group of heavy equipment owners and contractors. Some of the attendees looked like they were former bodyguards or "rent collectors" and the alcohol was flowing freely. Bill and I did the usual mix and mingle and posing for photos, and were frequently subjected to a lot of gross jokes. Out of the crowd, an obviously inebriated man came up to the Bill Clinton look alike and loudly berated him for everything from his political decisions to his "affair with that tramp you have there." He was ready to start a fistfight and no one looked like they were going to try to stop him. Bill and I broke character and tried to explain to the man that we were only look-alikes, not the real people. He paused for a second and then very loudly exclaimed, "Anyone who would impersonate that (expletive deleted) ought to be taken out and shot!! You and this tramp ought to be hung....." Bill and I very rapidly made our way to the opposite side of the crowd and kept a wary eye out for the offender for the rest of the evening. It seems funny now, but it was scary at the time."

Q. What was your funniest moment while mix and mingling?

A. **Richard Halpern as The FAKE Austin Powers:** "I was doing a job as Austin Powers at a gig at the Desert Springs Marriott Resort, and the DJ started playing my theme music, "Soul Bossa Nova," from the Austin Powers films. In the middle of the number, as I was running around the room to the delight (I hope) of all the guests, I took a flying leap up onto the stage. I heard this enormous *RRRRRRRRIIII-IIIIIIIIIIIIIPPPPPPPPPPP!!!!*, and to my horror, saw that the seat of my pants had completely shredded! It was my first Austin suit, and it was quite old to begin with, and very skin-tight, baby, yeah! Luckily, my coat covered my now-bare butt. No worries, though, I did have my Calvin Kleins on underneath! And nobody except me and the DJ knew a thing had happened. *Smashing, baby!*"

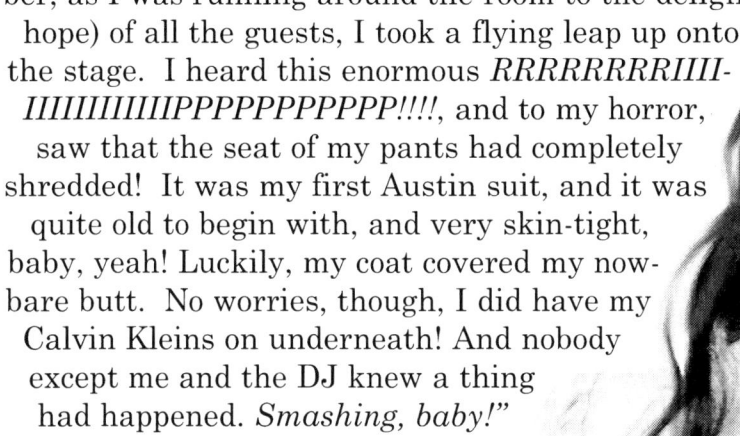

Q. What is the most common thing said to you while mix and mingling?

Lissa Negrin as Cher:
"I loved you in Moonstruck."
"My husband will die when he sees this picture" (of us together)
"My wife will kill me when she sees this picture" (of us together)
"Hey, you look like Cher!"

Lissa Negrin as Cher; Photography by Sonia Keshishian

Q. What was the most challenging situation you have been in as a look-alike while mix and mingling?

A. **Alli Spots as Marilyn Monroe:** "The most challenging situation I have been in as a look-alike repeats itself. Some men + alcohol + Marilyn Monroe = "inappropriate behavior." I can usually handle it through being sassy-but-firm. However, on occasion someone will find it hilarious to sneak a "goose." Once, I finished taking photos with a group of men and as I turned to walk away, I was "goosed" firmer than anyone had ever been. I didn't know who did it because the entire group played innocent. I felt humiliated and I wanted to leave the event, but I was the headliner and still had another couple of hours on the clock with hundreds more guests to meet. I spent the rest of the time trying to block out the incident. If I had been able to identify who did it, I would have asked if he had a wife or daughter, and how he'd like it if someone touched them that way."

Q. What has been your best job as a look-alike?

A. **Jade Roberts as Sylvester Stallone:** "I think my best gig working as a professional look-alike was being booked to work in Hollywood. I was sent a first class ticket to fly to L.A., and the producers I was hired by put me up in a room at the Beverly Hillcrest Hotel. The highlights were getting a nod from the security guard at the Twentieth Century Fox Studios, meeting Cybill Sheppard and Bruce Willis, shooting a scene for ABC's hit series *Moonlighting* and seeing myself credited as a guest star at the end of the show when it aired. P.S. I still get residual checks, even though they are minuscule!
This business has sent me to places and introduced me to people that I probably never would have experienced. And the pay isn't bad either! As a celebrity look-alike performer, you get to experience some of the glamour and pampering without the loss of privacy that the actual stars have to endure."

Q. What is it like to look like someone like John F. Kennedy, Jr.? Can you give advice to newcomers?

David Day as John Kennedy, Jr.: "John was a very respected and admired man, so it's always a compliment when people tell me how much I resemble him. Advice to newcomers: We all want work; however, don't sell yourself cheap!!"
How creative can you get? Going the extra mile to present yourself in a creative way will allow more agents more reasons to book you. I hope the following will inspire you...

Heeeeeeeeere's Johnny...

When Almost Jack (Robert Lemaster) does his mix and mingle as Jack Nicholson, he carries along a prop dog to resemble the famous little dog from the film As Good As It Gets. This is a great conversation starter and helps create the overall look for the role.

Robert Lemaster as Jack Nicholson;
Photography by Bill Solo and Ivan Doe

Can she talk...

Dee Dee Hansen as **Joan Rivers** carries a prop microphone with her as she mixes and mingles. This allows her to be "on" and instantly creates the talents Joan is known for. It allows an instantly identifiable look as well as a great way to perform her quick, witty conversations and comedy with the guests. The guests instantly feel like they are being interviewed by Joan, and this makes the guests feel special by putting the focus and attention on them.

And all that jazz...

Randy Caputo is an amazing jazz drummer, so with the creative suggestion to portray another famous drummer, **Gene Krupa**, Randy has put together a live tribute show and has dazzled the crowds at Disneyland and the Playboy Jazz Festival. He's played at private parties for Bob Hope and Michael Eisner. He recently put on a super show at the Hollywood Vintage Drum Show, performing as Gene Krupa against a Buddy Rich look-alike (Jimmy Ford). Randy brings the magic of Gene's famous drumming alive for all audiences, and gets paid to do what he loves most.

Ralph Chelli as Clark Gable; Photography by Marty Getz

Frankly my dear...

Ralph Chelli as Clark Gable is a great example of a look-alike who is able to provide agencies with an incredible impersonation of a Hollywood icon, Clark Gable, as well as offer the very well known, very recognized character Rhett Butler from the Hollywood classic film "Gone With the Wind." His dashing good looks and remarkable dead-on resemblance to legendary actor Clark Gable has allowed him years of work. At nine years old, Ralph dressed as the actor for Halloween, and now, over 21 years later, Ralph has been working full-time as one of the all-time great legends of the silver screen. "By honoring Mr. Gable in the most positive professional spirit, I am able to continue the tradition of the Old West with the creative energy of the present." If you look like someone famous, who is well known for having a famous partner, find a performer who can portray the famous partner. This is a great way to offer a more entertaining element to your "mix and mingle."

Posed as Madonna and Rosie from A League of Their Own

Denise Bella Vlasis as Madonna and Vicki Brown as Rosie O'Donnell; Photography by Michael Fiala

Get a sidekick: You can be sure that you can create more bookings for yourself when you take the time to double your act, so to speak. You can certainly double your bookings by finding a look-alike that can double with you to re-create a famous duo. Event planners and agents LOVE it when YOU do the work, in creating a new way to sell your look-alike act. Famous duos are a perfect and fun kind of booking for any event. Having a famous duo meeting and greeting together allows the talents to play off one another and gives the talents the opportunity to perform an improvisational acting scenario any time and any place. Guests seem to love duos, so get creative and begin to see how you can incorporate a partner into your act.

Some great duo examples: Tom Cruise and Cuba Gooding Jr. (from *Jerry Maguire*), Dean Martin and Jerry Lewis, George and Laura Bush, Madonna and Rosie O'Donnell, Clark Gable and Vivian Leigh, Austin Powers and Felicity, Mimi and Drew Carrey, and on and on…

Vicki and Bella create a whole new show idea by costuming themselves in the original costumes from the film *A League of Their Own*. By offering a themed idea to event planners, the two girls have since created their own one-hour show. They now perform their MO AND RO SHOW for corporate events nationwide!

Robert S. Ensler as Dean Martin and David Wolf as Jerry Lewis; Photography by Gerald M Craden

What's HOT now?

Looking like a celebrity who has a hit movie currently in theaters can open more doors for work. Once you know that the film (of your celebrity) will be a box office smash, you may consider having the right costumes made in order to achieve a similar look to your celebrity. Offer a "movie-themed character" to the agents you work for. Example: Kimberly Jones is a dead ringer look-alike of actress Nicole Kidman, and when Kim invested in a costume of Satine from *Moulin Rouge*, her bookings tripled.

Kimberly Jones as Nicole Kidman; Photography by Michael Carins

Putting your Stage Show Together

Putting together an entertaining show can also be your ticket to securing a lot of great jobs as a look-alike. Even a person who doesn't look like someone famous can often duplicate a live performance well enough to make a mark in the Impersonator Hall of Fame. Many well-known impersonators have cashed in on this idea by choreographing a performance that brings a celebrity completely to life. Whether it's a soliloquy, a lip-sync act, a live tribute band, a stand-up comedy routine, or a singing impression, a live performance can be just the ticket for a talented performer who wants to work as a successful celebrity look-alike.

Before putting your live show together, you need to decide whether you are going to hire live musicians, dancers, stage hands, and sound technicians as part of your ensemble. If you are going to perform with a live band, it will be up to you to find local musicians and put the band together yourself. Scout through the music trade papers and local music shops to find the right musicians and singers. Have your song list and sheet music ready for your musicians and/or singers to learn. When an agent calls you to hire your show, you need to explain to each agent how many musicians, back-up singers, dancers, or sound technicians will be performing with you, so your pay should include all performing members. It is not necessary to have a full band, as most corporate events have a hired band already performing for the evening. These are usually the musicians that can also play and perform your songs for your performance. Check with your agent and find out if you need to supply sheet music for each musician and be sure the band is already prepared to play your show. You can find sheet music at most music stores.

Karaoke tapes and CDs are also a great option for singing live. This way, you can save costs on hiring musicians and be ready to sing anywhere any time. Karaoke stores can supply you with music on cassette tapes and CDs without vocals. Most karaoke stores carry music by the most popular recording artists from past to present day.

Lip-sync performances are another way to create your own tribute show. We are living in a time where even our "pop star" singers make a living lip-syncing and singling over pre-recorded live tracks (no names mentioned) but these are well known singers who sell their act by lip-syncing at their concerts, award shows, and so on. Most people don't notice or care that performers lip-sync, as long as the show looks convincing, and has high energy, and is entertaining.

The art of lip-sync: There are specific techniques to lip-syncing (believe it or not), so you will want to learn how your celebrity pronounces their words, hear how they articulate the lyrics, listen to when they take a breath, and rehearse getting the timing the same. You should sing lightly over the music, to have a more realistic visual. Practice in a mirror and get every little hum, "owww", or "ya" right on time. You may wish to do what these well-known performers do so well and add a live microphone to your lip-sync performance, to allow yourself to speak in between songs, and give the feeling of a live show. Just be clear with agents that you are a lip-syncing impersonator that *speaks* in between the numbers. Live singers are expected to sing with a live band, so if you are not ready to sing live with a band, stick to lip-syncing.

With a live microphone, make sure to always have a sound check to check your live microphone and volume. Lip-sync look-alikes are requested as much as singing look-alikes for special events. Have a CD or cassette tape with three to five of the most recognizable songs professionally pre-recorded for all of your performances. Most events have a deejay that will play your CD or cassette tape for you. Make sure to have a few backup CDs with you at all times.

There are computer programs that allow you to burn CDs yourself, and this is a great vehicle for performing look-alikes who may want to have several pre-recorded shows (music) ready to go. Many of these CD-burning programs will allow you to mix music, edit music, and even create medleys all on one CD. You can even download many songs for free in MP3 format, from file-sharing sites on the Internet. If you do not have access to a computer, there are studios that can do this for you, or you may wish to ask around to see if anyone you know has a computer set up to do this.

Before telling agents to book your show, be sure that you have rehearsed sufficiently, memorized your routine, and arranged all the details of hired musicians, dancers, or sound technicians. When you arrive at the event, you will need to arrive early enough to have a proper sound check. Check the sound system, the lighting, and the stage. You are responsible for any required tapes or CDs, and in some cases, your own microphone. Communicate your needs to the sound and light people.

Have a printed list of songs in the order you will perform them, in case they need to stop the music or follow specific stage instructions for your performance.

When booked to perform a show, you should discuss the arrangements with your agent. Be sure to ask about a dressing room or a place near the stage to make any costume changes.

Your agent should be clear with you about what time your show is expected to go on. You will need to know if you should arrive in makeup or if you are to get ready at the event. I suggest that you do your hair and makeup at home and then change into your costume after you arrive at the venue. If you are provided with an unaccommodating changing area such as a bathroom or kitchen (which happens often), you'll be glad that all you have to worry about is your costume. Remember to collect your CDs, tapes, and/or costumes after your performance is over.

When putting a band and live show together, be aware of your focus and direction. Make sure that your performers have the same focus and dedication. Remember that stepping into the shoes of an idol, rock star, or legend can be a lot harder than it looks. The misconception of many people who watch impersonators is that an impersonator is instantly loved because of the star they emulate - but the opposite can be true. People will expect you to be *better* then the original. Even if you make the same mistakes as the artist, people may criticize you twice as hard. This is why it is so important not to lose who you are as you begin to impersonate someone else. In the end, you're just an entertainer who is portraying another entertainer. Like any kind of stage performing, if you're honest with yourself by keeping yourself grounded, then your humble intentions will more likely be embraced by your audiences.

Finding Your Band

You can find musicians by publishing an ad in your local band and music magazines. Newspapers and even the Internet all have classified advertisements for musicians and singers. It is best to not give your personal phone numbers or information, as you will need to screen the people who respond to your ad. A pager number and voice mail is best. When you do decide on possible prospects for your band, make sure they understand your vision clearly, so your concepts do not get changed by another's desire to change or control. A safe meeting ground is always best when coming together for the first few times. You will need to decide on a rehearsal studio and future details arranging your new band.

Once you get your musicians and performers together, you will need a cassette demo tape that will showcase your live tribute show for generating gigs and future booking agents. Find a multi-track studio (again, you can find one in your local musicians' trade papers or in the Yellow Pages) and record 1-3 songs with your band. Make sure your band is prepared before you go into the studio. Studios charge by the hour, so it is best to be totally prepared. Make arrangements ahead of time as to costs per hour. There are many people with home studios now, so shop around. Be prepared, strong, and grounded, but have fun! Remember - when you're on stage, let your light shine from within, and then you will enjoy the show as much as the audience.

Having a live Tribute Show can showcase all of your musical talents. Singer David Brighton performs an amazing live tribute to legendary singer David Bowie.

David Brighton as David Bowie; Photography by Lesley Bohm

Choreographing Your Tribute Show

Finding a choreographer:

54

Having a fully choreographed performance is a great way to get yourself and your show booked for work. Adding back-up dancers, singers, and musicians to your show will allow you to be a self-contained, ready-to-go tribute performer.

If you do not have the experience of choreographing a show, you will want to hire a **professional choreographer** to bring your vision to life. You can hire someone to help map out your ideas and make your show come to life with the expertise of steps, movement, and choreography to match your celebrity. A professional choreographer can also help you find the right backup dancers for your show.

I am an avid believer that the right choreographer can bring your performance to a new level of professionalism.

Having a choreographer is well worth the investment for any impersonator who wants a strong stage show or a better understanding of how to move like their celebrity. A choreographer can study a music video, film, or stage performance and have the ability to re-create the steps accurately for you, your cast, and your crew. A choreographer can also assist you by teaching the steps to your cast, allowing you to concentrate on perfecting the impersonation of your celebrity - and that is a great thing! If you are traveling with a tribute show, you may wish to add the choreographer to the overall budget of the show. If you have the original choreographer of your show with you through all of your travels, you will have their assistance and organization in keeping the backup dancers, singers, and musicians in check, in addition to having them help with the costumes, choreography changes, lighting, and communications between the impersonator, the producer, and the back-up crew. Some choreographers have a **dance captain** that they work with who can also take care of all of these details.

Musical celebrities and actors all use the aid of a professional choreographer, and some artists have become more famous because of the hard work of the choreographer. Brilliant choreographers like Bob Fosse, Michael Peters, Jamie King, and Tina Landin (my personal favorite), have paved the way to help create and mold celebrities into superstars through innovative, moving, and memorable choreography.

Like a great director, a professional choreographer can bring an artist to life and turn an ordinary performer (or song) into something extraordinary! A great choreographer has the skills to work with dancers and non-dancers a like and help an artist look like a polished professional even if the artist has never danced a single step before.

Being a dancer myself, I was aware of the importance of a choreographer for my Madonna tribute show. I wanted to bring my show to a level of professionalism that would allow me to get booked in the same shows with the leading "top impersonators." Impersonating an artist like Madonna, I was also aware that my visual performance needed the help of a professional to re-create the magic of Madonna live.

How I found the perfect choreographer: I was not sure how to look for someone to choreograph a look-alike show, so I went to the Debby Reynolds dance Studio in Burbank, CA, and asked if they could suggest a choreographer to work with me. They gave me the number of Heidi Anderson Jarrett, and explained that Heidi is a professional choreographer who has studied dance extensively. She has worked for many top impersonators, show producers, and even real celebrities that needed a "professional" to help bring an impersonation to life through movement. Heidi has even been hired to help actress Bridgett Fonda become Marilyn Monroe for a feature film. I knew Heidi had the expertise to bring out the best in my natural abilities as a performer, and I felt very comfortable knowing she was already skilled in her work.

Heidi worked one-on-one with me to improve my movements as Madonna and then helped in the hiring of backup dancers, the editing of music, the production of my show, and the overall choreography.

Heidi has created and personally choreographed my show(s) to emulate all of Madonna's greatest moments in film and stage. Her ability to pay close attention to detail has personally helped me get all the impersonation even more exact. I have hired Heidi to travel with my show and work as the dance captain and my personal business partner. She has also worked with me on video and film shoots, helping me with movement or dance steps. Heidi has the perfect combination of professionalism, flexibility, sense of humor, and (most importantly) brilliant, creative visions and movement for my work. We have a perfect balance of friendship and business skills together, and this allows us to continue to create all kinds of possibilities together. Heidi also brings out an enthusiasm in me with each new project, and this inevitably shows on stage.

If you are going to impersonate a celebrity who is known for full productions, dance steps, or specific moves, you will want to find a choreographer that you can work with, and together you can create a dynamic tribute show. Calling around to dance studios or talking about your needs to others in the industry will help get the word out that you are looking for a choreographer that best suits your needs. You will want to feel comfortable with this person and be able to share your thoughts and ideas to develop a show that feels right to you. You can contact Heidi with any questions you have about choreography and/or finding the right choreographer for you.

Rehearsing Is Part of Your Show's Success!

Bella, Heidi, and dancers;
Photography by Johnny G Photography

Heidi rehearses Bella and her dancers for the filming of a BBC documentary.

Putting On the Hits:

Q. How does someone put together a show that has lots of visuals, costumes, and choreography?

A. **Tatiana Turan as Jennifer Lopez:** "Finding a choreographer is an important part of the process in becoming a professional look-alike. You want to make sure that you and the choreographer understand each other and that you both are willing to develop and implement your vision. This is most important when you are putting a look-alike show together and you need the performance to look as similar to your celebrity's presentation as possible. I am fortunate that one of my dearest friends, Heidi Jarrett, is a choreographer (and a brilliant one

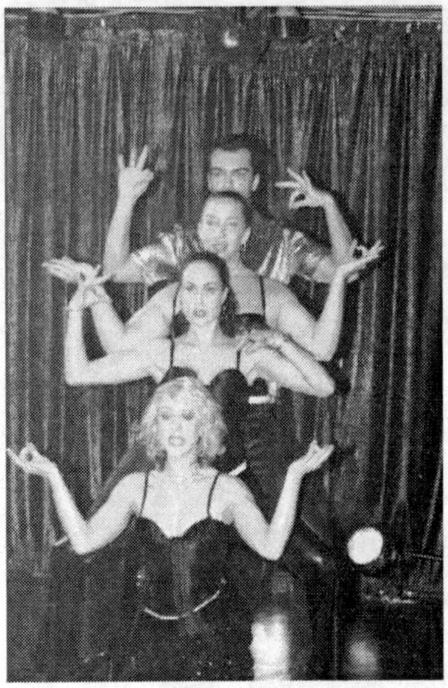

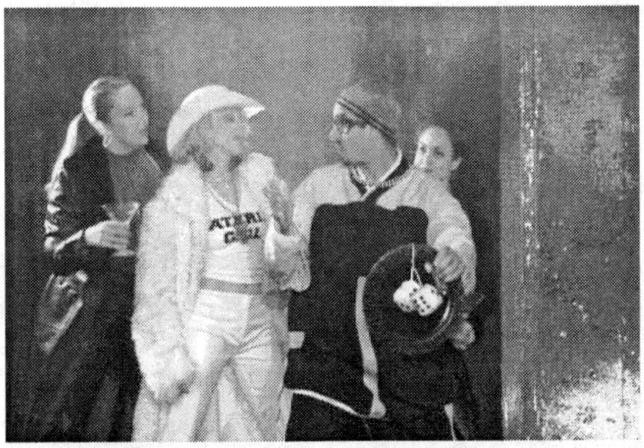

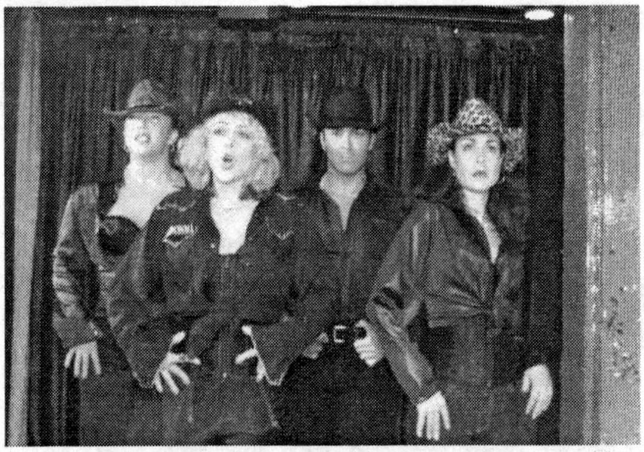

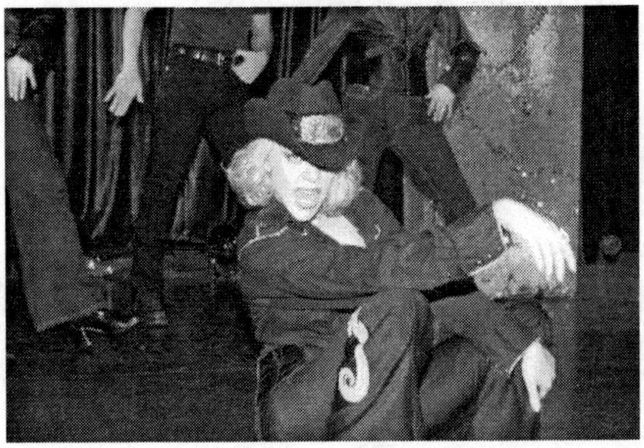

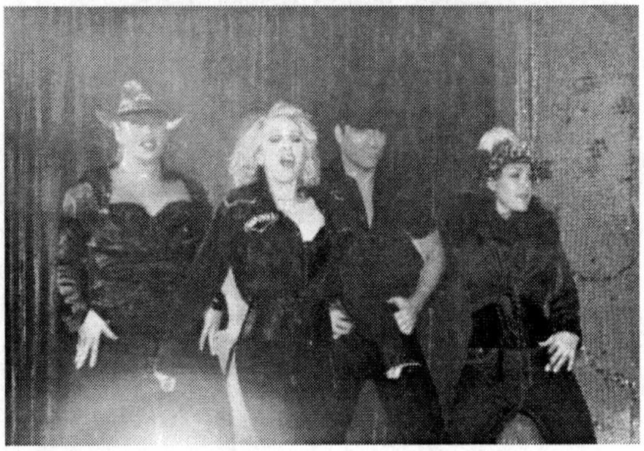

at that!) who has been hired by many of the top impersonators in L.A. If you don't have that luxury, however, referrals are always a good way to get in touch with a choreographer. Local dance studios are another great source for finding a professional. I would suggest going to a dance studio and watching their dance classes to see how they teach class, work with people, and share their general style. Most great choreographers are also dance teachers, and they teach classes in between choreography jobs to keep their craft sharp.

You will want to observe how they interact with their class and how they communicate their choreography. Notice how the students respond to the teaching and interact with the teacher. These are very important details you will want to pay close attention to. **Finding good dancers** is just as important as finding a good choreographer. Your dancers are very important to your success in making your stage show strong. Go to dance studios and watch a few dance classes to see which dancers have the performance quality and technique you are looking for. You may also consider putting up some audition notices on the billboards of the studios and/or holding an audition yourself. You may want to find your choreographer before you hold your audition, as the choreographer can be very helpful in the audition process, helping teach the dancers a combination or routine, and having the understanding to help you choose the best candidates for the job. Choreographers may also have dancers available that they already prefer to work with.

Before you begin to put your show together, you will want to have an overall vision and sense of what you want to come across in your show. For example, as Jennifer Lopez, I want to make sure my performances stay as authentic as possible to the original star! So my first step is studying and watching her concerts, videos, and interviews over and over again to ensure that I am staying true to her persona and energy. I want to make sure that it is lighthearted and fun, because let's face it, we are not that person, we are merely portraying them in as close a way as possible. That's what I find so entertaining about this line of work in the first place. The audience knows that you are not the real celebrity and so the closer you can get to being *like* the real thing, the more your audiences will get a kick out of your performances and feel they are really entertained!

Paying dancers: As a professional dancer who has been dancing for other look-alikes for years, this is a topic that is close to my heart and very important to cover. The best way to hire dancers is by looking for them in dance studios, word of mouth, or holding an audition with a choreographer when possible. However, I am more concerned with the "how to pay dancers" issue. One thing to keep in mind when paying the dancers is that they are there to enhance your performance/show, so they are an integral part of it and it is important to appreciate this about them and let that show in their pay as much as possible! Bella, whom I've been fortunate enough to work with for years, is a perfect example of a performer who recognizes her dancers as being just as important as herself!! You as the look-alike are the main event, so to speak; however, the dancers are working right behind you - or maybe even beside you - making sure that you shine that much more. Keep in mind, too, that they will have to rehearse a number of times to help put the show together. You will want to tack on some extra money for their rehearsal time. Often times, the dancers get the "raw end" of the deal or are cut out of the show all together due to budget, but when possible you should always try to keep in mind how much they can add to the quality of your show and quote a price for them accordingly. Selling your show as a package deal, where the dancers are already included, is strongly advised!! It is best to sell your show "as it is," so that when the agents call you for work, you can give the price of the SHOW and insist that your entire SHOW be booked, not just you individually. Once in awhile you may have an agent or producer say they have their own dancers, but your dancers already know your routines and show, and having to teach new dancers the show will take more time, energy, and money. If you are able to present your show complete with dancers, costume changes, and great choreography from the very start, you will be self-contained and agents will appreciate that they have one less step to worry about!

Advice: Study, study, study! There is nothing like popping in that CD, DVD, or video and just listening and watching your subject over and over again! You can have the look all you want, but if you don't move like the star, talk like the star, and carry the same essence as the star, ain't nothin' gonna help! Makeup, wigs, and costumes are great but you have to capture and
portray their star quality and let it shine through YOU!"

Tatiana Turan as Jennifer Lopez;
Photography by Johnny G

Q. Does being an impersonator hurt your career as a singer or musician?

A. **Romeo Prince as The Artist (Prince):** "Actually, no, it has done the opposite for me. It has opened many doors for me as a singer/performer. At first I was reluctant to work as a look-alike, because I had my own ambitions of performing and writing my own original music, but after taking the stage for the first time in the image of Prince, I was swept away by the energy and enthusiasm of the crowd. Even though they knew I wasn't him (Prince), they were able to appreciate what I did as a performer more than I had ever experienced. From that moment, I decided to commit myself to working as a live tribute performer. I began putting musicians together, arranging shows, and choreographing the dancers, backup singers, and musicians.

Essentially, this is how I learned how to work as a producer.

My experience as a look-alike taught me more about the music industry, and has allowed me to produce myself as an artist, writer, arranger and producer. I have recorded my own music and signed many other talents to my production company because of my years as an impersonator. I have had the opportunity to travel the world and see things I may have never had the opportunity to see. I have learned so much about life."

Q. Do impersonators perform Legend type shows for corporate events?

A. **Brenda Miller as Bette Midler:** "Yes, all the time. They are performed in a format similar to a Legend style show, with several impersonators in one big show. I've have been hired to perform in hundreds of one-nighter Tribute Shows. These shows are put together for corporate clients, and can be very intimidating to someone who may not know what to expect. You generally have one day to rehearse, and then you have to perform to charts that you provide to a band you've never met before. Very scary! The clients pay thousands of dollars and expect your "twenty minutes" to be the best they ever seen. Accommodations are not always provided, and you just may find yourself having to get ready in the restroom (along with all the guests at the event).

Brenda Miller backstage at the Golden Rainbow Foundation Mandalay Bay Storm Theater with dancers Andrew Branche, Linda Green, Scott Lockwood, Marlena Overbey and choreographer Scott Barnard;
Brenda Miller Photography

Q. What has been your best job as a look-alike performer?

A. **Betty Atchison as Cher:** "That's easy - performing for Celine Dion and her husband Rene, for an intimate party of family and friends on her private yacht for her 32nd birthday. Celine got so excited. She is even more beautiful in person. Celine and Rene are sweet, wonderful, loving people. It was an honor to be in their presence."

Barbara Hyde as Mimi Bobeck;
Photography by Sharon Hyde

Q. What was your worst stage nightmare?

A. **Barbara Hyde as Mimi from The Drew Carey Show:** "At an awards show several look-alikes were asked to go on stage for a group photo and I backed up to allow a fellow look-alike to pass in front of me and *Pow!* I was up to my nose in stage. I fell into a hole! I was in shock, but was I left to languish? No! The gentleman nearby got me out...not an easy task getting *Mimi* out of a hole!"

The Variety of
Work Available

The following listings are job descriptions that are standard samples of work available. As the industry grows, so do the opportunities for work.

You can begin to search for jobs that are already available to professional look-alikes for hire. You can also begin to create work ideas for yourself and either book yourself or have your favorite agent follow up on your creative booking idea. For the particular kind of work you're hoping to find, I always suggest finding an agent, a manager, or a person you trust to assist you and represent you.

- Acting
- Casinos
- Children's Events
- Charity Work
- Cruise Ships
- Drag Shows and Female Impersonation
- International Media
- Legend Type Shows
- Night Clubs
- Photo Doubles and Stand-Ins
- Print Work
- Telegrams
- Theme Parks
- Trade Shows and Conventions
- Voice-Overs

Let's go over some of these jobs in detail and hear what other experts have to say...

Acting

To BE or not to be...

You will need basic acting experience to book yourself for television, stage, and film work as a look-alike talent. Acting classes are a great way to learn the general techniques you will need to know. If you do not have any skills in acting, you may wish to find a local acting class at your local college or acting studio. In many situations, as a look-alike, the people who hire you will expect you to have these kinds of skills, and may just hand you a script to memorize at your next corporate event.

If you are an actor first, then this is a great way to open more doors. Look-alikes are sent to many television auditions, and the performers with polished acting skills will have better possibilities to land the desired role. Can you memorize lines on a moment's notice? Can you take direction? Interact with other actors on stage? Working as a look-alike, you will most likely get a call to go to an audition of some kind. It will be solely your decision if you wish to go to the audition, and I have added some basic "what to's" to give you an idea of what to expect.

At your first audition: You will need to bring 1-2 head shots, a resume, and the contact number of the person who called you for the audition. Be warmed up, and made up as your character, unless the director requested otherwise. You will be called into a private room, where the director and/or casting person will ask you some questions (name, availability, etc.). They may take a Polaroid photo of you and ask you to fill out a sheet with general questions.

• When you enter the room, you may be videotaped. This is for the director to study later. You may have only 1 minute, and probably no longer than 10 minutes.

• The casting people will ask you to slate your name to the camera (speak you name to the camera) and give profiles (stand to the left, center, then at right angles for the camera). At some auditions you may be asked to read from a script or for projects that require more acting, and you may be asked to prepare a short monologue for your audition. Many auditions are short and quick in time, and the most time consuming part is usually waiting in line for your turn. Some auditions may have you come to a call-back audition, which is a second audition for the same directors and casting people, so they can get a second look at you and your skills. Call-back auditions are for the remaining few selected performers that are all being considered for the same one role. Your agent will get a call (or not) if you are chosen for the part.

Remember, auditions allow you to hone your skills as a performer and they can be great practice, a way to meet new faces and most importantly *network*.

Try to remain detached from any outcome whenever you go to auditions. It is not uncommon to "get the part" and spend time to rehearse, get costumed and made up, and even shoot the film project - and STILL the project gets cancelled. Hundreds of film projects (daily!) get dropped, cancelled or shelved, so getting your hopes up after every audition will leave you feeling like a roller coaster. Choose to go to auditions for the experience, meet new people, and toughen up (and hopefully lighten up) to the process.

Auditions are part of a performer's experience, so keep your personal feelings aside and understand that the casting decisions have little or nothing to do with you personally. Casting decisions are determined on several factors, and are not to be taken to heart by you, should you not get the part you hoped for. Going to auditions will make you stronger in attitude and performance. If you can remain detached about the outcome of an audition, you will have the audition process mastered.

The opportunities and variety of acting opportunities for professional look-alikes range in type, and your professional acting experience will determine which kinds of acting jobs you can get for yourself.

The following are typical acting jobs available for the talented look-alike with acting experience:

- **Corporate events:** Corporate event acting jobs can include performing at a corporate event awards shows and working with other people from the company that has hired you. Many times, you will have a script with lines to memorize. Try to get your script in advance to memorize your lines before the job.

- **Film:** Working in film as a look-alike requires being hired as an "actor" first, and a look-alike talent *second* for **television, commercials, music videos, feature films, low budget films, independent films, student films, corporate videos**, and **international film projects**. Most directors prefer to hire professional actors rather than look-alikes, but if you can submit yourself for film projects as an actor, you may just have a better chance at landing the role for yourself. Many film producers and directors assume that look-alikes do not have acting experience and ability. We know this is not true, as many very talented look-alikes are professional actors FIRST and book jobs like feature films and national television shows because of their talents. As a matter of fact, the reason many great look-alikes experience great success is because they are actors first. If you are looking to do more acting in film, I suggest keeping your look-alike resume and photos separate from your regular acting promotion. You can use your look-alike skills to get you jobs, but keep the look-alike profession in its own separate place while working with industry people.

• **Special event specialty:** Special events and corporate events may ask you at some point to memorize names and/or information about the company you are working for. These can be spontaneous requests from your agent or client, but you may be asked to do some kind of sketch acting at any of your corporate event bookings.

• **Other situations for look-alike actors:** Other acting jobs available to the look-alike talent include getting hired to re-create a famous movie scene live for a special event, corporate event, or video. You should have your part memorized, and if you are booked to re-create a famous scene from a film or stage play, get your part down as close to the original as possible.

• **Stage shows:** Your acting request may be for a live stage performance. Stage productions, live musical productions, and even tribute shows may require some dramatics as part of the show. With look-alike work, you will want to be ready for just about any kind of acting request, especially for live theater and stages.

As a look-alike, you will (sooner or later) be requested to do some kind of acting, so be prepared as much as possible!

A clearer understanding from a working professional actor and exceptional impersonator...

Do you think doing look-alike work helps or hurts actors working professionally?

Kurt Meyers as Indiana Jones/Harrison Ford: "It's a double-headed sword. Sometimes a casting director will not cast me in something because I look too much like Harrison. If a director decides to cast a look-alike in something, then they may expect to get the same acting talent as the person that the look-alike resembles, and that may not always be the case. However, looking like someone can also be a blessing, such as the case when Diet Coke was looking for an actor who looked like Harrison Ford for a national television commercial. When I walked into the audition, the director of the commercial could not believe how much I looked like Harrison. I got the commercial. They used all the original actors from the first film *Raiders of the Lost Ark*, and me."

When you work as a look-alike, do you portray the actor, or the character from the actor's film?

"I prefer to work as the character Indiana Jones. Since Indiana is a character that Harrison has played in a film, it gives me more freedom as an actor to give life to the character the way I would interpret it. People already have a set idea of how Harrison would be, so playing Indiana is much more fun."

Are look-alikes expected to know how to act?

"I think that if you are hired for any kind of acting work, you are expected to be at least a somewhat believable performer, no matter what the job is. So you should be able to 'act your way out of a paper bag' in any circumstance. Remember, you are a professional entertainer, and a look-alike is no different from any other actor. In fact, I think you are even more under the gun to do double duty as a representative of a person in the entertainment field and as an actor yourself. Look-alikes are as much actors as any other actor out there and if someone wishes to work in this field professionally, they are going to have to act, in person or on celluloid, and they will need some kind of experience to do so. I find that directors and producers of non-union film projects are less picky about who they hire. With non-union jobs, you can have a little less acting experience. Union acting jobs are very particular when casting actors, and they expect experience and professionalism from the performers they cast.
I have been blessed to have worked professionally, both as me the actor and as a look-alike for film, commercials, and television. I look at it like this - if I get hired for a job or if I do not, I'm fine with that! I KNOW I can act my way out of a paper bag; after all, I've been doing it all my life."

- ***Trade Papers:*** Magazines designed for actors, dancers, and performers. These papers can be found at news stands, magazine shops and stands, bookstores, libraries, and on the Internet. There are several to choose from, most commonly *Drama-Logue, Daily Variety, Casting Call,* and *Hollywood Reporter*.

- ***Acting Break Down:*** A list compiled daily containing that day's casting needs by producers, directors, and casting agents. Most licensed agencies get these breakdowns daily and some look-alike agents also get them. You can also find casting notices and the breakdown listings on many casting websites on the Internet.

Casinos

Good as it Gets....

As a look-alike talent, you may find yourself booked at casinos for corporate events, special events, filming, or a Production Show. Casinos provide an exciting atmosphere for guests, and adding celebrity look-alikes is always a hit. When seeking work in ongoing Production Shows, you should submit your materials to the show's producers and/or casting departments. Word of mouth is always a great way to find out when auditions are being held, and then, of course, if you are an independent-thinking kind of talent, you can get yourself booked by taking the extra steps required.

The following is a great example of a talented guy who does just that, and he looks just like Jack!

Can performers find and create work opportunities for themselves?
What kind of advice can you give?

Almost Jack, Jack Nicholson Impersonator: "When promoting yourself as a Hollywood impersonator, you should begin by finding out where your character best fits in - where you can shine as a star, and where the celebrity you impersonate fits the theme of the venue you are performing at. Every venue is different, so you will want to work in an atmosphere that best suits your celebrity. Since I perform as a highly recognizable and likeable star, it makes it easy for me to perform almost anywhere. Agents and event coordinators can easily sell my act to all kinds of events such as corporate parties, Oscar parties, comedy clubs, cruise ships, theater openings, and trade shows."

In Almost Jack's many years as a celebrity look-alike, the jobs he's enjoyed the most were working in casinos as Jack. Here are some of his tips on getting those kinds of jobs:

Go to a bookstore and buy the latest casino guide. Every year there is a guide put out called *The American Casino Guide*. It costs about $15.00, and can be found in the games section of all major bookstores. This book is filled with phone numbers and mailing addresses for over 700 casinos. To get your act booked at a casino, start by calling the 800 numbers and find out who the booking people are at each casino you are interested in. Get the name and address of each booker, and send them your promo packet, along with a bio, a picture, and sometimes a video.

Follow up with a call about two weeks after sending your promotional pack. If they have never booked a celebrity look-alike, you can certainly introduce the idea to them and help the casino start a new addition to their hired entertainment.

You will be amazed by the huge number of casinos spread across our great country. I love Las Vegas, but thanks to a large number of Native American casinos, the elements of Vegas are now developing in more areas in all states.

Always provide a class act. Casinos usually hire look-alikes to help promote the casino, to promote a show, or to act as the featured performer in a Legends type show.

When you have been hired to work in a casino, remember that you are a temporary representative of the casino. I like to think of it as being a "goodwill ambassador" and an extension of the casino management. You will want to be comfortable with mixing and mingling with people. While you are working, you should be on your best behavior - entertain and involve the guests in your act as much as possible without ever interfering with casino guests while they gamble. Always be polite, even if the celebrity you're impersonating isn't. For example, when I perform as Melvin Udahl (Jack's character from the movie *As Good As It Gets*), I choose to portray the softer, more charming Melvin, rather than the rude, impatient Melvin - the nicer Melvin goes over better when dealing with the public.

Be sure to get the details of your contract in writing. Pay will vary depending on what you have been hired to do. When you are booked for more than 1-3 days, part of your contract should include that the casino provides accommodations of room and board, three meals a day, and your paycheck at the end of each performance (be sure to get this in writing in your contract). To work at a casino (out of state) for the whole day, I usually charge $800.00- $1000.00.

Promote the casino while you are working. If you have been hired to promote an event, you may suggest handing out literature or material that promotes the shows. I have handed out free tickets, roses, gambling coupons, etc. All supplied by the casino, and many times after I suggest it. You may be the casino's first look-alike hired, so your suggestions will be appreciated.

Picture taking is important. People love to have their pictures taken with their favorite celebrity. In some casinos, there are strict rules about using cameras in gambling areas. Make sure you find out the guidelines and rules from management before you start posing for photos. Many times, there is a designated area for just that purpose. A theater lobby or even the main casino lobby is usually the best location for photo shoots. Some casinos even provide a security guard to walk with you, and it actually helps bring more attention and makes for a more authentic act.

Almost Jack's final tip for casino success? "Have fun! I wish you luck with your career as a celebrity impersonator."

Children's Events

Young at Heart...

Performing for young people can be an excellent way to begin working as an entertainer. Performing for young audiences will allow you to experience honest feedback from your performances and help you practice and polish your entertaining skills with a more accepting audience. Children are mostly easy to please and accepting, and they love to get involved as you perform. Parties and celebrations for the younger audience is another fun way to get your feet wet, if you're just starting out. Bar and Bat Mitzvahs, Sweet 16 parties, Graduation, or Birthday parties are always happening. These shows generally require a lip-sync or live performance as well as photo opportunities with the party guests. Sometimes you are hired to be a "party starter" and you can end up being the "celebrity baby sitter" in so many words. You will want to be good with kids, and know how to entertain and interact with them.

Some performers begin a career by entertaining at children's events, and others excel and continue to specialize in creating work for themselves by offering a unique, loving way to give with their talents.

Before you begin to consider working as an entertainer for children's events and parties, listen to someone who is exceptionally talented and is a creative performer who is especially patient with young people. Become a kid again with these tips from Annette Pizza, Specialty Children's Entertainment:

"Ask yourself if you posses the following qualities:
- Patience
- A sense of humor
- An outgoing, friendly personality
- A love of working with kids
- A versatile set of characters you can perform
- Communication skills
- Creative ideas

You should understand that different age groups will generally require different kinds of entertainment.
Children between the ages of 1 and 10:

Performing a well-known character that children recognize from movies, books, and fables will go over best and always bring excitement to any party. You can create your own clown character or costumed themed characters such Belle, the Little Mermaid, Princess Jasmine, Barbie, Rag Doll, Peter Pan, and even the Easter Bunny.

Most costume rental shops can rent you these kinds of costumes for a reasonable price, so before you decide which character you wish to perform on a regular basis, renting a few different costumes can be a great way to figure it out.

Some agencies can train you and even supply you with costumes, but they will pay less for your performance.

Examples of my rates:
Clown: $ 55 an hour, and up to $125 for 2 hours.
Characters: $ 65 an hour, and up to $150 for 2 hours.

Costume tips:
When putting a costume together, make sure it is bright and colorful. You could get a bright wig to add to the costume. Children love color, sparkles, and things that they can touch. Avoid things like a white clown face, as most toddlers are scared of the white paint on the face. Create your own clown face by using bright watercolor face paint. You can even (after agreement of the parents) bring watercolor paints and paint the faces, hands, or arms of the kids. Watercolor paints are best because grease paint is very hard on the skin, it can be messy, and many kids are allergic to it.

Show ideas:
Basic entertainment for kids can include making animal balloons, performing magic shows, playing games, playing music, and teaching dance steps. Each party will vary depending on the age of the children, how many kids are in attendance, and the amount of time you are booked for.

Animal balloons are always a great opener for kid's parties. The best high-quality balloons are by qualatex. To blow up balloons, you will need a balloon pump, which you can buy from a catalog or at a party store. You can buy a book containing instructions on how to make balloons in various shapes. Practice making the balloons so that you can be fast at the party. The most popular balloons are hats, dogs, flowers, swords, and hearts. Making balloons can take 10 to 20 minutes of time for an average children's party.

A magic show can be a fun way to entertain. This can take up to 15 to 20 minutes of your act. Find a magic store in your area and pick up six or seven tricks. Most popular are the magic coloring book, magic crayons, shrinking glove, shrinking or vanishing card, needle through a balloon, disappearing ink, and a good magic deck of cards. Use the children attending the party as assistants for each trick. Have prizes and easy "give away" gifts for all the kids.

Games can take another 15 to 20 minutes of your act. Some games you may want to use are Pin the Nose on the Clown, Freeze Dance, Simon Says, Bean Bag Toss, Musical Chairs, coloring or drawing contests, or even the Hokey Pokey. Again, have prizes to give out to everyone.

Face painting is a fun way to involve each child. Remember to get a parent's okay with this in advance. Bringing Q-tips to apply paint is best, for sanitary reasons. If you use brushes, be sure to clean them between children, after each paint application. Having stick-on jewelry and temporary tattoos can also be a fun way to decorate each child. Eyeliners and lip liners are great tools to draw with. Again, swiping each liner with rubbing alcohol after each application is best when you are dealing with several children.

Some popular painting ideas: Clown faces, flowers, butterflies, spiders, turtles, hearts, and of course famous characters. Be careful when applying makeup, since small children can squirm or move unexpectedly. Bring a small mirror so kids can see the paint when you are finished. Always clean up your mess.

Ideas and opportunities:
If you know someone who performs for children, you may wish to go with them to their next job or party, so you can see how they interact and relate to the children. You can learn by observing, and then gather your own ideas on how you want to put your own performance together. Volunteering your time and performances to children's hospitals and/or charities will also groom your special abilities with children.

With teenage audiences:
You will want to perform as someone who will appeal to the 13- to 19-year old age range. Most teen idols from teen magazines, MTV, or television and film are the best suggestions for this target audience. In the case of teenagers, a celebrity impersonation is going to be best.

Pay: Generally ranges from $150 to $250. With many parties for children, budgets will vary. Some parties will be in private homes and in this case, budgets are much smaller. Sometimes a party will be held in elegant hotels and country clubs. In this situation the parents (or the people involved in hiring the entertainment) will have a bigger budget and expect a more elaborate performance. For these kinds of parties and events, you will need high quality music, costumes, and performances. There will most likely be a deejay who can play your music on a good sound system, and you may be on a stage or dance floor. By asking questions of the agent who calls you for the job, you will have a better idea of the party being booked. When performing a smaller-budget party, you will most likely need a boom box when traveling to each job so that your act is always self-contained. Always have extra batteries and/or extension cords so that your show can be performed just about anywhere. You should perform one to three popular songs, providing the music. You can involve the kids in your act as much as possible. You may wish to bring other popular music to play, once your show is finished, in case the kids wish to continue dancing.

Other ideas:
Write a rap, poem, or song about the guest of honor and perform it. You can gather information on the person by speaking to the parents or party planners ahead of time. Ask about funny personal stories and information that may be fun to include in your act. You will want the birthday person or guest of honor to feel special and have most of the spotlight on them. Young people love to learn, so teaching dance moves or allowing them to learn something from you is a way to hold their interest for a good amount of time. Remember, younger audiences will have a shorter attention span, so holding their attention by inviting their participation and giving them things to do, see, and learn are all great elements to incorporate into your act. After performing your show, you will want to stick around and pose for photographs, sign autographs (think of a fun way to sign your name rather than using the handwriting of the celebrity you are impersonating), and talk with the kids. Having fun and using simple "give away" items like costume jewelry or fan memorabilia of the celebrity you are impersonating can be calculated in your total price, and is a memorable way to give a little extra to the kids.
For birthdays you will need to stick around for birthday cake and sing "Happy Birthday." Be ready to answer loads of questions, and take lots of pictures.

Things to know:
Always call the agent the day before you are to perform. Go over details for the event; be sure you have exact directions to the party, and a phone number in case an emergency keeps you from getting there; if your appearance is a surprise, what time you are to check in vs. what time you are performing; and the total price and when you are to be paid. Note: Tips are not expected, and should not be expected; however, if someone is generous enough to offer, be gracious and discreet if you choose to accept.
When you arrive at the party, introduce yourself to the parents and ask where they want you to set up. They can then help to gather the kids. Your show can be entertaining for all the party guests, so encourage the adults to join in, too.

Bottom line:
Have fun and be a kid yourself! Performing for young people can remind you to discover the child-like qualities of your own life again. Remember to play, enjoy yourself, and become child-like again, even if it is for only one hour. Sometimes one hour of your time can mean a lifetime to a young child.

Annette Pizza as
No Doubt singer Gwen Steffani;
Photography by Johnny G

Charity Work

Practice Random Acts of Kindness...

Being able to work in entertainment is a blessing and a gift that all performers should not forget. When you begin to make money with your natural-born talents, then I suggest that you may wish to remember to share those gifts with all people. There are endless ways in which you can find a way to donate a moment of your time to people who may not otherwise have the opportunity to see and experience live entertainment.
Stop and think for one moment what it would be like to be bedridden or ill. If you could not do simple things in your life like dance, get out, and hear beautiful music or singers, wouldn't it mean a lot to you for someone to bring their performance to you? If you have been blessed by living well and being healthy and capable, it is so important to remember those who are unable to because of sickness or health reasons.

The look-alike world opened to me BECAUSE of this understanding. My very first request as a look-alike was to dance for sick and homeless children, and I will never forget the impact of how a simple visit and performance brought such joy to hundreds of young children. A simple request from Mom asking me if I could come to a Christmas charity event and "dance like that girl that people say you look like" broadened my understanding as a look-alike.
It was a challenge to understand this at first, as I thought "I am not the real celebrity - what can I possibly do to cheer up anybody?" After this event and my first visit to CHOC (Children's Hospital of California), I quickly learned that most of the children wanted to meet Madonna, and for some children it was a "last request" before they went into life-threatening surgeries.
None of the children understood that I was "only a look-alike," and the thrill of a "celebrity" coming to visit them in their Hospital room was a highlight for many.
As a look-alike, early experiences like these brought my awareness to a new level. What could be more rewarding to experience in this life than knowing that a moment of time could mean making a loving difference by bringing the experience of "celebrity" to someone who may never get the opportunity to meet a star?

By giving a personal visit, song, or dance, or merely signing an autograph, you can make a lasting impression on someone's life. Thousands of children's hospitals, retirement homes, and endless charities that need entertainment will give you an opportunity to make a small difference. Find a cause that you feel passionate about, and submit your promotional materials to their entertainment department or coordinator.

Charities and nonprofit organizations can be easily found on the Internet or in your local Yellow Pages. There are some charities that offer pay for entertainment, but after you have experienced selfless giving, money, fame, or celebrity pales in comparison to the joy you will feel in your heart in experiencing this kind of connection with people of all ages and conditions.

The law of cause and effect:

Irby Gascon as Elvis and Ricky Martin: "You can chase fame your entire life and you will never feel satisfied. Being a professional singer, there was a time I used to dream of an ideal for myself. I specialize in singing classic music from the 1940's and have a sincere love and respect for the music of that generation. I was not sure what it was I was searching for - money, fame, recognition - but (like most singers or performers) it was an unattainable search that never seemed to end, like a bottomless pit.

Then I met Bella Vlasis, the author of this book, and she gave me the idea of sharing my love for 1940's music with people of that generation who were in retirement homes, convalescent homes, and care centers for the elderly.

I was not sure how to begin this process, who to call, or where I could present this idea, so I decided to open up the Yellow Pages, close my eyes, and choose the first retirement home on which my finger happened to land. I made my first call and a warm voice answered the phone. He introduced himself as Father Paul and proceeded to ask me some questions. I explained that I was looking for a way to volunteer my services as a singer, and could he point me in the right direction.

Before I knew it, Bella and I were on our way to our first retirement home to "put on a show." Father Paul and his wife Mrs. June were so impressed with our offer to perform for free that they later explained that most of the retirement homes offered compensation to their performers.

Meeting Father Paul and his wife turned out to be a blessing in disguise, as they guided me with helpful suggestions and helped me to understand how working with the elderly could turn my life into a new, much more satisfying direction in every way. They made some calls and got my act booked at several more facilities for the elderly.

The support and encouragement they gave to me was something I will never forget. Mrs. June suggested that I make a flyer and send it to more homes and hospitals. She gave me a book called *New Lifestyles*, which is a guide of listings of housing for the elderly. Before long I found myself performing and singing for the elderly almost daily.

The experience of watching the faces light up, and the heartfelt gratitude for the music I brought to their lives seemed to open my heart as much as theirs. As I performed for more people I began to understand the universal connection people can share with music. Music breaks all barriers and reaches all people in all conditions. I saw people with Alzheimer's who I thought were "checked out" come to life just by holding their hand or giving them a smile - and that experience was life-changing for me. Having the vehicle of music has also helped me realize that music can be the last form of connection a human being can experience in this life.

Music allows all people to enjoy the now - THIS MOMENT - which is all any of us really have. It allows people to forget the pain they may be experiencing, escape into a wonderful memory or good feeling, and for one minute, feel young again.

I found that the more I put my energy into this kind of work, the more doors were opening in my everyday life.

This is a Universal Law...I believe, from experience, that when you live a life of selfless giving, then life can only be more positive and fulfilling. My understanding of performing has since broadened and now I sing with a different awareness. It allows healing to take place in myself as well as for everyone who allows healing to take place within themselves.

I now have a full-time career doing what I love, and have more insight into life's purpose.

I am able to take care of my own booking schedule, sing what I love to sing, give unconditionally, and even perform with my partner Bella!"

Special note from Bella: Performing at retirement homes with Irby has allowed me to receive incredible lessons of life.

I look at age differently as I am learning that what we perceive as "old" is relative. As I am holding the hands of a ninety-five year old man who is laughing, dancing and singing, I ask myself, "How can a number (our age) matter or define us?"

I have a constant reminder that beauty (as society recognizes it) fades and it doesn't really matter WHO we once were, HOW we once looked, or the MONEY we once had...we only keep the love in our heart and that is the only thing we take with us. Dancing in retirement homes has given me the blessing of being able to share a moment with somebody's Grandpa, and that is a great joy since I no longer have that opportunity for myself. The ability to receive lessons like this is priceless and available to all of us. Selfless service will change anyone's life for certain. The best way to get over any personal problem for yourself is to give unconditionally to someone else.

Retirement Home Connections
New Lifestyles contact: www.newlifestyles.com
Phone: 800 869-9549

Lyndal Grant as Arnold Schwarzenegger: "I have worked with and/or met many look-alikes in this business. Some are very good and others are, well, not as good. The ones who bother me are the look-alikes who blur the line their own identity and their celebrity counterpart. It's very intoxicating to the ego to be afforded star treatment. Especially since we all want to be significant in our lives and know that who we are made a difference. My advice is to maintain your own identity by making a real difference. Bella is one of the best examples of this that I know - her web site reads like who's who when it comes down to her involvements with charities. As far as identities go, if I ever met the real Madonna, I would hope she measured up to Bella.
In this respect, each and everyone of us should be actively involved in charity work".

Cruise Ships

The Love Boat...

Look-alike work on a boat? You bet! Some cruise liners have regular Legend type shows nightly, and talented singing look-alikes are often the live entertainment.

Many of these live shows are Legends type shows featuring celebrity impersonators. You will need to audition for these kinds of jobs, which can generally be found in casting and trade papers or via agencies that book live singing impersonators.

These kinds of shows can be hard work, with two to three performances a day, five to seven days a week. They may book your act to be part of an ensemble of other impersonators, dancers, and musicians. These shows will generally have a running time of two weeks to six months. After being part of a longer running show, performing the same show night after night, you will learn a lot about live audiences and become a more polished and refined performer.

You will need to have plenty of live singing experience before auditioning for these jobs, and you should have a professional promotional package with you at the audition. Cruise ships have contracts that you will sign and they all vary in length, commitment, and pay. Cruise ship work is a great way to hone your skills, doing what you love while seeing beautiful parts of the world.

The following is great advice from a talent who is on a ship at this very moment...

Tell me how someone can get work on a cruise ship. What can one expect from a job on a boat?

Harmony Dean as Britney Spears: "I've worked for Princess, Premier cruise lines, and I am about to get on a Celebrity Cruise ship tomorrow morning and begin my contract for another performing job. Cruise ships are not really for those who are "free in spirit." If you are used to doing "your thing" however you want to and when, then I suggest that performing on a cruise ship may not be for you.

But if you love to travel for free, have all of your accommodations paid for, work steadily for at least 6 months, get great benefits, and receive excellent pay (usually separately negotiated, but $1200 per week is pretty standard for a "solo act") then I would suggest a cruise ship for performers. Finding out about cruise ship auditions is actually very tricky. If you want to do a "solo act" (such as performing a cabaret act or even as a production singer) the best way is to contact the ship itself and try to speak directly with the head of entertainment. It takes a couple of phone calls, but it is not impossible to do.

Usually, with my experience, video/resume and pictures are adequate to get the job.

Most shows are: Two 45-minute shows a week. Some cruise ships have a nightly show (5-7 shows per week), and sometimes they provide two (2) shows per night.

The drawbacks of ship life are:
You always have to answer to somebody. There usually is a choreographer telling you what to do and when, and even though singers are treated royally (passenger cabins and other benefits) you are still considered "crew" - therefore, boarding times/drug tests/checking in and out/boat drills/safety meetings...all of these things apply!!!

However...working on a ship is an incredible experience. I think that getting paid to see the world, make friends, and do what you love to do is the BEST reward ever. I do suggest that everyone use their networking skills, and make their phone calls, so they can at least try to see if cruising is for them."

Drag Shows and Female Impersonation

You'd Better WORK!

Female Impersonation, Drag Shows, and Illusionists are a category of their own. In the look-alike world, these acts are generally separated from basic look-alike work, as Female Impersonators are considered "Specialty" performers. Once in awhile you may have an Illusionist at a look-alike corporate event, but more often you will see brilliant drag queens performing in Drag Shows and other forms of media and entertainment.

Drag takes extra special skills, as men becoming women (or vice versa) demands so many more specifics for the performer to meet. There are some extraordinary impressionists who have gone on to star in movies, commercials, print advertisements, and their own one-(wo)man shows. Ru-Paul, Frank Marino, Jimmy James, Viva-Sex, and Chad Michael are some of the finest talents in this industry.

Chad (A Diva Live) shares his detailed expert advice for anyone hoping to break in to Drag.

Can you tell me about female impersonation? How does one find work?
Chad Michael, Illusionist (Cher, Celine Dion and more): "I got my start performing as an Illusionist in 1993 with the help of a friend who was a performer at a local club here in San Diego, CA. After seeing my first drag show, I was hooked! It was not only a matter of "I can do that!" but "I can do it better!" After seeing how much fun the performers were having and how much love and money they were getting from the audience, I knew that some sort of performance art was in my future.

Chad Michael as Cher;
Photography by Sarah Lee

As a fledgling performer, finding paid work was difficult. I did a lot of free shows, but this is something that all performers must deal with in the beginning of their careers. It's called paying your dues - something I think we're all familiar with. There can be pressure on a person working for little or nothing, so it is an ideal time to experiment with makeup techniques, character mannerisms, hair, and costumes to see what combination of these things will deliver the best illusion. It is also a good time to establish a professional reputation with the people you are working with, and network as much as possible.

Your decision about which celebrities you are going to impersonate often hinges on natural facial features, body structure, and for the truly gifted, who you sound like. My face is long and narrow, I have a prominent nose, and I am tall and lean. These are very general descriptions, but they are the true core of what I have to work with. To render a good illusion, it is best to attempt characters with features similar to yours. Experimentation with makeup techniques is the next step, to see just how much your natural features can be enhanced to look even more like the celebrity you wish to impersonate. Also, let me add that it helps if you truly enjoy the work of the celebrity you choose to impersonate; it simply adds more guts to your performance."

Some of Chad's Most Useful Tips

Study: It is important to study a character's facial features and determine how to enhance your features to look like them. The shape of eyes, brows, cheeks, and lips are unique to each celebrity and you need to learn how to literally paint them onto your existing canvas. Pictures and videos of your celebrity are the best learning tools. Start tearing pictures out of magazines and build a scrapbook.
Keep a blank tape in the VCR and hit the record button when you see anything appear on television having to do with the celebrity you
have chosen to impersonate. Study the mannerisms, style, demeanor, and spirit of the celebrity. Only by observation and experimentation can you begin to perfect their illusions. Stay focused and practice, and these lessons will become second nature.

Makeup: Learning makeup techniques is different for everyone. It helps in the beginning to have a mentor or a talented, experienced person to give you a foot up on what to do with a case full of cosmetics. A consultation with a professional makeup artist or fellow illusionist can be very helpful. Once a performer grasps the basic concepts of how to apply their makeup, experimentation and practice are the only ways to really learn and develop their own independent style of character makeup. Choosing proper cosmetics for celebrity impersonation is important.
The following products are good enough for me: Dermablend Foundation, Coty Setting Powder, La Femme Eye Shadows and Blushes, Maybelline Very Black

Mascara, Revlon Timeliner Eye Liner, Prestige Lip Liners, Ultimate Lipstique Lip Crayons, Jordana Lip Gloss, Duo Lash Adhesive, and the standard blue box false eyelashes. These are the products I have in my makeup kit right now. They are inexpensive and deliver dramatic effects. Do not be taken advantage by cosmetic sales people. Look for less expensive products with strong color pigment. Intensity is the key to creating a good illusion on stage.

Where did you get that body? Body illusion is a technique that is just as important as makeup, especially for a man transforming into a female celebrity. Padding is key. I use 1-inch high-density foam to create my hip pads. Using a pair of new fabric scissors, I carefully edge down a piece of foam cut to the general dimensions of my outer thighs, from the hip to just above the outer knee, and wrapping around onto the outer cheek of my buttocks. Once shaved down smooth
and evenly around the edges, these pads can be inserted into a pair of heavy-weight tights to achieve jaw-dropping effects. Note that several pairs of tights are needed to completely hide the hip padding. There are many different types of breast prosthetics on the market. I suggest looking at all the options before you buy. I use both silicone and foam falsies, depending on the effect I wish to achieve. As for hiding your "assets," if you are a man wearing a skin-tight body suit, do what I did - ask a friend in the business!

Hair: Finding the right hair/wig for your illusion is crucial. If you have a friend who is a hairstylist, wiggerie and start by looking for a wig with the right color and style. Do not settle for a wig that "kind of" looks like your character's hair; you will just end up spending more money on the right wig later when you are still unsatisfied. Always ask to look at catalogs and color swatches. Special orders for the right wig are often necessary and worth the wait.

Lashes: I suggest you experiment with the standard "blue-box" eyelashes. There are many different styles and it might take a few tries before you find the ones that best suit your character.

Nails: My favorite glue-on nails are the French manicure by Nalene; they look great and are inexpensive.

Costumes: As for your costumes, have them custom made; you won't regret it. You may pay a little more, but they will fit well and be exactly what you want. It is important that your costumes are recognizable to your audience; this adds so much more to the reality of your illusion.

Shoes: Larger size shoes can be found by surfing the Internet and in stores like Nordstrom Rack and Payless Shoes. Sometimes it can be difficult to find the exact style of shoe you want in a women's size 11.5. All I can say is good luck!!

Getting hired and paid: Finding work as an impersonator on a regular basis can be challenging, but it is possible. I book myself out through an agent as well as independently, dealing with club owners and promoters. A sure way to make money as a performer is to work with an ensemble cast of impersonators on a weekly basis. Investigate the clubs in your city that have weekly or nightly running shows. Earning a spot in one of these shows will undoubtedly pay your bills if you apply yourself to your craft. There are also the larger production shows like *La Cage* in Las Vegas that provide a performer with a comfortable living. I find that a combination of regular weekly ensemble cast performances along with solo bookings afford the best living for an entertainer. Each individual will find their niche in time.

My feelings for the art of Impersonation and my colleagues run deep into my heart. I love what I do. I have come to the realization after many years of working as an entertainer that this is what I was meant to do. I thoroughly enjoy the process of creating and presenting my characters. I take pride in succeeding at my craft. Giving an audience a fleeting vignette of their fantasy icon is so gratifying to me. Knowing that I have made a group of people forget their problems, if only for five minutes, makes all these years of work and diligence well worth it. The service that an impersonator provides is unique and precious. I am blessed to be a part of this industry and I am grateful to the celebrities I impersonate. The people I have worked with during the course of my career are many and varied. They have all enriched my life and taught me lessons that I could never put a price on. As Illusionists, we create magic for the world to wonder at. Being a small part of that magic makes my life complete.

There are a few things to remember during the course of one's career as a celebrity impersonator. These are the lessons I have learned over time that keep me focused and grounded:
• Never forget you are an impersonator, never cross over the line, for it may eventually land you in a mental ward. First impressions (no pun intended) are crucial.
• It is important to deliver a pleasant demeanor and professional attitude along with your look-alike performance. Remembering that I am a man in a dress underneath all the costuming keeps me in check!!
• Having a sense of humor and humility can carry a performer through many a challenging situation and also
get them repeat bookings.
• Finally, be best at what you do and do it with grace and style. Set an example with the talent you have been granted. This is how we learn. This is how we inspire. This is how we perpetuate the art. This is how we keep making magic!"

International Media

Hurray for Hollywood...

International media is a big market for look-alikes, including documentaries, television shows and commercials, product endorsements, billboards, and live appearances. By considering international media, you increase your chance of finding work opportunities for your look-alike talent. There seems to be a constant request for Hollywood doubles for international television shows and media, and the call for celebrity look-alikes is an ongoing casting call for the most famous celebrity faces.

Many times these jobs are filmed in Hollywood (as many directors love Hollywood as the back drop for filming) and many times you may need to travel to perform for these bookings.

Traveling Internationally: For bookings where you are required to travel abroad, you will want to be very specific with job details (see Travel) and work directly with an American booking agent who can better protect you.

International Media can mean days of work or hours, depending on the booking request.

International Media means dealing with many different nationalities, so communications may be somewhat different than what you are used to.

Documentaries, television, music videos, and print advertisements: You will want to negotiate your prices with the directors of the projects for any international media jobs. You can base your pay scale to match these same kinds of jobs here in the US.

For any international television shows you are hired for, your price quote can match a day rate of what you would charge for a local job.

Example: If the SAG scale for performing in a television show here in the US is $550 a day for a "specialty performer," then you can stick close to that rate for any performance on international television.

There are hundreds of documentaries always being filmed about Hollywood and many times celebrity look-alikes are hired for performance, sketch comedy, or interviews.

As each job request comes in, you will want to know where the filming will take place (locally, or will you travel?) and every detail that will be requested of you. Ask for a copy of the script and sit down with the director to clearly understand the job description. International media is constantly requesting Hollywood doubles, so sooner or later you may find yourself on the set with many different cultures filming for some very different programs (other than American films).

Some typical look-alike jobs for International Media:

- Variety shows

- Documentaries and interviews

- Filming movies and television shows to film on location

- Billboards, magazine layouts, magazine interviews, print advertisements, Internet promotions, and product endorsements

- Commercials for television shows or advertisements

- Music videos for international (well-known) artists

- Live appearances, making a speech, taking a photograph, walking into an event

Documentaries seem to be the most typical request for look-alikes in the International Media category.

My advice on filming any documentary:

When deciding if you are going to participate in filming a documentary, you should find out as many details of the project as you can BEFORE agreeing to the project.

You will want to make sure that the film project is not insulting to you or your celebrity in any way. Certain media programs like to present look-alikes in an unflattering light (think daytime television), or give examples of inexperienced people claiming to be look-alikes as a way to prove that the look-alike industry is a joke. Be incredibly selective when making decisions about what projects you will choose to participate in.

Some filming situations can mean running you through the ringer, or having you doing stunts or having you in dangerous situations that you are not capable of pulling off. A director trying to save the costs of a stunt double by hiring a look-alike can put you and everyone else involved in a compromising situation.

Most documentaries are generally **no pay**, if done interview style. Find out what is being asked of you so you can determine if you wish to participate for free. If the documentary requires you to be "in action" as your celebrity, then you will want to negotiate pay.

Here is an example of how I do it: When filming international documentaries for myself as Madonna, I have decided to "interview only" for countless documentaries with the condition that:

- My name is in the credit with contact information
- I get a copy of my performance mailed to me
- Sometimes lunch and gas budgets are allotted for me
- They come to *my house* to film me

With each film project I decide, AFTER speaking with the producers, if the publicity would be worth my time to shoot for free. In the event of performing/interviewing for no pay, the exchange of publicity was worth the one to two hours of my time. It seemed that each job I filmed led to future work for me every time.

On the occasion I was asked to look like Madonna and perform, drive (through busy streets in L.A.!), shop, work out, run, speak, sing, or dance then I would sit down with the producers and calculate my charges (which were mostly close to SAG scale). Film projects where the producers want you to work like this SHOULD be paying you, and I suggest that this is how to draw the line for whether or not you should be paid for documentary work.

As a look-alike talent, jobs like these may come up for you, so you will need to decide each time when to do it as a freebee in exchange for publicity, and when to ask for money.

Ermal as The Duke, John Wayne; Photography by Phillip Ritchie

Working with Japanese Production Companies:

Ermal Williamson as John Wayne: "I was hired to perform with an entertainment group for a one-week job in Japan. I can say with authority that the Japanese people had gone out of their way 100% to make sure that our stay with them was enjoyable. There was no pressure.
We had our schedules, we had meetings with the producers, and we had the rest of the time for rehearsals, sightseeing, and simply enjoying ourselves.
The events were of the magnitude that one would expect in Las Vegas, the audiences were appreciative, and the house was full for each performance."

As a performing look-alike you may experience that your international audiences are more expressive and impressed than American audiences with your look-alike show or appearance. Audiences in the US can be used to seeing celebrities and may not respond as enthusiastically as people from other parts of the world.
This is another reason that international media is one of the biggest ongoing jobs for look-alikes.

Many International groups like to book "Rock Stars" and Political figures

DL as Bono from U2, Amber J as Bette Midler, D. Bella as Madonna,
Irby as Ricky Martin, and Tatiana as J.Lo; Photography by Johnny G

Some thoughts of portraying an ICON:

DL as Bono (from U2): "It's about midnight, and while sitting at a dark bar in a restaurant on the edge of Sunset Boulevard I enjoy a draft out of respect to my character and a good night's work. To my right sits Madonna, Ricky Martin, and J.Lo. Bette must have slipped outside to catch a smoke. I thumb through the appetizer menu, trying to decide between a shrimp quesadilla and a macho nacho, when the friendly voice of a kind fan speaks out: "Excuse me, I don't mean to bother you, but I just wanted to say I really love your work! You guys are awesome, I've got all your CDs."
I'm flattered with personal amusement yet an outward sincerity. I reply in a soft whisper, "That's wonderful." He asks if he can buy me a pint and I graciously

decline, shaking his hand in thanks. As he leaves, I release my grip and let it fade into a "peace" sign. He smiles, walks out the door, and (in his own mind) was excited, having met a Legend. I smile, too, hoping I lived up to the fan's expectation and the Legend's integrity.

I feel that with great celebrity comes great responsibility, and part of that responsibility transfers to a look-alike. Many of the real celebrities who are lucky enough to warrant a look-alike have worked hard honing their craft and making their image and likeness marketable. In fact, the harder they work usually means more work for the look-alike. I have so much respect for my character's inspiration that any off-color portrayal of him is not something I would ever consider.

I am not the celebrity. To verbally state that I AM the real celebrity is illegal, and in the situation of hanging out with fellow look-alikes in a dark restaurant after a show, I am sometimes left with a split second to decide how to deal with an awestruck fan, hopefully without crossing the line."

DL as Bono from U2
Photography by Zanek.

92

Legend Type Shows

Viva Las Vegas...

You may have seen "Legend" shows that feature live singing impersonators in Las Vegas, Reno, Laughlin, and various casinos and nightclubs. To get hired for these kinds of live shows, you will need to be a strong live vocalist and have had a great deal of live performing experience before you audition. These shows are generally long-running shows (months or years) and usually they require the performer to sign an exclusive contract. You will need to be able to perform up to three shows a day, five days a week. You may need to relocate your living situation to accommodate availability for the show. To find out about which show is holding auditions, contact the show producer, check trade papers and casting magazines for the next auditions, check the websites of each show, network with other impersonators, and find out which agency can submit you for the next opening.

Legends In Concert™ is one of the very first look-alike impersonator shows ever. Show director/producer John Stuart has opened the door for hundreds of talented singing impersonators. The show Legends In Concert has become quite infamous and is a *must-see* for anyone visiting Las Vegas.
Legends has several talented casts of characters from past icons to present day superstars, and Legends has several different shows that travel as well. From Legends on Cruise Ships to Legends for corporate events, Legends has made its mark in the look-alike world. To audition for Legends, you will want to send your promotional package to their offices and later schedule a live audition with John himself.

The Stratosphere in Las Vegas is another wonderful Legend-type show that features talented rock star impersonators of the current day, including Madonna, Michael Jackson, Ricky Martin, and more. Another *must-see* while in Las Vegas!

What about Legends In Concert? How does someone get a job performing in this show?

Anonymous live performer from Legends In Concert: "First you send them (the show producers) a promotional package (photos, video, resume, cassette tapes) and then after about a week, you follow up with a call...and be persistent!

The show producers get a lot of people calling and it's hard for them to keep track of everybody - it's the "squeaky wheel gets the grease" idea. In order to get a spot in a show like this, you used to have to have been in the impersonator or entertainment business for a while. Now, a show producer may find a karaoke singer in a local bar here in Las Vegas, and if the producer thinks they are worth a shot at being in the Legends show they'll hire the bar singer. The singer may get bottom scale pay (the lowest pay possible) for having no previous experience. Of course this all depends on who's looking at the act. In my opinion, many of these show producers are not qualified for picking acts or talent. Show business really all boils down to the same old saying - it's *who* you know, not *what* you know!

The audition is held at the main office and you will be performing for the show's producer and sometimes whoever is involved in the show. The Producer may not always know who the character is that you are portraying, but he will still advise you and give a critique of your performance. Shows are generally presented two times a night, six days a week.

The traveling show is pretty well organized, except sometimes the sound systems are not what they should be and whatever sound you get that night is what you get. The travel expenses are taken care of and the hotel is paid for. The money used to be great, but they've cut down a bit. It's still great for a night here and there, though.
Being that I worked for them for a while now I can tell you that working for Legends is great, but a lot depends on who is your production manager.

Something else to be aware of is that after your three months is up (or however long they hire you for), they might not tell you they do not have any work for you until the last day or so. This may leave you out of work for a while until you can find something else. It's a stressful time when "change over" comes around! That's when the producer says, "Don't worry. I have work for you. I'll keep you working." Not always a guaranteed promise, though.

General pay: Starting rate used to be $1000.00 for the week but I know many performers who are out of work and are working for a lot less per week. If you do go to Legend venues other than Vegas, you will only be put up in a hotel if you are a headliner act! (Unlike the dancers, who have to move to the location and pay for their own place.)

Working in a show like this, you can really get to know what this business is all about.

Q. What's it like to put a Legends type show together?

Gary B as Frank Sinatra: "I am having the time of my life as Sinatra. However, stepping into the shoes of a famous talent is a great responsibility. I have been doing Sinatra all of my life but never as much as I have in the past 3 years.

My dream was to create and produce a "Rat Pack" type show while I was doing Frank around the country. I had these pals of mine Bill Whitton (Dean Martin) and Lambus Dean (Sammy Davis Jr.) who I worked with in the past on other projects, and I knew these were the guys for the job. It turned out great! The continuing friendship and teamwork along with the appearance, ambiance, sound-alike capabilities, and our musical director Mr. Ned Mills make for a very successful show.

It is a thrilling experience to emulate these great artists and bring their musical talent to life and feel the love and response from the audience, as well as reliving the excitement of the Rat Pack!" -

Our Way with Frank and Friends. Gary B as Frank, Lambus Dean as Sammy and Bill Whitton as Dean; Photography by Major Entertainment Prods.

Night Clubs

Strike up the Band...

Some look-alikes have live tribute shows and just need a place to showcase. Some look-alikes work as professional singers, and decide to put a Tribute band together to double their money and work opportunities. If you are putting a band together and need a place to start gigging, look for local clubs or bars that may be hiring entertainment. You may also wish to submit your promotional materials to the club owners and management, as many agents don't book clubs and bars as regularly as events.

The following is from a guy who has mastered a Legend...

How does someone get booked in a club or bar?

John Mueller as Buddy Holly: "Send them your promo and then follow up with a call. Actually meeting the person responsible for booking talent really helps as well, so they can place your face with your promo. Include good reviews of past performances and good audio.
Scout out the places you'd want to play, the places most suitable for the type of music you're doing, and then try to meet the person in charge. Give them your best promo, audio tape, or CD and bio/reviews. If you have a following, it doesn't hurt to inform them that you can draw a crowd. (It is always a good idea to have a fan list or a mailing list to start a following for your act). In order to book these kinds of gigs, you can do it yourself and/or work in conjunction with an agent/manager. It is up to you to decide if you wish to have a manger represent you and your tribute act. One of the best elements of playing and performing in a club or bar is that it allows you to practice your craft and develop a new audience for your music.

Some of the challenges include: The playing conditions can be less than desirable (like bar noise and smoke), audiences may not be interested in watching the show, and the pay is much lower than most corporate jobs.
For American performers, I find overseas audiences to have a greater appreciation for Americans and they are much more expressive and appreciative of your live performances.
For a performer who is looking to start a careers as a tribute performer, remember that you will need perseverance, perseverance, perseverance. Don't wait for someone else to handle your career - do it yourself and create your own opportunities. Never wait."

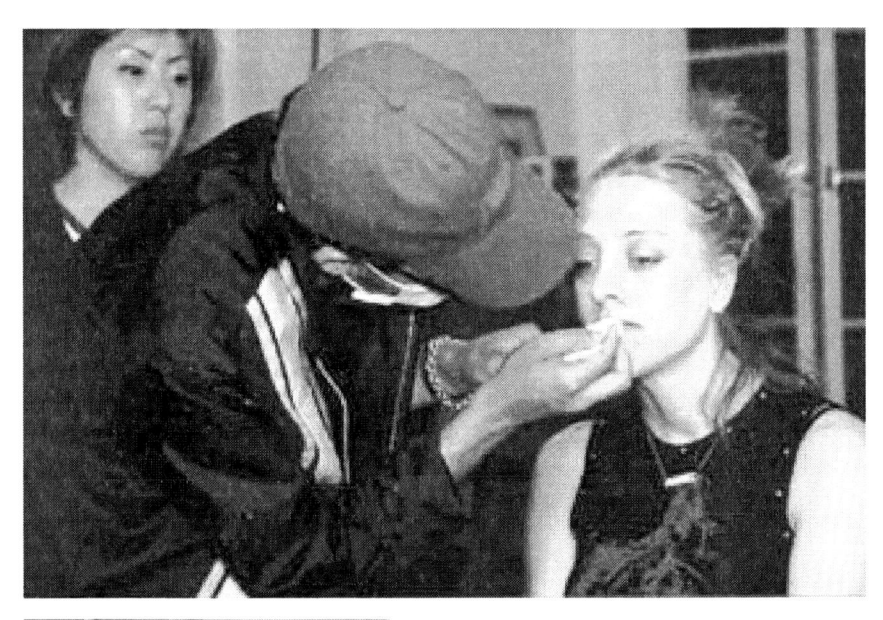

Working as a stand-in/photo double is not always a glamorous job. Denise Bella Vlasis has done numerous stand-in jobs as Madonna where she is hired for her likeness, voice, mannerisms or body parts. These photos show make-up artist Klexus Kolby apply black eyes and bruises for the video/Geisha segment for Madonna's Drowned World Tour 2001.

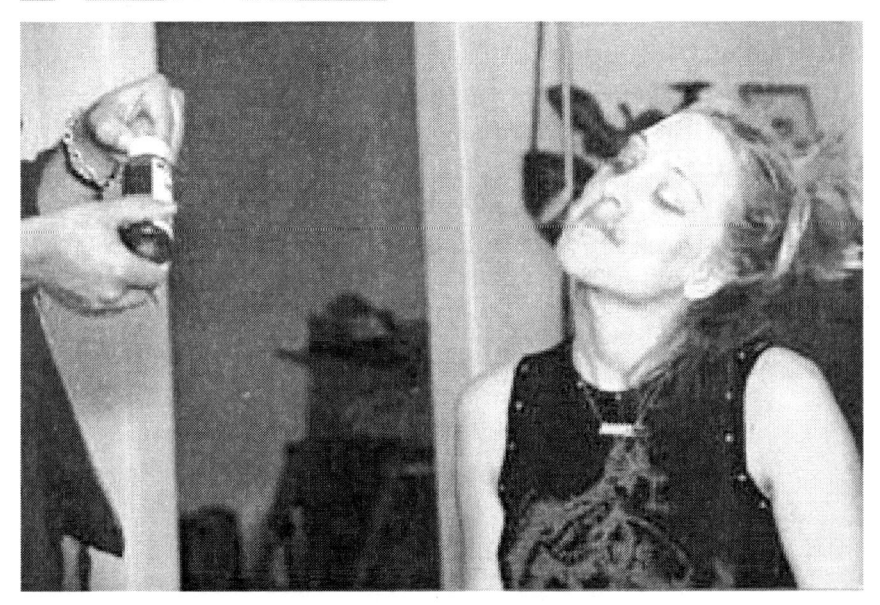

Photo Doubles and Stand-ins

Double Vision...

Photo double work can be ideal for the professional look-alike who has very similar features to a celebrity. You may also be hired just for a body part such as lips, back, hands, legs, etc. You may be hired for your walk or gestures to be used for the filming of a television show, movie, or music video. Again, these jobs tend to be long full days with early call times (like 6:00 a.m.) and wrap up to finish sometimes at 1:00 a.m. Photo Double jobs are generally union jobs, and you will most likely get this job from an agent submitting you for them.
Pay will most likely be union scale (see Unions).

How did you get your start as George Clooney's double?

Bill Piper as George Clooney: "I live in Cleveland, Ohio. I was looking for part-time work as an extra and heard there was a casting call for extras for the "Welcome to Collinwood" production. I went down to the audition and got in line with the hundreds of others. When I got to the casting director he looked up at me and said, "Wow - you know, you look just like George Clooney!" I said, "Yes, I've heard it many times; I once met his Aunt Rosemary years ago and she said the very same thing to me." The director explained they were just discussing that they needed a stand-in and photo double for George and were wondering where they would find one. Talk about timing! They asked me if I'd be interested in the job. I said of course!

George was very nice. He introduced himself. We even played basketball together during a lunch break on the set. The newspapers wanted to do a story about George but he wasn't giving interviews. William H. Macy told the reporter she should interview me since I look just like George anyway. So they did!! It was on the front page! They asked me about the supposed relationship between myself and Jennifer Lopez (tongue-in-cheek). My quote was, "Don't tell my wife."
Another time the local ABC-TV affiliate asked me for an on camera interview since George wasn't granting them. I asked George if he minded me doing it since I didn't want to step on any toes. He said, "Sure, go ahead. I don't mind. Just remember - any money you make from it, you have to give it to me." We had a good laugh. I have to admit it was pretty weird, though. Everyone on the set kept saying how remarkable the likeness was and they were surprised they found me. I gave him my phone number after the shoot and told him anytime he needed me for stand-in work I'd be glad to oblige. I've been invited to the premier of the movie in October (probably in case he doesn't show). I may be working on the

"Intolerable Cruelty" shoot next month if the scheduling can be worked out. I just got off the phone with the casting director for the day players a few hours ago. Note: I got only scale pay for the stand-in work. But the benefit has been the look-alike work I've been getting since by being able to say I worked as George Clooney's double in a motion picture! For that I've been getting between $1500-$2000 per day for a meet and greet."

A Look-alike Anecdote and great example of a great photo double job possibility:

Agent Jeffrey Briar: "A young fellow by the name of Kevin Holloway was (I think) selling toner (ink for printers) when he started doing a few "personal appearances" (photo ops at corporate parties) portraying actor Michael J. Fox. I think he had done only three or four of these when he was cast to be the photo double *for* Michael J. Fox, in TWO major motion pictures: Back To the Future, Parts 2 and 3. These two films were shot back-to-back (with only a two-week pause between them).

Kevin was on-screen often. Between takes, he often hung out and played basketball with the real Michael J. Fox (who appreciated a basketball opponent that was about his size). Kevin got on-screen credit (rare for a photo-double), and a 50% salary increase between the first film and the second. He worked with prestigious director Robert Zemekis, and even dabbled with stunt work. That year he worked practically solid, on *two* major motion pictures. His income approximately tripled. And for a year, he got to tell his friends he was a full-time, working movie actor.
Not bad for your 4th gig!"

Send in the Clone...

Stand-in work is for people who look very much like the real star. For some jobs you may not necessarily need any performing skills. You need to be close in height, weight, body type, hair, eye color, and mannerisms as your celebrity. Some jobs (such as the following example) require a sharp, skilled, and professional actor to pull of the job's success.
Many jobs include long hours on a set and standing in place of the celebrity. (It is not as glamorous as it seems). Many times, the celebrity you are doubling for is not there, so the stand-in is placed where the celebrity will be when filming begins. You may be dressed in the same wardrobe and makeup as the celebrity, so the director will be looking at you through the camera and matching the angles and lighting accordingly. Acting break-downs or agents must submit you for this work.

There are several kinds of jobs for look-alikes as the stand-in or photo double in Hollywood.

Here are a couple of examples of the good, bad, and ugly of Hollywood and the treatment of performers in general, with great advice from the best in this business.

Can you share your experience of being a stand-in (and more) as an example of the kinds of work you can do?

Jeffrey Weissman- Professional actor and impersonator of several characters: "A few years ago, I costarred in two films that I had been cast in as a stand-in/photo double. These jobs were for Universal Studios for the film sequels *Back To The Future 2* and *Back To The Future 3*, playing the role of George McFly. The producers of these films had had some disagreement with the original actor, Crispen Glover, and the producer and actor could not come to a mutual agreement in order to have Crispen, the original actor, return to play the role. At the last possible moment, I was told that I would be more than just a photo double. In fact, I would be hired to re-create the role in prosthetic makeup to resemble the original actor, yet with much of the part reduced due to the makeup being too obvious to the discerning fan. Most of the shots in the film I appear in, I was intentionally kept turned away from the camera, or at distance far from it.

Close-up shots of the original actor would be inserted to supplement my performance, especially in the return to the 1955 scenes, where I played young George McFly, age 17. When I walked onto the set the first time in the George McFly makeup and costume (1955), Michael J. Fox looked at me and said, "Oh no, Crispen's not gonna like this." It made me feel the job was almost scab-like. However, I wanted the work. It was a Screen Actors Guild contract and I thought it would be a challenge and a gift. In the long run, it was both. Frustration reared its head often. My agent was forced into accepting a very low rate for my services and producer's discretion on my billing. As well, I was never invited to be a part of any script readings or rehearsals that took place before shoots on and off the set.

Bob Gale, the writer/producer, did offer me a role in Back to the Future 3 sans all of the prosthetic makeup, so I could appear in the film with my own face. I suppose this was the reward for the many hours of torture I endured (three to four hours a day getting in and out of makeup, being hung upside down for days, and being unable to promote myself publicly). Unfortunately, he did not come through on his promise. Everything seemed to get stranger just as soon as I tried to get some help on my billing (credits in the film). Much evidence made it seem that I wasn't going to be working in my trade or getting anything out of my "break" from co-starring in the sequels to the highest grossing film of 1985. I was still somewhat unknown as an actor. To this day, most people still don't realize that there even was a George McFly look-alike in the films. As frustrating an experience as it was, being in that movie, it gave me an understanding of how Hollywood can treat performers. I have continued my career in film, television, theme parks, environmental theater, and stage work. I currently work as one of the most requested look-alikes impersonating Groucho

Marx, Stan Laurel, Charlie Chaplin, Roberto Benigni, Pee Wee Herman, and others. As well, I have trained and directed look-alikes and actors internationally.

My advice to performers cast as a stand-in or photo double is: Do not get so excited by the offer that you act blindly and rush the details of your employment. An agent that gives you little to no details or offers you a contract for any work that is not union work is not representing you correctly. When you are being hired as the stand-in, and the producers want to hire you, you may have more power than you are aware of. Take the time to see the big picture. You are important to the project and the producers should be prepared to pay a fairly good wage for you. Most look-alikes make $750-$1500 or more for a day of working in television or feature films, with billing and residuals. Your agent should be a franchised agent with the Screen Actors Guild, and he/she is entitled to 10% of your earnings. If you work on a non-union shoot, make sure you have protection in writing. It is best to pass on non-union work or work that does not meet your worth and requirements.

Once you get all of the business settled, go have fun. Develop a relationship with the creative team on the project so you can be involved in the development of the moments in the shoot. Keep your professionalism, and you will develop a good reputation."

Jeffrey Weissman as Charlie Chaplin;
and as George McFly from the feature films Back To
The Future 2 and 3
Photography by Chuck Smith

Print Work

Got Look?...

Look-alikes are often hired like models, to advertise products. Your look-alike agents will call you for these kinds of jobs. There is generally no modeling experience necessary.

The pay will be negotiated and determined by you and the job offer. You may wish to have your favorite agent represent you for larger-scale print jobs.

Print jobs can vary, from catalogue work to billboards and advertisements, magazines, books, newspaper layouts, or product endorsements. With print work, there are fine lines that go hand in hand with a celebrity and any endorsements.

When getting hired for any print job, you will want to clearly understand all the details of the job before signing any contract or endorsing any product as your celebrity.

It is always great for your portfolio if you can obtain copies of all of your print jobs.

Jade Roberts as Sylvester Stallone: "Working as a print model (as a look-alike), I was hired for the most unusual print assignment. I was flown to Italy, where the photographer of the job took shots of me with a "bride" on cross-country skis in St. Peters Square. During milder weather, I was asked to look serious while posing with topless models in such locales as the Roman Aqueduct and the Coliseum."

Telegrams

There's no Business like Show Business...

Telegrams can be a great way to earn quick money; however, your comedic skills and quick wit will be one of the most necessary skills to have as an entertainer. You can develop your own characters, and put an act together with material that YOU write. If you have more comedic abilities, and wish to perform in a more lighthearted atmosphere, telegrams and singing telegrams may be for you. You can get away with being a character of a star and even present your character in a satirical kind of way. Your costumes, wigs, and makeup can be less extravagant than if you were working at an elegant corporate event; however, your impromptu skills and sense of humor must be sharp. These kinds of jobs can be booked in the middle of public areas, so if you're bashful about being outrageous in public, you may not want to do this kind of work. If you are creative and spontaneous, and can have fun with putting people on the spot, this may be a great creative outlet for you. Your local Yellow Pages will list companies specializing in Singing Telegram entertainment. Give them a call so you can send your promotional materials and/or arrange a meeting with the company's booking agent.

Breaking it down with an extremely talented gal that has it down to a science...

Singing Telegrams- How did you start, and is this the same as look-alike work?

Gina Bacon- Singing Telegram Specialist: "I got started in the singing telegrams business in 1982 by answering a newspaper ad in the local paper. I was petrified of performing or even speaking in public. I thought this would be a great way to break my stage fright. I went to the audition, sang "Happy Birthday," and got the job. I started out doing basic singing telegrams with basic costumes (Playboy Bunny, Nurse, French Maid, Cop, etc.). As customers started requesting other characters, I was willing to buy the costumes to add to my list of characters (which is currently over 100 costumes). Customers sometimes request something other than a singing telegram. I have been a golf caddy for a golfing event dressed as a Playboy Bunny. I have worked conventions dressed in various outfits passing out literature. I have dressed as a celebrity impersonator like

Marilyn Monroe to meet, greet, and pose for photos.

I work full-time as a professional entertainer, and I have learned that there is a way for any good entertainer to find full-time work. If you are looking into the possibility of becoming a telegram talent, begin to get an idea of characters you can do well. When you feel comfortable with your act, start looking for the companies in your area that book telegram talent.

I have owned my company, Artistic Singing Telegrams, since 1991. I book 50% of the shows I do and I also work for at least 27 other agencies. I work almost every day.

If you are more skilled at improvisational acting and being spontaneous with people than looking exactly like a celebrity, telegrams may be a perfect job for you. In some cases, with telegram work, you can look less like a celebrity than with corporate look-alike work and the impersonation can be more of a caricature or done in a satirical light. When performing a singing telegram, you have certain freedoms in your performance that you do not have in straight look-alike work. With telegrams, you can basically act and say anything you want because you have created the character you are performing. When impersonating a celebrity, you must stay in character and act just like the celebrity.

The general pay for a 15- to 20-minute singing telegram is $50.00 for a basic telegram and $75.00 for a celebrity character.

My pay scale is as follows:

- 15-20 minutes $75.00
- 30 minutes $100.00
- 45 minutes $125.00
- 1 hour $150.00

For driving costs, the first 25 miles are free and then I usually charge $1.00 for each mile thereafter.

The kinds of jobs one can do as a telegram talent are endless. For myself, you name it, I've had it requested! Let alone what has happed AT the events: the crying baby, the deejay's system blows up, the birthday boy leaves to go to the store, the propane tank catches on fire, cell phones and beepers go off, trying to avoid the drunk, and avoiding dangerous dogs. (I always make sure now that dogs are out of the house while I am performing.) People doing telegrams should be ready for anything. It's all part of the job.

Telegram work certainly has its perks, like tips. I get tipped 90% of the time. General tips range from $5.00 to $100.00. I never *expect* a tip, but I sure do accept a tip. I don't count the money in front of the customer, but when they pay me or slip me a tip, I immediately thank them and tell them I appreciate it very much.

I find most of my material from quotes or jokes on the Internet, books, friends, and even from party guests at shows when they fire off a cute joke.

Advice: Remember, each job you are booked for will be different. Your audiences and circumstances will change from job to job. Keep this in mind as you begin to see the differences in each booking. You can perform the exact same routine at one gig and have your act go over as a hit of the party. The guests will love you, applaud and compliment you (and possibly give you a huge tip). Yet on that same night, you can go to another party, repeat the performance, and get a cold response with no tip. Don't sweat it! Chances are, they either are the type of guests that do not show lots of emotion, or they really loved you but are so surprised at how good you are that they are speechless.

Final comments: Learn to improvise, go with the flow, and have fun. Be willing to travel, be available anytime, and be willing to purchase costumes to make your performance even better."

Theme Parks

Thrills and Chills...

Many theme parks hire look-alike talent for ongoing shows or walk-around meet and greet. Universal Studios, Knott's Berry Farm, and state fairs have all hired celebrity impersonators. These jobs have advantages and disadvantages like any job, but you may find the benefits to be enticing. Theme park work can mean long hours and less pay than corporate jobs, but the regular work can be a nice balance to other look-alike work. You will need great people skills and patience.

To find a theme park in your area that is hiring look-alike talent, keep your eyes open to trade magazines and ask your local agencies to notify you when and if they hear of auditions.

Here is further information from a diva, who has been hired to perform at several theme parks...

It seems like so many great, talented look-alikes (like yourself) work at theme parks as look-alikes; can you describe your experiences with that?

Betty Atchison as Cher: "I was hired to perform as Cher for my first theme park look-alike gig at Universal Studios for a New Year's Eve Show in 1995. Cher is not a regular celebrity (meet and greet character) used by Universal at their theme parks, so this was a rare chance to perform there. Most of the time, Universal hires the "classic" look-alike characters for meet and greet or live shows - typically, the Legends like Marilyn Monroe, Charlie Chaplin, the Marx Brothers, etc. are used.

Universal is the only theme park where I have worked as a celebrity look-alike. Since the opening of Universal's City Walk in 1999 I have had more opportunities to work as Cher in nightclubs such as The Groove and The Jazz Club. Performing full shows on their stages has really been fun.

Theme parks normally hire look-alikes for conventions, special events, and themed parties. These events are cast within the special events department on property and talent is cast according to what they have on file. That is why it is important to have a good promotional package. On rare occasions, they hold auditions if their files lack the talent they require for a special show or event.

I was originally hired by Walt Disney World to participate in the All-American College Workshop Program during my senior year in college. It's a great summer performance education/work program for aspiring entertainers. It was the first time I was able to experience working professionally as an entertainer and I absolutely fell in love with Disney and the experience of performing there.

The pay for performers really depends on the type of performer you are. Singers, dancers, and actors are usually paid a higher hourly wage ($10-$12 starting, usually) than atmosphere characters who usually begin at a rate of around $6 -$8 hourly.

When you are hired for regular (ongoing) work, this means you then qualify for health insurance, workman's compensation insurance, paid vacation time, and annual park passes. Theme park employees are often given discounts at many restaurants and shops as well. These are all nice perks.

Theme park gigs are a great way to find full-time or part-time work and still allow you to perform other look-alike jobs in between. If you are scheduled to work at a park and another look-alike job comes in for you, it's important to plan ahead and schedule days off or find someone to cover your shifts. Most of the time there is enough flexibility to make any adjustments necessary to work an "outside" job.

I find working as a look-alike performer at theme parks to be a great way to experience the feedback and reactions of the guests up close and personal. People are very casual and relaxed and will say most anything to you. Because of this, it takes extra effort to remain professional and maintain the integrity of the celebrity you are portraying. With time and practice, you get better at coming up with good responses to outrageous comments.

This business has provided wonderful opportunities that I would never have enjoyed had I not impersonated Cher. I am grateful to Cher for the hard work she put into her career. Without her talent and persistence, I would not be talking to you today about my fantastic experiences as Cher!"

Betty Atchison as Cher; Photography by Michael Carins

Trade Shows and Conventions

Spicing it Up...

Look-alikes always bring excitement to long and boring conventions. Look-alikes are hired by the hour to promote products, companies, and corporations by appearing at a booth or mingling around a convention center.
A look-alike agent will submit you for this work. Convention and Trade Show jobs are usually a great booking, and many times the agent will request you to perform one to four days of work at the convention. There are daily conventions at most convention centers and these jobs seem to be ongoing, resulting in employment many look-alikes.

Some convention work may take place in another state, so remember to add travel costs to your overall pricing for these job bookings. When working at a convention for an all-day booking (5-8 hour day) you will need to take lunch and dinner breaks, and bring eyedrops, breath mints, and comfy shoes for in between breaks and working.

Don't forget to remind the agent (if you are working 5-8 hours a day) to book you to work only 45 minutes *on* with 15 minutes of break-time every hour. Convention work can mean sitting in one booth taking photos or walking through the entire convention center. If you are to meet and greet throughout the entire convention hall, you will need to be extra animated, so that the hundreds of people attending will understand that you are a hired look-alike.

When working at a booth, you may wish to suggest to the agent or client that bringing music, photos or themes that represent your celebrity, can make for a more enthusiastic atmosphere. Convention work is generally easy, but there are long days of work, so make sure you are well rested and energetic before doing these kinds of jobs. Your energy level may need to last eight hours, and in look-alike years, that is a lot of hours to be in character!

Trade Show and Convention tips from Betty Atchison as Cher:

To succeed in convention work, you MUST be flexible. I have yet to see an event go exactly as planned.

Once you are on location, be professional at ALL times. Whether you are on stage or not, you are still representing the agency that hired you.

At the job, NEVER bad mouth anyone for any reason.
It's a good policy to follow up and call the agent the next day and let them know how things went from your end. Agents can't always be there to see the events they book and especially appreciate knowing when they go well.

I always bring my own drinks and snacks in a thermal bag, since many events last 4-5 hours (and sometimes more) without a meal break. Don't expect the client to feed you. It's a privilege when they do. Come prepared and you won't go hungry!

Voice-Overs

Imitation is the Most Sincere Form of Flattery...

Having a unique voice or singing ability is another example of impersonation. Most people are familiar with famous voice impersonations, and many comedians perform using their voice talents of impersonation in their stand-up comedy routines. If you have a voice that is flexible, and you can emulate many kinds of voices, voice-over work may be for you. Film, television, and commercials use voice-over talent all the time. A producer may hire a talent for his or her ability to emulate the voice and sound of a famous personality. There are many talented impersonators who began their careers in impersonation by realizing that they have the ability to use their own natural voice to impersonate someone.

Having a dead-on sound identical to a celebrity is a skill that many great actors, comedians, singers, and voice-over artists have mastered. There is always a demand for voice impersonators, and utilizing the voice takes practice, skill and technique.

As a look-alike talent, you may get a job offer to use the talent of your voice, be it a singing job or speaking job, as a specialty talent. You may just get this job over an actor since you specialize in impersonation.

I have listed some job possibilities for voice-over talent, and then later asked a voice expert how to master the voice...

Here are just a few examples of work available:

Singing jingles: Voice-over entertainers are hired to sing and/or speak for television commercials, radio, film, corporate videos, theme songs, and cable network programs.

Voice-overs: Again, using your speaking voice to record for movies, commercials, radio spots, television, live broadcasts, announcers for television programs, and game shows.

Studio work: Some singers are hired for their ability to sound just like the original artist. Some artists actually look for singers who can match their voice and hire them to sing on their tours and albums. Another form of studio work is being hired by companies that make karaoke recordings. Again, a sound-alike talent is necessary.

Voice telegrams: Some companies provide singing telegrams over the phone.

You can find voice-over agencies from SAG or by searching the Internet. Some look-alike agents may get calls for sound-alikes, and they can submit you as long as they have your promotional materials. Acting breakdowns will also list some voice work. Voice teachers can also help you network.

For soliciting work as a voice talent, you will need a recording featuring your voice.

For speaking voice-overs: You will want to include several voices of your own original material. A total of about 15 minutes in length is sufficient. An agent will want to hear how versatile your voice is and how well you can read and enunciate. Remember, with any kind of entertainment, it is critical that you write your own material. Do not use the same stand-up comedy routines as your celebrity. If you cannot write comedic materials, you should find a writer that you can work with and hire them to write material for you.

For singing demos: Your demo should be a recording of your voice (either with your band or karaoke) singing at least three to four songs (only using about 30-60 seconds of each song). The recording should be no more than a total of 5 minutes long.

You will also need to include your headshot, photos, resume, and cover letter.

Pay: Will depend on the type of job you are hired for. Some voice-over jobs for film or television will go through the correct Union (SAG or AFTRA) and your pay will be on the standard scale. If you are signing a "buy out" contract, this means that the company is hiring you to perform your voice-over and will pay you a one-time fee. They are then free to use your voice as much as they wish, without you receiving a residual check. Your buy out price is up to you to negotiate. Basic day rate can be determined by calling SAG offices. (Telephone numbers are listed in the back of this book).

Can someone make a living just using his or

her voice and does someone have to be a singer to impersonate a star?

Irby Gascon, Look-alike, sound-alike, and voice expert: "Yes, there are many options available for work using your voice. Many actors with distinctive voices (James Earl Jones, Joan Rivers, and hundreds more) have made successful livings by establishing their own unique tones and becoming recognized as a voice personality. Other entertainers who have become known for their own sound and voice (such as Pee Wee Herman, President Clinton, Barbara Walters, Austin Powers, and many others), have paved the way for impersonators to emulate in comedic satire, so in these cases, you do not necessarily have to be a singer, although having voice training can be very helpful.

It is much easier to impersonate someone who has a similar background as yourself.
Example: I am from the South and can swing into a Southern accent naturally, so learning how to bring correct sound and diction to sound very close to Elvis Presley, in impersonating and speaking, comes natural. Because I'm a trained singer, it is easier for me to emulate how someone sings, so singing like Ricky Martin is easy for me; however, speaking with a Puerto Rican accent takes a lot more practice and concentration.

If you are a Whitney Houston look-alike but you have no singing skills, you are probably better off with a lip-sync act. Impersonating a celebrity's stage performance and emulating their energy will make for a stronger, more believable impersonation without the distraction of an inaccurate sound. On the other hand, if you feel you can match your voice fairly close to that of a celebrity, with the instructions from a voice teacher you can learn to sing and develop your voice to match your star, while learning to sing correctly.

Irby Gascon as Ricky Martin;
Photography by Bella

Here are some techniques for the voice:

Listen to your star's voice and notice where the singer is focusing the sounds in their mouth. Do they place their vowel sounds in the front or back of their mouth? Do they have a nasally, throaty, or breathy sound? Pay attention to the tones of their voice. Practice on your own, by recording your voice speaking and/or singing like your celebrity. Record and listen to your voice repeatedly and objectively until your voice matches theirs. The tape recordings of your own voice can be the most honest and valuable tool for perfecting your sound. Should you choose to take voice lessons, you can learn more in-depth techniques that can develop your skills, such as proper pronunciations and diction, breath control, singing from your diaphragm (even when your celebrity may not be), microphone techniques, and ways to preserve and strengthen your voice for years to come."

Real World Examples from look-alike professionals:

Q. What was your most unusual booking?

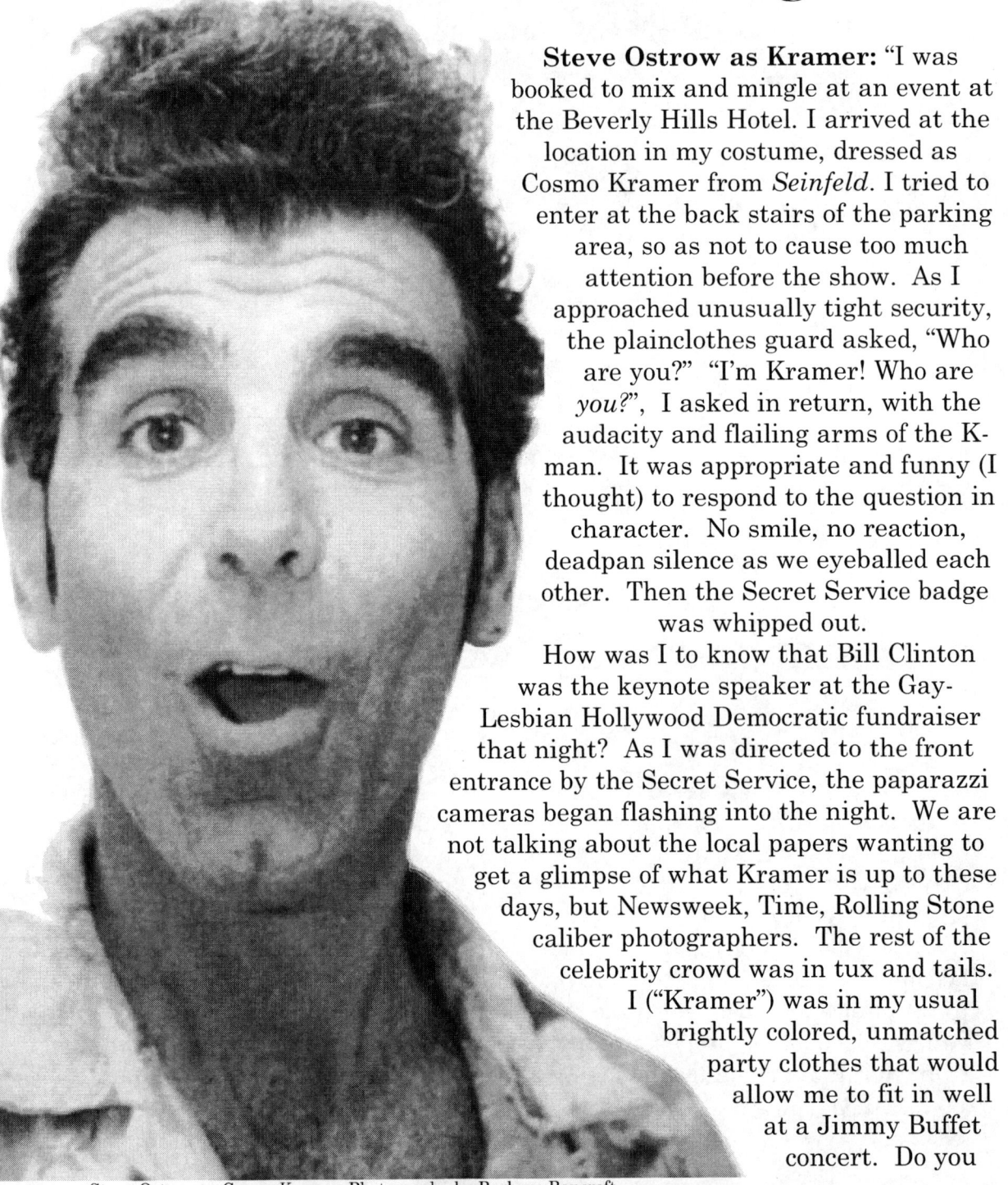

Steve Ostrow as Kramer: "I was booked to mix and mingle at an event at the Beverly Hills Hotel. I arrived at the location in my costume, dressed as Cosmo Kramer from *Seinfeld*. I tried to enter at the back stairs of the parking area, so as not to cause too much attention before the show. As I approached unusually tight security, the plainclothes guard asked, "Who are you?" "I'm Kramer! Who are *you?*", I asked in return, with the audacity and flailing arms of the K-man. It was appropriate and funny (I thought) to respond to the question in character. No smile, no reaction, deadpan silence as we eyeballed each other. Then the Secret Service badge was whipped out.

How was I to know that Bill Clinton was the keynote speaker at the Gay-Lesbian Hollywood Democratic fundraiser that night? As I was directed to the front entrance by the Secret Service, the paparazzi cameras began flashing into the night. We are not talking about the local papers wanting to get a glimpse of what Kramer is up to these days, but Newsweek, Time, Rolling Stone caliber photographers. The rest of the celebrity crowd was in tux and tails. I ("Kramer") was in my usual brightly colored, unmatched party clothes that would allow me to fit in well at a Jimmy Buffet concert. Do you

Steve Ostrow as Cosmo Kramer; Photography by Barbara Bancroft think I stood out in the crowd? By the way, my gig wasn't the Democratic fundraiser, but a telecom company that may not even be in business today."

Patience, patience, patience... advice from The King

Mark W. Curran as Elvis: "When you first begin to work as an impersonator, you may feel really self-conscious, but then you build your confidence. As audiences really begin to react favorably and give you encouragement, it empowers you to build on your act, to practice more, and to get better and better. Also, there are guys who work as Elvis that have been working for years and years. Give it time, and understand that the work will come. You have to realize that it takes a lot longer than you may expect. It takes time to establish yourself in any business - to get known, to make contacts, and to get a referral network going. No matter how hard you work, it takes time. I didn't start getting referrals till I was out there doing it for a full year, full time, and then it took another year for it to really get rolling. Also, don't listen to negative people. They can destroy you. Stay spiritually grounded and believe in yourself, and above all have fun. If you can't have fun with it, it isn't worth doing. (And of course, buy many extra copies of Bella's book for your friends and family as gifts!)"

Ross Seymour as
Maximus The Gladiator;
Photography by Amber Collie

"Take life by the horns! Don't be the person who later in life say's; *I should have done that, or I wish I would have tried*".
Ross Seymour as The Gladiator

115

Q. What are your thoughts about this business in general?

Julie Sheppard as Judy Garland: "I believe that we bring a lot of joy, nostalgic memories, and lighthearted entertainment to regular folks who marvel at what we do! I think we are blessed to be able to do this. It is a gift, an art form, and not something I trivialize or take for granted. I have always loved the characters I impersonate, since I was about five years old. What incredible fortune that I can look like, sing like, and act like my idols and give others a glimpse of what it might have been like to see them perform LIVE!"

William Peterson as Rodney Dangerfield;
Photography by George M Loring Studios

This guy does GET RESPECT!

William Peterson as Rodney Dangerfield: "Never believe you *are* your celebrity. You are a professional impersonator and should respect the image of the celebrity. Do justice to your celebrity by being pro!"

Just a quick word of advice from an expert with the track record to prove it:

"I have been impersonating ALAN ALDA as DR. HAWKEYE PIERCE since 1978. I continue to work as a professional impersonator because it gives me numerous opportunities to experience incredible ways to do what I love. When I work as an impersonator, I may be simply doing improvisational comedy acting while greeting a crowd, mixing and mingling, or posing for photos with guests from all over the world. I have been hired for stage performances, television, print advertisements, and mostly corporate stage productions.

I have found it is one thing to resemble a celebrity, and it is quite another thing to be able to impersonate that celebrity and hold the attention of an audience at the same time. I get a lot of satisfied clients calling me back over and over year after year, so I must be doing something right.

Many of those people have stated: Marv, without question you are definitely the very best Alan Alda/Dr. Hawkeye Pierce celebrity look-alike impersonator ever!

I'm not trying to brag, but if I go to my grave with simply being the very best in that category, I would have to say that's not all bad! Many people strive for perfection and never achieve it.

By entering this profession you do, in fact, have that unique opportunity to become the very best at what you do!

Take it seriously, but have fun with it!! You will be amazed at where it can take you!!!"

Best always,
MARV "HAWKEYE" CLINE

What is a Union?

Used with permission from Abbas Bagheri - **MY Entertainment WORLD**

The Screen Actors Guild– (SAG) covers actors performing in motion pictures, prime time TV programs, most TV commercials, industrial and educational films, student and experimental films and anything else shot on film. You may become eligible for SAG membership under one of the following conditions:

Principal Performer Employment: Performers may join SAG upon proof of employment or prospective employment within two weeks or less by a SAG signatory company. Employment must be in a principal or speaking role in a SAG film, videotape, television program, or commercial. Proof of such employment may be in the form of a signed contract, a payroll check or check stub, or a letter from the company (on company letterhead). The document proving employment must provide the following information: applicant's name and Social Security number, the name of the production or the commercial (the product name), the salary paid in dollar amount, and the specific date(s) worked.

Extra Players Employment: Performers may join SAG upon proof of employment as a SAG covered extra player at full SAG rates and conditions for a minimum of three workdays subsequent to March 25, 1990. Employment must be by a company signed to a SAG Extra Players Agreement, and in a SAG film, videotape, television program, or commercial. Proof of such employment must be in the form of a signed employment voucher (or time card), plus a payroll check or check stub. Such documents must provide the same information listed above.

Employment Under an Affiliated Performers' Union: Performers may join SAG if the applicant is a current paid-up member in good standing of an affiliated union (AEA, AFTRA, AGMA, AGVA, ACTRA) for a period of at least one year or longer and can prove that they have worked as a principal performer in the jurisdiction of that union at least once. Performers may also be eligible to join SAG provided they are currently paid up.

Joining Fee: The joining fee is $904.50, of which $862 represents the initiation fee and $42.50 the basic semi-annual dues. In addition, new applicants may be required to pay 1.5% of any SAG earnings over $5,000 that were earned during the year prior to their joining. No personal checks are accepted for joining fees. Fees may be lower if you join in some branch areas, or if you are a paid-up member of an affiliated performers' union.

Dues: SAG dues are based on SAG earnings, and are billed twice each year. Each SAG member will pay basic annual dues of $85.00. In addition, those members earning more than $5,000 per year under SAG contracts will pay 1.5% of such income in excess of $5,000 to a maximum of $150,000. Members who are paying full dues to another performers' union, and earn less than $25,000 per year under SAG contracts, will receive a reduction of $20 per year and $10 per year thereafter. Members whose SAG earnings exceed $25,000 per year will pay full dues, regardless of other guild affiliations.

Legitimacy of Application: Your application and proof of employment will be fully investigated by the Guild. Your application for SAG membership will be denied if you have falsified your credentials, or if your qualifying employment is not bona fide. While it is your responsibility to ascertain the validity of your qualifying employment, the Guild will be the sole arbiter in determining whether the employer was legitimate or bogus, and whether the qualifying employment which you performed was actual production work or work created solely to enable you to gain Guild membership. Please be aware that false representation or deception on your part will jeopardize your chances to join the Guild. Further, if after your application has been granted, the Guild discovers such misconduct on your pat, you may find yourself subject to disciplinary proceedings which could result in your being fined, suspended and/or expelled from SAG.

Appointments for Admission: If you are eligible under the conditions previously stated, please contact the nearest SAG office before going in so they can advise you of the amount of your joining fee and arrange an appointment for you with the New Membership Department.

The American Federation of Television and Radio Artists– (AFTRA) covers live and taped TV shows, some TV commercials, announcers, disc jockeys, newspersons, singers and specialty acts, sportscasters, stunt persons, all radio commercials, soap operas, and anything else shot on videotape.

AFTRA Facts: AFTRA is a nationwide organization of more than 70,000 members. It is chartered by the Associated Actors and Artists of America (commonly known as the 4 A's) and is affiliated with the AFL-CIO.

Members: Every performer who speaks, sings, or acts before a microphone or television camera. Additionally, people engaged to make transcriptions, videotape commercials, recordings, and slide films.

Benefits: AFTRA can negotiate a legally binding contract, protecting and securing the rights of radio and TV performers through collective bargaining. If you are employed on a staff basis, it guarantees you vacations, holiday pay, sick leave, and termination pay; also freedom from onerous hours, split shifts, unfair scheduling, and unjustified discharge. AFTRA promotes improved labor-management relations and good will. You as an individual member attain the dignity warranted your profession as a result of AFTRA's enviable position in the broadcasting and TV field. It has a history of good relations with management, battles fought fairly and openly, and agreements lived up to. AFTRA always keeps its word. You are backed by an accepted national organization.

Initiation Fee: An initiation fee is the only method, tested through the years, that enables the newcomer to AFTRA to share in the past achievements of the older members in securing improved working conditions and better wages. It is payment in lieu of time and battle, which older members of the organization contributed to secure the benefits, which the new members receive at once. This initiation fee entitles an active member to rights and benefits that accrue to AFATRA members anywhere in the nation.

Dues: Dues are assessed on the basis of your earnings in AFTRA's jurisdiction. Dues dates are the first of May and November.

Member Responsibilities: You must:(1) Live up to the intent and terms of AFTRA contracts; (2) Bring to the attention of your shop steward or executive director any infraction of AFTRA codes, agreements or rules; (3) Refer questions of interpretation, application, or fees to your executive director; (4) File membership performance reports for every transcription and video tape engagement; and (5) Keep your current home address and telephone number on file with your AFTRA office. You must not: (1) Accept an engagement to perform for an unfair agency or producer; (2) Pay any agent commission in excess of 10 percent; (3) Pay any commission which reduces your compensation below the established code, contract or agreement rates. You are expected to: (1) Attend AFTRA meetings, to express your opinion without fear or favor, to vote as your reason and conscience direct; (2) Read and be familiar with the subject matter of all AFTRA communications; (3) Pay your dues on time; (4) Take your suggestions and complaints on AFTRA administration and AFTRA affairs to your executive director or your officers, not to management or into a gripe session; (5) Be thoroughly familiar with the contract provisions under which you work; and (6) Work to strengthen the position and bargaining power of your union through active participation in all AFTRA affairs.

Contracts: You have the advice and assistance of experienced AFTRA representatives, but the basic elements of the contract demands are up to you. Of course, the terms of the completed contract depend on the final results of negotiations with your employer.

AFTRA Local Administration: Each Local schedules regular membership meetings, at which all members are expected to be present and participate in making decisions and framing the policies of their union. In addition, the membership elects officers (president, vice president, secretary and treasurer) and a Local Board of Directors to carry on the affairs of the Local between membership meetings. Also, each Local has an executive director - a paid representative who is in charge of the administrative day-to-day operations of the Local.

Over-Scale Artists: If it were not for the AFTRA minimum, you could not be over-scale. By raising the starting point from which you bargain, AFTRA has made it possible for you to reach a higher standard. In addition, there are many clauses in the AFTRA Codes other than those covering fees that work to your benefit, such as clauses covering arbitration, protection against unfair producers, health and retirement, etc.

AFTRA/Employer Relations: It will probably cost an employer a little more money, but in the long run it will help. A satisfied performer is a better performer, and establishing a definite scale of fees and clearly defined obligations will help your station manager or an agent in his dealings with clients. The majority of the thousands of their employers who are signatories to AFTRA pacts will agree with this statement. AFTRA has a reputation for being firm but reasonable.

Transition: If you are going to be out of the media for a period of time in excess of six months, send written request to the AFTRA office for a suspended payment. This will relieve you from paying dues until such time as you resume activity under AFTRA auspices. However, if you return to active status before six months have expired, you will have to pay the interim dues. Any paid-up member moving to the jurisdiction of another Local should request a transfer from the AFTRA office. Keep in touch with your AFTRA office.

Actors Equity Association– (AEA or "Equity") covers live stage performances, stage managers, and under some contracts, covers choreographers and directors as well. Priority is given to all performers who satisfy the following criteria, whether or not they are members of Equity, and they will be treated in the same manner with regard to the scheduling of auditions. Performers who qualify for audition priority must provide proof that at least one of the following standards has been met:

> (A) The performer was employed solely as a stage performer and has earned as salary, in any one calendar year, for performing onstage before live audiences (other than in an amateur or community theatre), for at least four consecutive weeks, a sum at least equal to four consecutive weeks' *bona fide* minimum salary plus health and pension benefits ("eligible rate"), or the dollar equivalent, as established in the Theatre for Your Audiences Agreement in effect during the applicable year; provided, however, that employment secured in excess of four continuous weeks (including rehearsal) must have been compensated at a uniform weekly rate of compensation (which rate is not less than the "eligible rate") for each week of employment; OR
>
> (B) The performer was employed as a performer in motion pictures, TV, or radio, and has, in any one calendar year, earned as salary in that medium the equivalent of the formula and rates set forth above; OR
>
> (C) The performer has completed, since 1981, no less than 40 weeks of stage performances in professional theatres, before live audiences, as an apprentice performer, under the training of, and as a performing member of, a company of stage performers, the majority of whom have met the qualifying theatre criteria, as set forth above.

Application Procedures: Information sheets and application forms are available from any Equity office either in person or by mail. Applications must include a self-addressed, stamped envelope. Processing of applications will take place at the New York Equity office. The Auditions Department will verify the information supplied and, if it determines that the applicant meets the minimum standards, the applicant will be so notified, billed the appropriate fee, and upon payment, be issued the qualifying credentials. Processing of applications should be completed approximately two weeks after receipt.

Documentary Evidence: Together with the completed application, the applicant must provide actual proof of employment as outlined in the application. Eligibility will be approved on the basis of the documentation provided. Letters from producers or employers are not sufficient documentation. You must show proof of four consecutive work weeks; salaried work at the eligible rate; payment to the performer as a performer; and/or performance on a live stage, in a film or on TV. You must submit such proof for (1) theatre employment by a contract stating full employment dates and salary information; and a playbill/program with performance date(s) and role(s) played; and pay stubs showing four consecutive weeks of employment, together with adequate proof of payment for fringe benefits (paid bills, checks, receipts, etc.); and (2) film and/or television employment by a *bona fide* film/TV payroll company W-2 form or 1099 form, or a contract or employment voucher accompanied by a copy of the payment check.

Appeals: If it is determined that an applicant does not meet the minimum standards, the application will be denied by written notice to the applicant. The applicant will be supplied with information with regard to the appeals system. Appeals determinations will be based solely on the evidence provided. Final determinations will be made by a neutral arbitrator.

Fees: A current annual fee of $17.00 will be charged to any performer who is eligible to audition. Payments made in person will not be accepted after 3:00 pm. No personal checks will be accepted. Do not include payment with your application.

Eligibility Rates: You need only meet the applicable rate in any one year. Example: $322 x 4 weeks = $1,288 (Rates may change from year to year, so contact AEA for the current applicable rates.)

Actor's Equity Association Addresses: 165 West 46th Street, New York, NY 10036; 203 North Wabash Avenue, Chicago, IL 60601; 6430 Sunset Boulevard, Los Angeles, CA 90028.

The American Guild of Variety Artists– (AGVA) covers live performances in musical variety shows, performers in Las Vegas cabarets and club showcases, comedy showcases, magic shows, dance revues, and amusement park shows.

The American Guild of Musical Artists– (AGMA) covers performers in operas and other classical music productions and concerts, and dancers.

Q. Do I need to belong to a Union in order to work as a look-alike?

You need to belong to a union ONLY if you are hired to work on a union show. Look-alike work varies, and corporate events, stage shows, or personal appearances (most of the typical look-alike jobs available) are NOT union jobs. ONLY with union work (like television, film, or radio) will you need to join a union. If you get regular union bookings, then you will need to join the right union. If you get a call to audition for a union show, and you get the part, you may then decide to join the union to be legally able to work on the show you have been cast for. You will then go to the union offices to officially join the union, fill out your paperwork and pay your dues. After becoming a union member, you will pay yearly dues. You will also have all the union benefits and membership opportunities.

Q. What about the Look-Alike Guild?

If you should decide to join the Look-Alike Guild, I suggest that you ask a lot of questions and understand what the Guild can offer you as a performer. The Look-Alike Guild is a fairly new organization to this industry, so learn as much as you can about it and make decisions based on the variety of services offered. As a look-alike performer, it will be your resume, reputation, and work ethic that will allow you to continue to get hired as a professional, and not necessarily your status as a member of unions or guilds.

Q. What are your thoughts on the Look-Alike Guild?

Lyndall Grant as Arnold Schwarzenegger in The Terminator; Photography by Rochelle Richards

Lyndall Grant as Arnold Schwarzenegger:
"I believe the Guild is a practical necessity of our business. In many respects it is the ultimate network for anyone in this business. The Guild is too new to predict how well it will work; therefore, I feel the future value of the Guild will be a function of the persons who collectively are the Guild, meaning all of us. The Guild will be a viable force, but only if we declare it so."

Julie Sheppard as Judy Garland: "I think it's just a way to give more control to people who shouldn't have it in the first place. It seems to me that any attempt to organize a field as varied and - unfortunately - as distrustful as ours, can only lead to more problems...not solutions."

Working Your Look

Hair and Wigs

As a look-alike, you must keep in mind that about **80% of the accuracy of a convincing look is your hair**, so it is extremely important that your coif matches that of your celebrity as closely as possible. Many celebrities have a distinctive way in which they style their hair, and that is the first feature that causes people to recognize them. So as a look-alike, your hair will be one of the first things people notice that will make them recognize you as your star. So what do you need to do to create *the look*?

Where to go:

First, you need to determine whether you will be using your own natural hair or whether you need to prepare a hairpiece, wig, bald cap, or hair extensions. These can all be found at wig or costume stores. Search through your local Yellow Pages to find the closest shop available. You may want to call in advance and speak with a representative. Tell them what you are looking for, and ask if you need to make an appointment for a consultation.
Before you contemplate dyeing or cutting your own hair, consider the fact that investing in wigs may save you lots of time and energy, as well as make it easier to leave your character behind when you want to be yourself again. Wigs are fairly priced and can be worth the investment, since they are easily set and styled and can be much more time-efficient for you. The stylist can also help you with bald caps, hair extensions, hair sprays, and temporary hair colors.

What do you need?

Do you need hair spray, mousse, gel, color sprays, clips, barrettes, ribbons, or other items to complete your look? These can be found at almost any drug store or beauty supply store, and sometimes even at local grocery stores or discount stores. Study your celebrity's hair and determine what you will need to have available *every time* you are getting ready for a show.

Bring your photographs:

You can show the stylist exactly what you need, if you have good photographs that show your celebrity's hair clearly. Most of the time, they can cut and style a wig to fit your needs. You may have to pay a little more to have your wig designed the first time, but this will be part of your investment and well worth it. Tell the stylist that you'd like to watch as they style your wig, so you can learn the techniques for yourself.

Using your own hair:

If you decide to use your own hair, you may want to consider taking a trip to your local beauty salon and letting a professional show you how to best achieve your look. Don't forget to take along photographs that show your celebrity's color and style clearly. You may want to take notes and/or videotape as the stylist shows you how to manipulate your hair to achieve the hairstyle of your celebrity.
If you choose to do your hair on your own, **practice at home** in front of a mirror several times before your first job. By the time you are getting ready for your first appearance or show, you should have practiced arranging your hair enough times that you are comfortable with how it looks and sure that it will be easily recognizable as the hairstyle of your celebrity.

Try different techniques with your hair and know the results with each new attempt. Remember, each job you work at will have a different setup, so be prepared to be in an outdoor setting (which may be windy) or in humid climates (which flattens hair). The weather will affect your hairstyle, wigs, or hairpieces. Be prepared to make necessary adjustments so you won't have *hair stress*.

Special Note: You may wish to have a stylist that you can count on, for the times when you need your look to be perfect. Finding a hair stylist in *advance* can alleviate any possible stress when you are getting ready to film, photograph, or prepare for an upscale booking. Finding a stylist who understands how to transform you into your celebrity will save time, money and regrets. Even though most studios provide professional makeup, hair and wardrobe stylists, even exceptional stylists may not understand how to create your look. Look-alike makeup and hair is very specific and should be applied distinctly differently than "glamour" makeup. Many makeup and hair stylists will give you a generic made up look, and may actually make you look *less* like your star, by applying the wrong applications and hairstyles. I strongly suggest that you find an experienced, capable makeup and hair stylist for jobs that you want your look to be dead-on. You should be able to bring your hair and makeup person to the set or backstage area of your job. Make the extra investment by having your stylist with you, to make sure you look just right.

Learning the hard way: I have been on over one hundred television, film, and video sets, where I have had well-known makeup and hair stylists make me up as Madonna. Most of the time, I have been made up completely wrong to transform into her. I have been stuck with *blue eye shadow and big hair* for shows that I wanted to look my best, because of a stylist that did not know how to change my face to look more like Madonna. It is very discouraging as an impersonator to have bad hair and makeup and still try to give a good performance. If you don't feel right with your look, it makes it much more challenging to feel good about your performance.

My solution: Take the time to search for a personal stylist that you feel comfortable with, someone who understands artistically what needs to be done to your hair and face to transform you into your celebrity.
I have been blessed in finding my own personal stylist, Michael Dorian, who is an expert in Madonna makeup, hair, and costumes. Michael has prepared my Madonna looks for several television shows, films, and personal appearances. Michael has studied Madonna extensively, and knows my features precisely. He understands how to utilize his crafts to transform me with a more accurate look. He has come to my rescue for many important bookings, and this has directly affected me as an impersonator, in helping me achieve a better live performance. I am confidant in his abilities and continue to bring him with me to photo shoots, etc.

Suggestion: Network and search for a stylist that you can connect with. You may wish to meet with a stylist beforehand and practice your looks a few times (without time pressure). Sometimes it takes a few tries to get your look right. By finding your own "Michael," you can guarantee a fabulous look every time.

How to find the right stylist for you: Ask around for a great makeup artist, hair stylist, at your local cosmetic and beauty supply. When you go to studios, ask for references from photographers and agents.

Keep a stylist "on call" for all of your bookings. It is worth the investment for you to get your best look, and it will ease your stress, so you can concentrate on your performance only.

Michael Dorian putting final touches on Bella backstage at The Jenny Jones show

Some of Michael's favorite makeup products are: Ben Nye (Aqua glitter) Benefit (Benetint), MAC pro, Bourjois (dual mascara), Nars (their entire eye shadow line)

Michael: "Working as a celebrity look-alike, your hair is about 80% of your overall look, so try to get exact colorization and style to match your celebrity. I suggest finding a stylist that understands your needs. Have photos of your celebrity, and speak to a stylist that understands what kind of hair you have, versus what kind of hair your celebrity has. Shop around for a stylist at your local beauty shop or by word of mouth, and see if you can find someone who is willing to work with you. The stylist can help you decide on using your real hair or investing in wigs. They can also help you to achieve several different looks for photo shoots, filming, or important appearances. All celebrities rely on their personal stylist to look and feel good, so why shouldn't you? I don't believe in "rules" for applying makeup, and you should have fun - after all, you are creating a fantasy. I also believe in investing in good tools (i.e. brushes). Good makeup brushes will affect how your makeup is applied, so make it part of your overall investment. celebrity look-alike, portraying a "celebrity" means part of your job is to portray the famous "style" as well."

Makeup: Giving Good Face

Applying makeup is a skill that you must learn in order to achieve success as a celebrity impersonator. Spend some time with a mirror and pictures of your star to discover what you need to do to your face to turn yourself into that person. Remember that your celebrity may have different bone structure than you. You will need to learn how to color and shade your face accordingly, to create the illusion of having the same curves and angles as your star.
I suggest that you work with what God naturally gave you, and take your own natural, beautiful face, and enhance it with colors, pencils, or whatever you need to do to make your celebrity come to life on your face and body. I strongly urge anyone NOT to consider plastic surgery so that you can work in the entertainment business. You do not have to try to change your face or body to achieve success! (More on plastic surgery and alternatives later.)

Where to go and what to do:

Upscale department stores usually have makeup artists that are knowledgeable in makeup application and can take the time to sit with you and help you learn to apply it correctly. When buying makeup, you should meet with a representative and clearly explain what you need and let him or her help you with your purchase and application.

Beauty supply stores are equipped with many of the items you may need, such as false eyelashes, applicators, pencils, foundations, and proper colors of contour powders and creams.

Art classes are a wonderful way to learn the tricks of shading, by learning to paint faces and figures. You can learn how to recreate your appearance using the techniques of painting to restructure the lines and contours of your face. This is a great skill to have if you are impersonating someone whose bone structure is very different from yours.

A makeup or theatrical class is something to consider if you want to learn how to perfect your makeup skills. You may find a class like this at your local college or theater. Discovering what you can achieve with makeup may even inspire you to recreate another character to impersonate.

Again, you may want to hire a professional makeup artist. By networking and asking around for someone who specializes in theatrical makeup, or even by looking in the Yellow Pages, you can locate an expert who can show you exactly how to apply makeup to achieve the look you want. Consider bringing a video camera and having friend videotape the application, so that you have a reference to study to become an expert yourself. Again, you may wish to keep the makeup artist's number for future jobs when you need your makeup to be perfect. Choose someone who has worked with you before, and knows exactly what you need to transform, quickly and easily.

You can also teach yourself by studying and practicing in front of a mirror. Keep photographs of your star next to you as you try new techniques, so you can quickly refer back to them. It may be a good idea to have a friend take pictures of you after you've applied your makeup, then compare the pictures with those of your star to see where you need to make changes. With enough practice and observation, you will learn what works best on your face. You absolutely must learn how to do your own makeup, so spend as much time as you can teaching yourself how to apply it before your first job. The more you look like your celebrity, the more confident you will feel about your performance.

Learn your own facial structure and try experimenting with different types of makeup applications. Try something new each time you go to your next job or scheduled photo shoot. This way you can feel what kinds of colors, shades, applications make you feel most like your celebrity.

Practice each version of your makeup applications. You will need to know how to apply your **mix and mingle makeup**, which will be fairly heavier than day makeup, yet light enough to look good when you have people looking at you from close range.

Photography makeup: When you are shooting your look-alike shots, your makeup will need to be applied heavier, and with foundations that are designed for specific lighting.

Stage performance makeup will be the heaviest applied makeup, as you will be farther away from your audience, with strong spotlights being placed upon you. If your makeup is not exaggerated, your look will get lost on stage. You can be bigger with your presentation when you're on a stage by the addition of false eyelashes, darker shades of eye shadow, lip colors, shading, and contouring.

If your celebrity does not wear much makeup, find a way to wear your makeup in a way that appears natural, but heavy enough to make it an impersonation of your celebrity.

Experiment on Halloween or costumed parties. When you try your makeup out before your first look-alike job, you can get some feedback from friends, and get a feeling of what people recognize and respond to.

What about false teeth, mustaches, beards, sideburns, teeth blackouts, scars, moles, etc?

If your character needs one of these items, you will need to go to a costume specialty store, Halloween store, or beauty supply store to find these kinds of items. Practice with beards and mustaches before your job, as they require sticky glue that will take some practice to get used to using. There are liquid paints that create a blackout tooth or create a gap. There are also makeups that you can buy that can actually create scars, moles, or in some cases prosthetic cosmetics, which (if you learn how to apply properly) will allow you to sculpt a new nose, teeth, eyelids, face shape, and more (more about this later).

Makeup Resource Books:

These gorgeous books describe specific makeup application techniques for look-alike applications, glamour, and practical makeup tips and application. All are available at most bookstores.

° Devon Cass - **Double Takes**
° Kevyn Aucoin- **Making Faces**
° Nars - **Makeup Book**

Sue Quinn as Boy George; Sue Quinn Photography

Makeup Advice (and More!) from Makeup/Impersonator Expert Sue Quinn

Since you can transform yourself into a male character, then you are an example of un-believable transformation possibilities utilizing makeup! Can you give us tips for makeup application?

134

Sue Quinn- Master Impressionist/Makeup Artist: "Work in a well-lit environment - best if the light is filtered or above and in front of you. Don't work under fluorescent lighting. Warm, bright, even light is best. Make sure that no harsh shadows are being cast on your face and the light is even on both sides of your face. Have a table for your makeup easily in hand's reach and it's best if you can sit down and are comfortable. You should be able to see your reflection clearly and in detail. But I also suggest a hand mirror for close up work for the eyes. You will need to be able to see close-up detail. Also, have a surface where your photos of the celebrity you are working from can also be easily seen. Have several taped in front of you next to the mirror for reference and at different angles of the star's face. Keep in mind that your reflection is your face in reverse - note which side the distinguishing marks might be on in that photo and repeat them accordingly in reverse on your own face. All of your makeup should be out and easily accessible. Have at your fingertips a damp rag or washcloth to keep your hands clean in between applications (as I often find myself doing) in case you need to blend make-up. This will avoid transferring different shades of makeup to areas where you don't want it. Keep a trashcan close by for pencil shavings. Have plenty of Q-tips on hand to fix mistakes. I definitely suggest you work in a cool climate, as this will keep your makeup from being too soft or oily (especially pencils, as they can loose their sharp point easily in heat). Try not to put too much powder on your face, as that can make it look dead or muddy. Using a clean puff, lightly dusted, can help to keep you from being too shiny. Makeup will always activate oil and sweat glands, so try not to apply makeup too thick. Doing light layering is the best method. Occasionally touch up areas that may experience wear or friction, such as lips and nose, to wipe smudges away. Always bring an extra hand mirror with you and touch up makeup.

When applying your makeup, it is essential that the photos of your celebrity be clear and taken from all angles. Their facial structure should be easy to see. Closely examine your own face and then your celebrity's, and try to observe where the two are similar and where they are different. Be objective and keep in mind that the mirror is an opposite reflection of what the world sees. Be aware which side of the face might have a distinctive mark or mole, and which side the hair is parted, or a scar or raised eyebrow is situated. Then through the careful application of quality theatrical makeup, by shading, contouring, and highlighting, you can re-create the celebrity's face on your own, using your face as a canvas. Match shadows and colors where the face has depth, and the same for the areas where the face stands out. If you can actually re-create that color, you can create false definition, widening and or narrowing your features, making them more deep and receding, or highlighted and pronounced. It takes some time to get used to applying makeup, especially if you have never done it before. Looking in the mirror and using hand to face coordination can be awkward at first, but with some practice one can usually learn.

It is best to have a professional makeup artist who is familiar with these types of celebrity transformations work on you first, and let them design your specialized makeup just for you and your character.

Ask your makeup artist what makeup you will need to have in your own kit, and then make a chart to follow. They can teach you how to apply it in various techniques. Some people may require more makeup than others, depending on how much they look like their celebrity already.

What makeup products do you use yourself?

I think Joe Blasco is probably the most dependable brand for easy application and accurate coloring. Their products are of high quality and can be somewhat expensive, but they also last a long time and should not irritate the skin unless one has a particularly sensitive condition. They have an extensive color selection and many different types of make up to choose from, depending on the skin type they are being used on. Different skin types will require different kinds of makeup. The age of the person requiring the makeup may also be a determining factor. They even have makeup to cover up scars or tattoos, deep facial marks, and rough texture. Re-creating an age of a person is an important detail. You may be younger or older than the celebrity you are transforming into. In addition, some performers may have had very long careers, like Frank Sinatra, for example, and have changed a lot over time by ageing, or body weight and hair fluctuations, but they may have distinct looks during those years that pinpoint a specific era for them. So you may opt to re-create several age periods of that person if at all possible. Here is where having good quality makeup and the knowledge and technique on how to apply it can really be of great help. Joe Blasco does provide a makeup school for such technique and training. You might wish to inquire about this if you are really serious on accuracy. You should be able to acquire Joe Blasco makeup at any well-stocked beauty or theatrical supply store, especially where film, TV, and local theater studios are close by.

  I have met Mr. Blasco in person, and I mark it as one of my most memorable experiences. I was rather awestruck in his presence, as he has been a great source of inspiration for me and something of a hero in my eyes. Sometimes working as a look-alike has its rewards, as in the case of meeting Mr. Blasco. To my surprise, he presented me with a most generous gift - a complete makeup kit that was quite valuable! I was absolutely bowled over with his generosity and kindness! I highly recommend Blasco makeup and products to achieve the perfect look for performing as well as daytime makeup.

Hair: Hair is a whole other chapter. Wigs are best if constructed of human hair. Human hair wears better, can be styled and colored accordingly, and looks much more natural. Synthetic hair, unless it is the very finest available, can be too shiny and then can look dull if overworked. You can't apply heat to it, as heat can melt it or change the texture permanently. Fake hair can also appear mono-colored and real human hair has subtle differences in the hair strand coloring. It also catches the light in a different way than fake hair. False hair can be stiff-looking or not move as softly as human hair. It can get frizzy easily and it is difficult to return to its original texture once it tangles. Falls and hairpieces such as sideburns and moustaches should also be made of human hair. They can range in price, but you can find good quality ones at a reasonable price range if you take the time to investigate. Facial hair should be on flesh-colored netting and can be applied in various ways. If it is going to be worn close up and for long periods of time, it is best to apply it with spirit gum, a tacky theatrical glue that dries clear and solid but is flexible once the hair is held in place for a while. It is a bit difficult to remove, as it can stay tacky after you remove the hair. But there is special solvent designed just for that purpose of removing the glue from the face and the hairpiece. It is a mineral oil-based solvent. Once the glue has been softened, then you must wash your face several times afterward with a good soap to remove the residue and oil. Also, keep the facial hairpiece clean and you can reuse it many times over, especially if pinned to a Styrofoam wig head and carefully reshaped while still damp. Hair tape for styling can also work to keep the facial hair's shape, once restyled and allowed plenty of time to dry.

Facial hair: Another way to hold facial and theatrical hairpieces in place is with hair tape, a double-sided tacky tape that adheres to both the face and the net side of the facial hairpiece. It is easily removed from both surfaces of the face and hairpiece, and will stay put for a good deal of time after application as long as the subject doesn't sweat too profusely. But it can be detected by close inspection. So it is best for distance usage or quick changes before an audience.

Many celebrities will have a variety of distinct hairstyles they are known for throughout their career. You may wish to invest in several wigs that are prestyled and set for a few distinctive periods or well-known looks for these characters. When I was impersonating Austin Powers, I noticed that his hairstyle and the color of his hair changed quite a bit from the first movie to the second. So I have two different wigs to represent both films and the costumes that go with them.
If you really look like the person you are representing, having your own hair cut and styled like them can work both in your favor and against it. It can be a huge help, as it will be very convincing as the character and easy to maintain, depending on how extreme their hairstyle and coloring is.
Performing as several different characters and keeping my own hair color can be a challenge. When I kept my hair colored to impersonate Cyndi Lauper's, it was costly and my hair became damaged with all the bleaching and dye, although it did make it easy for me to do costume changes into her character. For other shows, I had to cover and conceal my "Cindy" bright hair with a wig and brown mascara to become Boy George. So the washing out of the mascara and retouching took

quite a beating on my hair, as I had to do two shows a night changing back and forth to each character. You need to decide for yourself if wigs will best suit your needs or if having your own hair styled to match your celebrity will be best.

Makeup secrets: All my makeup is just that, painted or applied, and then I simply work and contort my features to bring the character to life. I will put a bit of cotton padding in parts of my facial cavities to add fullness or change the shape. I have done this for when I portray Elton John (for the mouth and nose). My ability to work my facial muscles to contort to match a characteristic facial expressions is a highly concentrated effort that requires many hours of close studying of video footage of these people talking, singing, mugging and just relaxing or reacting to different situations. It is time-consuming and requires tremendous control and concentration. Using the mirror to help guide you in re-creating expressions is an essential part of the illusion process by tying together all of the parts - makeup, hair and costume.

Face parts: For gluing on a facial part like a nose, for example, derma wax works best. First, one must apply a bit of spirit gum and allow it to dry to a tacky consistency. With clean dry hands, take a small bit of derma wax that has some color to it (light and not too pink), and knead it and work it between your fingers. This will make it pliable, and then form a ball. It is easiest if you have some baby oil or mineral oil to keep it from sticking to your fingers. It is easier to shape, too, but only a very small dab of oil on your fingertips is all you need. Then place the ball of wax on the tacky glued area of your face or nose and begin to smooth and shape it until you have the desired shape. Look at it from all angles to make sure it's even and smooth. Lightly powder it, and then with an oil-based makeup, try to blend it to match your skin color. Powder it and lightly dust with rouge or give texture with a sponge. Each application can be as varied as there are noses and facial scars in the world, so you may wish to practice different techniques and textures.
Actual pre-made latex prosthetics, it is best left to the professional makeup artists and FX specialists. It can be a rather involved process that requires a cast made of your face. It can also run you a lot of money and is very time consuming to apply. So I would suggest using them only in extreme cases or for things like a false double chin or an exaggerated nose.

Teeth: A celebrity's mouth can really be a distinctive feature. Sometimes all that is required is a bit of tooth blackout to create a notch in the front teeth for celebrities such as John Lennon or Lauren Hutton. Other characters may require more extreme measures if your own teeth are very different from your star's. If the teeth are a defining factor to the character (like Austin Powers) one may have a set of overlapping false teeth professionally made that snap and fit neatly over your own teeth and stay in place with suction. Latex prosthetics can involve a costly process that requires a cast of your teeth, made by a proper dentist, and then the fake teeth must be hand molded and cast of a hard and durable denture plastic. These can be somewhat difficult to speak through as well. Keep in mind that it is fairly easy to build outward on teeth but almost impossible to reduce the look of teeth that are too big already or protrude. In that case it just requires flexible mouth skills to hide obvious teeth - unless you decide to invest in actual cosmetic dental surgery!!

Getting ready and in the mood...

To get in the mood for a performance, I listen to music by the artist, or a soundtrack, as I work on my makeup and costume. I watch some videos of them. I prepare my costume and set it out, carefully checking each item over to make sure all is fine, and I make whatever repairs are necessary. I begin to make the faces of that person while I start applying the makeup and I keep this up throughout the entire makeup process. I also make sure I am wearing something that can easily be removed, without having to be taken off over my head, once the makeup is finished. I never wear t-shirts, as they have tight necks and can smear the makeup while being removed after the makeup is finished. A button-down shirt, loose-fitting and comfortable, is best. I also make sure my hair is tied back and out of my face. I can do any under-wig clipping down after the makeup is finished. A wig cap is also a big help, but must be secured to your own hair before you put on a wig, or else it can make a wig slip and shift if it slips back on your hair. And finally, I put the costume on and begin to walk, talk, act, and become that person completely, never breaking character until it is time to take it all off. Nothing will destroy the illusion of a character more quickly than for one to go in and out of character during the course of a night with the audience. It's okay to take a break away from them, and with people you know, but then return to the character once you are rested and refreshed.

Costumes: It is vital that your wardrobe is accurate, and is clean and well-fitting. Making your costume comfortable, as well as accurate, is important. You can add Dr. Scholl's pads in your shoes. Add heels if you need lift to be closer to the height of your character, and likewise, wear flats if you are much taller than your character.

Tips to live by: Be respectful of your character and never behave in a way that would not be appropriate to their public personality. If the character is extreme, use discretion and only portray the ideal and positive side of that person unless you are specifically booked to play the character in an extreme fashion. Never get drunk or use drugs!! Remain in control at all times. Never say you are really that person. Don't autograph their name. You may just write a first name or the character's name like "The Terminator," but be aware that you can actually fool people and you legally may not pass yourself off as the real article. Have fun and try to interact with your audience. Stay loose and try to have set routines and key phrases you can use to remind people of who you're trying to be. Use distinctive poses that make you appear more like that person, poses that you can strike at a moment's notice when a camera is angled in your direction. Be aware what angles are best for you. Try to keep your weight the same as your character's. If you are a smaller body type than your celebrity, you might consider padding your costume. Refrain from swearing and be aware of the type of audience you are playing to - religious, older, corporate, hip, adolescent - and act accordingly. Have appropriate and accurate props! I never use my fake gun for an adolescent crowd. Just have fun with the character and the audience, and you will be appreciated and rewarded for a job well done. This is a way to get great referrals from your client and guests alike."

Surgery and Skin Care

Q. What about plastic surgery? Is it necessary for entertainers to have surgery to look better or more like a celebrity?

Answer: Working in the entertainment business, even as a celebrity impersonator, one can certainly expect to experience some of the same pressures (and sometimes more!) that actors or models experience on a daily basis. Having a perfectly shaped body, a perfect photographable smile, perfect skin, or an oversized bust line are the images that Hollywood seems to bombard us with over and over in magazines, television, and film. Since our society seems to worship what the media dictates, we find ourselves in a time where girls in their 20s are going to have face lifts (and more!) in hopes of achieving that perfect Hollywood look. Worse, there are some look-alikes who have felt the same pressures to look perfect, and decide to have plastic surgery in hopes that having surgery will bring more work opportunities. The sad truth is that it is not uncommon nowadays for entertainers and performers to make the choice to nip, tuck, or go under the knife to achieve the right look for the camera. Performers may ask the question, "how can a look-alike talent attempt to impersonate a celebrity who has had plastic surgery"? Is there a way to impersonate someone who is known for having plastic surgery without having to have plastic surgery? The answer is YES! And here is why.

First: When working as a professional look-alike talent, it will be your outgoing personality, performing abilities, and/or act that will get you bookings, not the fact that you have the same nose job as your celebrity.

Second: There are ways to achieve distinct lines on your face, using shading or contouring with makeup to change the shape of your features. You can achieve an instant change of look without having to make permanent alterations to yourself.

Third: It may seem like a great idea at the time, but you need to think about how you will feel in 10 years about permanently changing your appearance now. Your concept of your celebrity may also change as years pass. I know plenty of Michael Jackson look-alikes who decided on plastic surgery in the highlight of Michael's career, then later regretted alternating their faces when his popularity had slowed. With or without surgery, there are several very successful Michael Jackson impersonators who still work regularly who have chosen not to cut their face(s). Most audiences would prefer to see a strong dance, singing, or lip-sync performance rather than a doctored-up face surgery anyway, so be more creative in putting a look together that does not require you to go under the knife. It IS possible, even for The King of Pop look-alikes!

Fourth: Before getting into entertainment of any kind, I suggest that you develop a strong sense of self, so that when you find yourself in scrutinizing situations and people picking your look apart, you can remain completely self-confident and centered. You should feel convinced in your talent and impersonation so that a critical comment does not make you immediately insecure. **Plastic surgery will not make you a better impersonator.**

Fifth: There is no turning back should you decide (after surgery) that the surgeon and surgery made you look less like your celebrity than before you started. Once your eyes are cut, you are stuck with that look. This has caused some people to keep cutting, in hopes that each surgery will result in a better look. We all know what too much plastic surgery eventually ends up looking like.

I want to personally say that if you feel like plastic surgery is something you are seriously considering to help in your self-esteem, then that is a personal choice for you to feel good about; however, I suggest that you take the time to investigate the idea, and the surgeon. Get many referrals!

However, if you are an entertainer who is trying to fit the casting breakdowns then I am here to tell you, you do not have to give in to the idea that you have to "cut and paste" your body parts in order to work in Hollywood. If you wish to redefine your look, body, skin, or face naturally, then I have several other options for you to consider.

Skin and face solutions: There are some products on the market that I have recently discovered that seem to be improving my skin from the inside out. In all my research for the perfect products, treatments, and therapies for the face and body, I had tried just about every product that one could find at department and beauty supply stores. With the understanding that my face is part of selling my act, I wanted to care for my skin and attempt to preserve it as much as possible. It was important to me to find products that would improve and heal my skin without having to resort to plastic surgery or sticking needles in my face. As I began to read a variety of articles and books on skin, I started to learn why certain people seem to have a beautiful natural look over the obvious surgically enhanced look. As I searched through some women's magazines, I found an interesting article in *In Style* magazine.

The article was on a product called **Epicuren**. Many well-known performers, models, and actors were using this product Epicuren and choosing to have Epicuren treatments INSTEAD of plastic surgery. Some of the actors listed were impressive enough for me to look further into this product and try it for myself.

As I looked into alternatives for plastic surgery for this book, I met **Leslie Sloane**. Leslie is an expert in skin care, and is a highly sought-after healer who works in energy balancing, acupressure, aromatherapy, and therapeutic reflexology. She works hands-on as a rep, trainer, and educator with Epicuren and has done so for 13 years. Many top facialists, massage therapists, and holistic practitioners study under Leslie's trainings and workshops. Who better to get an education from than Leslie! Here is what Leslie sat down to explain to me.

Natural Facelifts: There are actually products that heal your skin from the inside. Anyone can actually have a natural facelift without damaging layers of skin or going under the knife. Leslie insisted that there is a cure for people who would like to have a healthier look or younger skin without artificially altering their skin or face.

She explained that Epicuren is an enzyme-protein treatment genetically reproduced to be recognized by our human skin cells. Most cosmetic products are derived from plants, fruits, chemicals, or acids. Because we are human, the DNA in our cells does not recognize these structures and therefore can only be stimulated to a certain degree. The missing factor is that because of this, they do not get the message from our cells to feed through our blood and oxygen which maintains the source of their life, much like you or I exercising without eating or drinking. The end result is physical exhaustion and dehydration. This is what happens to the cells. Thus, they die and dissipate, leaving the skin to continue to age, wrinkles to remain and worsen, and scar tissue never to fade or possibly disappear. In order to see a change in the skin, the cellular memory must be changed at the very root, which is the source of all of these mutations.

This is why the skin industry is so bent on pushing glycolic acids, which are so dangerous to our skin, which is our LARGEST ELIMINATIVE ORGAN. All acids stress the skin by causing the cells to "mechanically" exfoliate, meaning to die before their time.

What happens when you stress any organ? If you stress your heart, lungs, or kidneys too much, they give out. With the skin, if you stress it too much it becomes thinner, dryer, and eventually will speed up the aging process. There is no amount of surgery that can make the skin thicker or healthier. It begins with the cell, in the dermal layers underneath the skin.

Each dermal cell carries a memory and copies the cells on the epidermis. This is why when a person lives in the desert and spends a lot of time outdoors, they age much more quickly, because their cells are not being fed properly by a product that causes them to feed from our blood and oxygen, giving them strength to stay healthy. So the cells continue to age as the skin continues drying out from over-exposure to the sun.

The definition of aging is THE SLOWING DOWN OF ALL CELLULAR ACTIVITY. This begins to happen basically when we approach our late twenties. This is 50% due to our genetics, and the rest is a result of how we take care of ourselves.

To change any memory in the body, you must change your habitual way of life. When you do this, the cells will have no recourse but to follow the new path you have chosen for them, whether or not it has to do with skin. This is where Epicuren is a *must* - to keep the skin from aging well as the treatments given by the aestheticians, which are non-surgical facelifts and lift the skin from 20-30% depending on the genetics. For any Epicuren products and procedures, you must contact a licensed Epicuren trained professional. You can contact Leslie to find an Epicuren professional in your area.

Product Ideas To a More Beautiful You for Men and Women

Products to be applied under stage makeup:

NOTE: Because this is an "alchemical" line, all products listed for different skin types will be mixed in the palms of the hands like a "facial cocktail" and applied all over the face, eye, and neck areas. Each and every formula is designed to keep the cells oxygenating under heavy or light makeup, since it is the makeup that suffocates the cell and causes the skin to age rapidly. Consultations for the exact amounts of each product to use should be done through Leslie or one of her trained aestheticians (facialists), as this is a professional, scientifically based treatment.

Ultra Dry Skin:
Protein Spray Mister, Pro-Collagen III, Evening Emulsion, and Rose Oil OR Colostrum. Also great for "on the road" gigs and traveling work.

Normal/Dry Skin:
Protein Spray Mister, Pro-Collagen III, and Ultra Rose Treat.

Non-Problem Oily to Normal Skin:
Protein Spray Mister, Pro-Collagen III, Facial Emulsion, and if your skin is more on the oily side, Aloe Vera.

Light Acne/Oily:
Protein Spray Mister, Pro-Collagen III, Probiotic Emulsion, Aloe Vera, and SRT OR Facial Emulsion.

Heavy Acne/Oily:
Acne Astringent, Probiotic Emulsion, Botanical Elixir, Aloe Vera, SRT, and Acne Gel to spot treat on infected areas. (A suggestion to help those of you with chronic acne - go to an acupuncturist/herbologist to help clear out your intestines, which is where the problem generally stems from other than being hormonally based. If you are interested, contact Leslie for the holistic practitioner nearest you.) Going to a regular medical doctor is an option; however, you may end up just getting a shot (or antibiotics, which will actually make your situation worse by simply "covering up the problem" and not getting to the actual source of it).

- **Products that take off heavy stage makeup**: Crystal Clear Makeup Remover followed with an antibacterial cleanser and possibly a scrub for your skin type.

- **Treatments to give a natural facelift**: Pro-Collagen III, Instant Lift, Concentrate, Gel Plus, and an enzyme-protein emulsion for your skin type.

- **Products to hydrate over worked skin**: Pro-Collagen III, Colostrum, and Ultra Rose Treat or Evening Emulsion mixed with Rose Oil.

- **Products to take on the road, on the set, and to the show:**
Since everyone has different skin, a personalized "kit" can be prescribed in two-ounce sizes and put in a small plastic Epicuren traveling bag to make it easy to travel with. This will usually last for about one and a half months, and is perfect for the artist on the road or on the set everyday.

Having clear, vibrant skin can make a world of difference as to how you look on stage, in photographs, on film, and in your everyday life. Consider looking into products like Epicuren before having plastic surgery. I suggest that you do your homework and search for products that work to heal your skin from the inside out, rather than burn and destroy what you have.
Being a performer means that your appearance is an important part of your product - you. So taking care of your skin is vital. Whichever way you decide to care for your skin and body, consider looking into finding an expert like Leslie to better educate yourself about all possible solutions for your needs.

Solution for achieving extremely different features on your face with makeup and NO knives or surgery: Master makeup artists like Sue Quinn have studied painting and art, and have a great deal of experience in drawing contours and shades that can literally reshape the face by painting onto the skin. Finding a makeup artist that understands shading and shape can help you achieve the proper techniques to redesign your face to resemble another face shape. It is possible to create a look that is close enough for you to work as a look-alike so that plastic surgery does not have to be considered as an option or solution for success.
Prosthetics can also be used, such as clay materials that mold to your own face to create new features. You will need to scout your area to find the right makeup artist for your needs.

Sue Quinn, Master Impressionist/Makeup Expert: "Performers that do not closely resemble a celebrity simply should not impersonate that celebrity. One should be able to create a close look utilizing hair, wardrobe, make-up, and performance and not go to the extreme to have plastic surgery. I perform as many different characters, including Austin Powers, Cindy Lauper, Boy George, Elton John, Madonna, Willie Wonka, and several more. I am proof that being good at your craft will allow you to get professional work as a celebrity look-alike without having looks that are identical to a celebrity. I would not suggest anyone go to that extreme for the accuracy of a character. Having plastic surgery to look like a celebrity (in my opinion) can border on fanaticism, and if this is the case, then a psychological analysis of yourself may be necessary before delving further into becoming a look-alike impersonator talent."

Body and Fitness

Solution for the body: What about the body? To impersonate an actor or singer who is well known for their great legs, curvaceous hips, big biceps, or muscular tones can be just a tad intimidating if you're not in the same condition yourself. Celebrities have the advantage of hiring personal trainers, chefs, or personal gurus, or investing in home gym training equipment. You need to decide for yourself if you are going to impersonate someone with a famous physique, and realize that you will need to look passable, but it is not necessary to have 32" biceps to be a Terminator look-alike.

There are many alternatives for reshaping the body:

For slimming midsections: Many corsets and girdles are made for both men and women. You can usually buy them at department stores. When worn tightly enough, they can slim you at least one size less than your normal size.

If you're looking to increase a bust line: many lingerie shops now sell items like water bras or gel cups to insert into a bra. These bras and inserts can increase your bust line up to three times its normal size. No need to worry if you look like Dolly minus the obvious; try Victoria's Secret or Fredrick's of Hollywood to find padding for your hips, bust, or behind.

Tips to alter your physical shape:

To slim your overall look, dark colors are best. Black is always most flattering. For skirts or pants, a high waist style is always a more flattering, lengthening look. Choose muted or small-patterned fabrics, and avoid horizontal stripes or fabrics with large patterns.

If you need to show off your legs, but they just don't look as good as Betty Grable's, try wearing control top, extra support panty hose underneath your fishnet stockings. Extra support pulls legs in and keeps them looking tight.

For someone needing to appear larger or taller, I suggest shoe inserts. These can raise your height about 1" you can find these inserts at most shoe repair shops. Taller shoes and taller hair also can contribute to a taller look. To appear larger, try adding several layers to your costume. Layers can bulk your appearance and help you to appear larger. Horizontal stripes and busy patterns are also a way to give a bigger illusion.

If you want more results with your body: You may wish to consider a personal trainer and/or a more serious workout program with a professional. Regular cardiovascular exercise and weight training can and will reshape your body type, and when done with the aid of a professional certified trainer, you will ALWAYS get results! I highly recommend some kind of regular exercise to people of all ages. It increases oxygen to the brain, stimulates the nerves, gets natural endorphins running throughout the body, helps you sleep more soundly, and will absolutely make you feel better every time you do it.

Weight training will change your body type and shape, so if you are serious about wanting to look better without surgery, weight training will allow you to maintain your results as long as you stick to a program regularly (unlike liposuction, which can have temporary results).

Find a gym in your area and call around for a personal trainer that you feel comfortable with. Be selective and make sure this person inspires you to work. Do they have a great shape? Are they focused on YOU and not looking around the room distracted? Are they certified in training? Get to know who is training you and tell him or her the results you desire.

Remember that the basics of a healthy diet and regular exercise of three to five times a week will allow you to achieve fat loss and overall better health and appearance.

If you decide to train without the direction of a personal trainer, it is best to understand the basics of cardio exercise and weight training. For any kind of weight loss program, you will want to do at least 30 minutes of cardiovascular exercise three to five times a week. Walking, running, biking, stair stepping, boxing, jumping rope, aerobics, power yoga, or whatever feels right to your body. Find a cardio workout that feels right, and stick to it. Change it up once in awhile so that your body does not become too used to the same thing. With weight training, it is best to understand what you are doing so you don't waste your time or injure yourself by training incorrectly.

Costumes: Let's Go Shopping!

When putting your costumes together, remember to bring photographs of the star you are impersonating. Look for distinguishable colors, fabrics, patterns, and styles that your celebrity is known to wear. It is essential to invest in at least two costumes, and preferably more.

Where to go:

Start by looking at **secondhand, thrift, Salvation Army, and Goodwill stores**. Take the time to browse through vintage and used clothing stores before investing in brand new clothes for your costumes, especially if you are going to impersonate a celebrity who is known for wearing elaborate gowns, distinctive shoes, or designer clothing. By searching through secondhand stores, you may find exactly what you need without having to pay full price. When shopping for costumes, meet and speak with store managers or owners and let them know what items you are looking for. Often they will be willing to keep their eyes open and contact you when certain hard-to-find items become available.

Be sure to check for stains or tears in a used garment before purchasing it, and be sure to wash or dry clean it before wearing it.

You may also want to **check garage, estate and yard sales** for clothing, props, or jewelry.

If you live in a big city, don't forget to check with **garment district shops and outlets**. This is an excellent way to purchase designer items for much less than you would pay at a retail store.

If you are not sure you are ready to invest in buying a costume, try a **costume rental shop**. There are many stores that specialize in renting costumes and wigs for an evening. Tell the shopkeeper what you are looking for, and they can put a costume together for you. This is a great way to get ideas for putting your own costumes together. Consider consulting a costume rental store for your first photo shoot or job. Renting a costume and wig may be a great way to try out a look before you invest money in your own costumes, and it allows you to try different things if the first costume doesn't turn out to be quite the look you wanted. Check your local Yellow Pages for costume rental shops.

If the costume you want proves to be impossible to find, you may need to have it sewn and/or designed from scratch by a **costume designer**. Ask around at your local tailor, dry cleaner, or fabric store to find a person who specializes in costumes. Look in the Yellow Pages for costume designers or tailors. Remember, your costumes are your most important investment as a look-alike, so you need to be sure they are exactly what your star would wear.

Have a back-up costume at all times. If you need to dry clean your costume, you will need a second option if you get a last minute booking. You will need your costumes available on a moment's notice, so make sure you have **more than one option**. By having more than one look to choose from, you won't get bored with the same costume, and you may find a look that becomes your perfect look-alike signature look. Be certain the costume you choose is instantly identifiable as your celebrity. You may want to invest in legendary costumes that your celebrity is famous for wearing, and has been seen wearing in public on more than one occasion.

Many events you will be booked for will have a "Hollywood" or "Oscar" theme, so make sure you have costumes that are appropriate for those kinds of formal occasions. You should always bring at least two costume options with you to a job, if not more. The client may not approve of your costume (which they have the right to do), and if that happens you must have another outfit to change into.

As a look-alike, you should be immediately recognized by the overall look of your costume, hair and makeup. Your costume should be instantly identified as something your star has worn (or would wear). A distracting costume can take away from your look, and no matter how great a look-alike performer you are, if your costume does not read right, people may not "get" your impersonation.

Look-alikes can bring an excitement to people and situations by creating a magical illusion with their look, voice, and presence, and an impressive costume certainly helps create that magical illusion. Take the time to put the right colors, fabrics, and style together that clearly identifies your celebrity. Remember the color and styles of fabric will make a huge difference in how you feel as your celebrity, and you will want to pick colors that make YOU feel best, as well.

More creative ideas:

Browse through fabric and craft stores and catalogs for creative ideas for your costume or accessories ideas. Craft stores carry inexpensive beads, fabric glue, glue guns (my personal favorite), rhinestones, fabric paints, and easy-to-sew costume ideas. If you are a fairly creative person, you may have some fun in creating your own one-of-a-kind costume. Hand-making costumes or costume pieces will allow you to create something original, and it can be much more cost-effective than buying a costume retail. You may wish to add a few beads or feathers to a costume you already have, and thereby turn your ordinary costume into a theatrical masterpiece.

Custom Costumes

Costume expert Shon LeBlanc of Valentino's: "Having the perfect costume is absolutely a must for any impersonator to achieve a great look and get hired by the agencies as a pro!
Finding an expert who can customize a one-of-a-kind costume to custom-fit your body is one of your greatest investments."

Costume Designer Shon LeBlanc is the proprietor of Valentino's Costumes, a full service costume house located in Los Angeles, CA, specializing in impersonator and look-alike replica costumes. Valentino's provides costumes for theatre, television, video, print ads, schools, Halloween, and special occasions. The costume stock at Valentino's contains over 40,000 costumes and accessories, including items from the Egyptian and Roman era all the way through the 1970's, with many available in hard-to-find larger men's and women's sizes.

Shon has been designing costumes for theatre, film, video, and television for over 16 years. He has created wardrobe items for many varied productions including *Titanic, Guys and Dolls, The Elephant Man, The Merry Wives of Windsor*, and *Dinner at Eight*. Shon has honed his skills and developed an attention to detail that has become his signature of the "complete picture." This attention to detail has earned him 9 Dramalogue Awards, 3 Garlands, and numerous nominations from the Los Angeles Drama Critics Circle, Ovation, L.A. Weekly, and Robbies.

If you wish to rent a costume for a job or have one specially made to keep, Shon can personally help you with all your costume needs. Although he is located in Los Angeles, he provides custom costumes worldwide. Feel free to call Shon or visit his website for any of your costume needs. He is very reasonable in price, is available for rush orders, and has helped some of the best look-alikes and entertainers with last-minute requests and hard to find garments.

Promotional Materials

Photographs: Strike a Pose

To be hired professionally as a look-alike, you are going to need some basic promotional materials. The most important element in all of your promotional materials is a great photograph. Many times you will be hired (or not) depending solely on this presentation. It is extremely important for your photograph to look professional and capture the look of your celebrity as closely as possible. You need to bring to life the essence of your star in one quick moment frozen in time. Your look-alike shot will be used for many different jobs and will be seen by many people. You may not get the chance to make a new or better impression (as the commercial says), so if your first look-alike shots are not convincing, it may be challenging later on to change a closed mind. Once you send your shot(s) out to agents, you may be making or breaking future work for yourself, so take your time and get your photograph exactly right before distributing it. You may wish to strike a famous and recognizable pose of your celebrity. Make sure you practice in a mirror before you take any pictures, so you can recreate that image for your photo shoot.

On the day of your photo shoot, give yourself plenty of time to get your makeup and hair exactly how you want it to look. Sometimes being a little nervous can interfere in the application of makeup, so allowing yourself plenty of time to get into hair and makeup without feeling rushed will help you to get a cleaner, more polished look. Decide ahead of time which poses you hope to capture, and know in advance which are your stronger sides, angles, and poses.

Taking your own photos:

If you are unsure about investing in a photo shoot and think you can create a professional quality photograph with your own camera, or with the help of a friend, then find a location with a clean background. Find locations that will give you sufficient lighting, with nothing distracting in the surrounding areas. Another suggestion is to have a digital photograph taken of yourself. Before investing in photos, you may consider trying your first photo shoot with a digital camera. With a digital shot, you can see instant results, and even e-mail them to your agents. With regular photos, one hour photo labs can get your shots done quickly and allow you to view which shot(s) you will blow up to 8x10. If you are not quite ready to invest in professional photographs and decide to let a friend take your first look-alike photographs, make sure the quality *appears* professional. You will eventually need to get professional photos done.

Having your shot duplicated:

Once your photo shoot is complete and you have chosen one or two shots that look the most like your celebrity, you will need to have 8x 10 copies made. A printing shop that specializes in duplications is the most cost-effective choice. A smart idea to have on the front of your look-alike shot is **JOE SMITH AND HIS TRIBUTE TO ELVIS** or **JANE DOE AS MARILYN**. It's best to have your name on the photo, so that people can remember who YOU are. It can get confusing to an agent when there are six Madonna look-alike photos in the file, but they all say "Madonna" and each photograph looks fairly close to one another. Let the agents begin to know who you are separately from your celebrity. Do NOT put your phone number or contact information on the photograph, unless you have a personal manager or agency. Agents send your photograph out to prospective clients, so they do not want your phone number on the photo if they are representing you for work. Your photographs may be sent to clients along with your resume or bio, or they may be included in a promotional package. So if you need to send out a photograph with your personal information on it, you should hand print your name, address, and telephone number on the back to avoid possible problems, rather than having the photos printed with your information. In deciding how many copies to order, remember that each agency you work for will need at least ten.

Going to a professional photographer:

I highly suggest having an expert photographer take your look-alike shots. It's your main investment to sell yourself as a talent, and a convincing photograph can instantly open doors. Following are some tips from an exceptional photographer who understands how to photograph impersonators and help them achieve the perfect shot to re-create their celebrity best.

The right look-alike shot can open many doors...

Professional Photographs

Advice on having your photos done right by expert look-alike photographer,

– Johnny Garcia.

The difference between having a great photo shoot and having a great *look-alike* photo shoot!

Considering that there are many professional photographers, choosing the right photographer to take your photos can be frustrating and time consuming. However, I've written a ***tip list*** that will alleviate the frustration and confusion involved in finding the right photographer.

Step One:

Are you really ready for a photo shoot? Before contacting a photographer, you should be prepared with your "look." Have your outfits ready, including accessories such as wigs and props (hats, cigars, eyeglasses, mustaches, pointy-coned bras, etc.).

Know which poses you'd like to use for your photos. Look for photographs of the celebrity you look like, and practice those poses in front of the mirror.

One of the best ways to find a professional photographer is by word of mouth. Do you know someone who recently shot with a photographer and was satisfied with the results? Have you driven by a photo studio and seen photos on display and liked the photographer's style? Can your local agency/agent refer you to a photographer? If not, remember that your local Yellow Pages will list several local photographers that specialize in portraits or headshots.

Step Two:

Calling the photographer

Before you make the call, review the following guidelines that I have put together:

Does the photographer have experience shooting celebrity impersonators?

Your photographer should have some experience or understanding in capturing a look-alike shot. Shooting a look-alike is different from shooting a regular person. The photographer should be aware of the "cheat" angles that will help you in nailing that celebrity's look. The photographer should also be aware that a picture that is not necessarily flattering to you could actually flatter your character. The photographer should take the time to study and recognize the facial structure and body type of both your celebrity and yourself. They should know what poses are going to photograph most like your celebrity.

How much does the photographer charge and what do you get for that price?

Normally, a photographer will charge per roll of film or give you a package deal for your photo session, which is usually less expensive in the long run. You'll want to inquire about black and white photos, not color (unless you wish to make the more costly investment). Black and white pictures are normally used for publicity and headshots and it's rare to see promotional photos in color. In Los Angeles, the average price for headshots done in black and white is between $75.00 to $250.00 per roll. This fee usually includes the price for film and developing, the proof sheets, the photographer's fee, and in most cases, the negatives. There are some photographers who keep the negatives. This might be an inconvenience for you in the future if you need prints made from those negatives. You'll have to track down the photographer and wait to get your prints developed. In the end, it's always best for you to keep the negatives. Try to work this out with the photographer beforehand.

When does the photographer get paid?

This depends on the photographer. Most will prefer a deposit before the shoot and the balance paid in full on the day of the shoot. Others might be more flexible and more willing to work with you in terms of paying for their services.

Does the photographer work with someone who does hair and makeup, and if so, how much extra would that be?

Some photo studios do have in-studio hair and makeup artists. Their fees are generally included in the price of the session or they will be quoted separately. One thing to remember is that you're having your photos made as an impersonator, and the makeup artist will need to create that look for you. They might be talented at creating "glamorous" looks but lacking in the skills of creating impersonations. You might want to search for a makeup artist skilled in impersonator's makeup, or even learn to do the makeup yourself. With practice, you can create the looks that *you* want. Plus, when you're booking gigs, you'll most likely be doing your own makeup. So the more you practice, the better you'll look.

Where does the photographer hold the photo shoot?

Photographers will shoot either on location, in a studio, or both. Figure out how you'd like to style the photograph. Indoors or outdoors? For instance, if you're impersonating Marlene Dietrich, would her character look better sitting on a chair in a studio or lying on a bench in the park? Obviously you'd want the studio shot. If you're impersonating Madonna and want to do shots resembling recent tour photos of her leaning against a trailer, do you do those photos in studio or by an actual trailer? You'll want the photos to capture the celebrity's essence as closely as possible, so the location of the shoot is an important element of your photos. Discuss this with the photographer. If you're set on doing a studio session but the photographer does only location shots, you want to make sure they can replicate what you want. If they can't, don't settle for second best - keep looking!

Can you schedule an appointment to see the photographer's portfolio?

Before shooting, it's always an excellent idea to meet with the photographer and get to know their work. Look at their portfolio and discuss work they've done with other impersonators. Discuss how you want your photos taken and ask how the photographer sees you being photographed. During this initial meeting, get a connection going with the photographer. Remember, you'll need to be able to trust the photographer so you can feel open and at ease as they photograph you. If you feel uncomfortable or uneasy around them, this will show in your photos. If you can't feel at ease with the photographer, keep searching. There will be a photographer with whom you'll click.

Can the photographer guarantee their work?

So you get your photos back and because of the lighting and angles the photographer picked, you look more like Jay Leno than Tom Cruise, the person you had intended to impersonate. What happens then? Discuss re-shoots and money-back guarantees before the shoot. Some photographers guarantee your satisfaction with their work, and others don't.

What's the turnaround time for getting back your photos or proof sheets?

This is where patience comes in handy. It can be a long process from the time you have your photos taken to the time you're mailing your photos to agencies and potential clients. Sometimes it can take anywhere from two weeks to a month and a half to be able to start sending out your pictures. Don't try to rush this process, because it will show on your final product. Ask the photographer when you can expect to have the proofs from your shoot. Because some photographers develop their own film and others send the film to specialized labs, the turnaround time varies, but still you should get a date on which you can expect to see proofs from your shoot.

Will the photographer help you pick out the winning photo(s) or will you need to do that on your own?

Find out if you can sit down with the photographer after the shoot and get his/her opinion on which shot(s) will represent you the best. Photographers have the experience to help you make the right choices. If they're unable to sit with you, an agent or an unbiased friend can also help you choose. You could do it on your own, but someone else's eye can usually catch something you don't see.

Are there any hidden costs?

Example: A photographer may charge $35.00 a roll, which seems like a great deal, but he may not communicate to you that he keeps the negatives. When you want your first photo blown up, he may charge an extra $95.00 just for that one 8x10 photo. The second 8x10 blow-up will cost you an additional $75.00, etc. Some photographers actually do business this way, and as you can calculate, this can get costly. Be clear from the start on all costs and expenses.
Keep in mind that the costs of the photo shoot, a hair and makeup artist, and getting your photos reproduced can add up, but these are all important details for a successful photo shoot. Try not to cut corners to save yourself a few pennies.

For example: If you decide to shoot only one roll of film, but hope to change your costume six different times, you're less likely to get the one or two perfect shots you need. If it's your first time in front of the camera, you might not warm up to the camera until the end of that one and only roll of film. It takes most people at least one full roll of film before they loosen up, so expect to go all out for your shoot so that you can get the best results.

Once you've decided on which photographer to use, what should you expect from the photo shoot and what should the photographer expect from you?

Step Three:

On the day before the shoot, give the photographer a call to confirm your appointment. This will also give you a chance to ask any last minute questions.

On the night before the shoot, have everything ready so you're not stressing on the day of the shoot. This means have your clothes hanging so they're not wrinkled, and have your accessories/props ready to go. If you're shooting black and white photos, pick clothes that are not black or white because these two colors are not good to wear for photos. Those colors can contrast harshly against your skin. Colors such as navy blue, burgundy, beige, and light brown are great alternatives for black or white clothes.

An important tip: Get solid rest the night before the shoot. Try to avoid salt or alcohol, as it will make your eyes bloodshot and puffy the next day as well as make you retain water.

On the day of the shoot, show up on time. If you're doing your own makeup, show up ready to shoot. If the photographer has another shoot scheduled for that day, your session might either be rushed or cancelled if you are not on time. If the photographer is late and you have a time restraint, don't hesitate to reschedule the shoot. Being late can result in not-so-good photos, and who wants that?

Come to the shoot relaxed and confident. Be prepared to *be* the person you're impersonating. The more you become that character, the more you'll give to the camera. Bring music that will help you *feel* in character. Strong, moody, or melancholy music may ease you into your character quickly. You may wish to bring a friend along who can help bring a smile or sincere laugh to your face.

If it's your first time in front of the camera or even your tenth, you might feel nervous. That's perfectly normal. While shooting, if you need to take a breather to calm your nerves, that's okay. When nerves arise, the first place they will show is the mouth, so when posing for a photograph, take time to loosen your lips, smile, and stretch your mouth and tongue in between each pose. This will help relax tense smiles. Think of something that makes you smile, and reflect on this image as you take your shots.

During the shoot, have your touch-up items on hand: lipstick, hair spray, eye drops, powder, safety and/or bobby pins, and baby oil. Keep a mirror handy so you can check your poses to ensure that you're doing them correctly. Without glancing in the mirror occasionally, your pose might be a little off. The photographer may take many shots of the same pose with only a slight change. This may feel strange, but it will give you many variations of one shot. Sometimes a slight angle change will give you that perfect shot. The simplest poses are sometimes the hardest to imitate. That's because in photography, there are many spontaneous moments that are very difficult to replicate. So when you're imitating a "spontaneous" shot, a simple tilt of the chin can make the difference between seeing *you* in the finished photo or seeing the *celebrity* you're impersonating.

Now you're finished with the shoot. Congratulations! Make the appointment to go back and pick up your proof sheets. Hopefully, the photographer can review the proof sheets with you. This would be a good time to ask for referrals to places where you can get your photos reproduced. Once they're reproduced, you'll be ready to start mailing them out and getting work!

So the message here is to be prepared and expect only the best. The better prepared you are, the better the results. The photos that you'll be submitting to agents will compete with impersonators who have been doing this professionally for sixteen years or more. Your photos are your first impression to many reputable agencies and casting companies. If they don't look professional, then *you* won't be taken seriously as a professional. If they look as professional as the rest of the elite impersonators, then you're ahead of the game and on your way to success.

Below, Johnny takes extra time and care to get the perfect pose for Bella to become Madonna.

Johnny Garcia poses Bella; Photography by Frankie Shammas

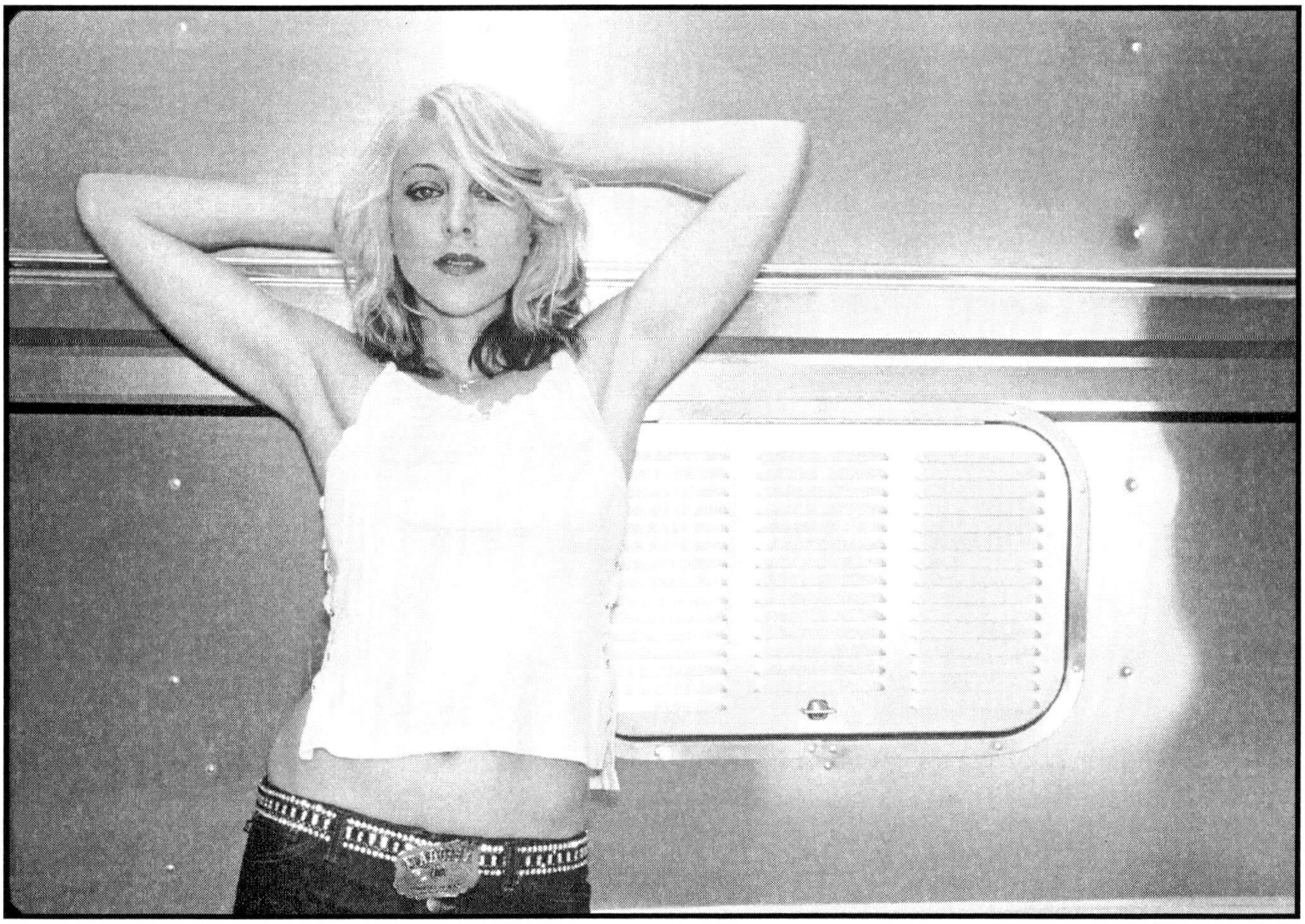

Mike Vitrano as Bruce Willis; Mike Vitrano Photography

Mike Vitrano as Bruce Willis: "Becoming a professional look-alike, you will want to get at least four professional photos of yourself, as your celebrity, that look as close to your celebrity as possible. Do not accept "close enough" as an answer from the photographer. You pay them for their services, and it MUST be as close to perfect as you can get! There are too many great look-alikes working, so your success comes down to **first impressions** and in most situations, all you have to offer is a photograph to convince an agent or client. These clients have nothing else tangible to base their opinions on but your photographs, so be VERY particular.
Now the oxymoron: I was called by producers to work as a stand-in two times based on *my driver's license photo!* (Go figure!)"

Cover Letter

If you're just starting out in entertainment and do not have impersonation credits to list to create a resume, a cover letter will be sufficient for submitting your photographs to agents. **The cover letter** should introduce yourself, stating who you are and what you do, and describe the kinds of jobs you are hoping to have booked. Provide detailed contact information in this letter so that the agent can reach you immediately. You may also wish to include a cover letter with a resume, for a complete promotional package.

I have enclosed a cover letter that I put together for television show producers to view, in hopes of booking myself on their show and to promote myself as an author, look-alike, and agent for other look-alike performers. When putting your own cover letter together, you can refer to this sample for possible ideas.

Tribute Productions   Your address here...

August 27, 2002

Receiver's address

12345 Sunset Blvd. Suite 50
Los Angeles, CA 90049

To Whom It May Concern:

    I would like to personally thank you for your time in reviewing our promotional materials for your future television show ideas and entertainment needs. Let me first introduce myself. I'm Denise Bella Vlasis, a professional double for Madonna, with over 17 years of professional experience.
    My years as a double for Madonna have allowed me to travel the world, perform on top television shows, and work with many great celebrities including Madonna, Christina Aguilera, Seal, and countless other industry greats. I have written an entertainment book that teaches people HOW TO become and work as a celebrity look-alike, which was recently published and is now in bookstores.
    I am considered to be an "expert" in this field, and I am now looking to present this instructional manual/ resource guidebook, which features great advice from many of the top agents and impersonators nationwide, to audiences that may be interested.
    You may already know the magic and excitement look-alikes add to any show, by adding that "star" element and excitement. My desire is to teach ordinary people how to become and work as a celebrity look-alike. It would be fascinating and entertaining to pull an audience member out of the audience and talk them through the process, using my step-by-step instructions. In addition, we can provide several top "stars" to be featured on your show (there is no limit to the number or type of celebrities desired - I have at least one look-alike for every top celebrity) to perform live, or just appear in their best "look."
    Since I am an agent as well, I see the demand for celebrity doubles here in L.A., as well as across the United States. I like to tell people, "It's is the easiest way to break into show business, without having any entertainment experience." With Madonna's latest film right around the corner, it may be a perfect time to book this show. As you probably already know, Madonna brings top ratings every time!
    I would love to work with you and share some creative ideas to make your show a super success and a memorable good time. Feel free to call me at the above number, or you can visit me on the Internet at
    I look forward to working with and for you today!

Sincerely,

Denise Bella Vlasis
  Tribute Productions

Your Resume

A resume is a listing of each job you have done as an entertainer. It also states your personal information and any other information that you believe will make an agent want to use you. Each time you do a job, be sure to add it to your resume. Keep precise records about your work, detailing each job, who it was for, what type of event it was for, and with film or television jobs, the name of the director, producer, and studio. As you get more and more jobs under your belt, begin to keep a separate log of the more impressive clients or jobs in which you were the featured entertainment, and give those jobs top billing on your resume. I have enclosed a sample resume to give you some ideas about how to put your own together.

You may want to include each job description, the client, and the location of the event.

For television, film, and cable: include the show title, the part you played, and the director and/or studio name.

There are professional resume-writing services that can craft a polished resume for you, and there is also great computer software available to help you to create professional resumes and letters. Check your local computer stores for selection and availability.

* **Note:** A look-alike resume can be different from a standard acting resume. With look-alike resumes, you can list corporate jobs, nightclubs, and specialty jobs. Acting resumes should be presented in a standard acting resume form. For more resumes, I recommend browsing through books like *How To Be a Working Actor* by Henry & Rogers, or any basic acting book.

Creating your Acting Resume

Here are suggestions of what a professional resume should contain:

- Name
- Address and phone (if you don't have an agent or manager)
- Height, weight, sizes
- Hair and eye color
- Training: Include your formal education, courses you have taken in modeling, acting, dancing, etc.
- Experience: Live shows, commercials, acting, television, motion pictures, special events, etc.
- Special talents

Have your printer cut your resume to measure 8x10 to fit with your headshot. Attach your resume to your photograph using two staples at the top.

You can have two separate resumes:

Your **acting resume** that lists your regular acting work only. Use this resume when you are submitting yourself for regular (non-look-alike) acting jobs.

Your **look-alike resume** to submit to agencies that book look-alike work.

Sample Look-Alike Resume

Jeffrey Briar
SAG/AFTRA/Am. Fed. of Musicians

Height: 5'7"
Weight: 135 lbs.
Hair: Light Brown
Eyes: Blue

FEATURE FILMS
Who Framed Roger Rabbit - Spielberg/Zemeckis
Sunset - Blake Edwards
Frances - EMI/Brooksfilm
Personal Best - Geffen Co.
Alice Through the Looking Glass - Bidue Films (Italy)

TELEVISION
Growing Pains - NBC
Matt Houston - ABC
Totally Hidden Video - Fox
A Celebrity Celebration: Voyage to 1939 - Disney
Break the Bank (3 times) - Hollywood
The Bozo Show - Chicago

COMMERCIALS
Tikkurila Paints (Finland - starred in 3-year ad campaign),
GMC, Toyota, Dodge, Anco/Champion, Chicago Sports Show, "Looking Good' promo spots for CBS

THEATRE
"The New Stan Laurel" – since 1979, internationally, over 1000 performances
"The New Charlie Chaplin" - since 1981; (Universal Studios Hollywood, Knott's Berry Farm, almost 2,000 performances)
"The New Inspector Clouseau" - since 1984; (California Mystery Train)
"Hollywood Follies" (Jerry Wilde, director)
"A Night in the Old London Music Hall" (Milt Larson, Producer; Gerald Gordon, dir.)
"H.M.S. Pinafore" (San Francisco)
"Tango" - Spquel,CA
"Deadwood Dick" – Showboat Dinner Theatre (Beau Rabb, Producer)
"Cock and Feathers Comedy Troupe" – co-founder, since 1972; Renaissance Pleasure Faires, international appearances

NIGHT CLUBS
At My Place, Comedy Store, Troubador (L.A.); MGM Grand Hotel, Imperial Palace (Las Vegas); Tramp's Cabaret, I Lena (NY); Resorts Intn'l Casino (Atlantic City); Goldenrod Showboat (St. Louis); SS Norway (Cruise Ship, England to NY)

SPECIAL SKILLS
Clown, mime, juggling, yoga, aikido, t'a I chi chuan
dance comedy, dialects
conducting, singing, piano (since 1962), silent movie/melodrama accompanist
organ, harpsichord, xylophone, clarinet, recorder, ukulele

"A real live wire, bringing joy with him wherever he goes."
  — Anthony Reveaux, Film Curator, Oakland Museum

Video/Audio Tapes and Promotional Reels

Consider making a **videotape** of yourself and your act. If you're a performing look-alike, you will have many agents requesting a videotape of your act, so my suggestion is to have a professional videotape made. This is a very important investment for many look-alikes, and sooner or later you will have an agent that will request your video. Many agents cannot actually book you until they view your video, and furthermore, the client who wants to hire you will also ask to see a video performance before making a decision.

To have a professional video reel made, you will need to call around to professional studios in your area. You can find studios in the Yellow Pages or on the Internet, and most larger cities have several to choose from. When calling the studios to reserve a time to film your act, make it clear that you are putting your demo reel together and speak with someone who can take the time to hear your needs and quote you an overall price. Most studios charge by the hour, and if you are not clear with what you need, this can get costly. Some studios have an "in-house" stage or performance area, and many have a "green screen" (a solid color green or blue backdrop to film in front of). You can do your act or show in front of the screen and later, the director or graphic artist can insert other background ideas. See if the studio can film you on location, and bring their crew to your next job to have your performance filmed live. You can also stage a live performance at an event, but make sure to get permission first from the agent, the client, and whoever is in charge of the event booking.

If you can find a local stage in your area, such as a high school or night club (most preferably during the day), you may be able to use the stage for free, and get your live performance on tape using the stage for your performing area. Get creative and map out a plan to get the best footage you can of yourself and your show. Later, you can have your tape re-edited as you get more footage of yourself. Prices to have a professional video made will vary, but be ready to invest some money, as filming, editing, and dubbing adds up.

If you are just starting out and are not sure you can invest in having a professional video made, have a friend videotape you during a staged or live performance. Your videotape should showcase your talent in the most favorable way possible. It should look professional and be clear, crisp, and of good quality. It doesn't need to be more than 12 to 15 minutes in length. It should feature your talents of singing, dancing, music, acting, or comedy in a polished, professional performance. If it is a tape of a live performance, make sure the sound is clear and the lighting is sufficient and flattering. If you need to, you can take it to a studio to have it dubbed so your voice is crystal clear. To get the best jobs and the most work, you should have a high-quality videotape. Again, your first impressions are critical. If you make your own videotape with your own camera, be sure the quality is sufficient. If you have a professional video done in a studio, make sure all details are worked out before the day of your filming, and get them in writing if possible.

An audio tape/cassette demo is also an important tool in booking a live singing act, stand-up comedy routines, and voice-over talent. If your voice is your strong feature as an impersonator, I suggest that you find a studio in which you can record your voice on a professional demo, 12 to 15 minutes in length, featuring highlights of your best sounds, skits, or singing. If you are preparing a voice-over tape, you will want to feature quick highlights of several voices. Remember to write your own original material when preparing a routine.

CDs as a demo: There are computer programs that you can buy that will allow you to burn your own CDs. You can get your singing demo burned onto a CD and then burn several copies on your computer program to mass mail to agencies. If you do not have a computer, you can call your local studio or computer expert to inquire about getting your demo on CD.

Promotional Package

A promotional package consists of:

Your head shots, full body shots (if requested), and any other professional 8 x 10 photographs

Your resume and/or cover letter stating who you are and what you do

A business card

**Your videotape
(for live performers or look-alikes showcasing their talent)**

Your cassette tape (for voice-over and/or live singing)

Any press clippings, media, or tear-out sheets (for print work)

Letters of recommendation

A folder to put all materials in

Be sure to ask the agent you are submitting your materials to whether they need a complete promotional package or just photographs. Each agent will need several copies of your photos, so it is not unusual for agents to request photos only. They will need your resume and video on file.

Jobs and Networking

Depending on where you live, your potential for work will vary. The amount that you work will also depend on how much focus you are willing to have and how creative you are at finding work possibilities. Until you find agencies that will hire you, you can create your own work by offering your talents to stores, nightclubs, and parties in your area.

Finding agents:
When searching for companies that hire entertainment, keep in mind that if a company does not currently book celebrity look-alikes, sending them your promotional package could spark in them the idea of a new talent to offer.
Once you have found companies who hire celebrity look-alikes, be aware not to sign any exclusive contracts with them. You should contract each new job separately as the agency hires you. Look-alikes are independent contractors. This means that no one agency can be the only one to get you work. You are free to work for many. I've listed several of my personal favorite agencies in the back of this book.

Note: Working for an agent is always better, even if you have made a contact on your own. When you have an agent representing you for a job, you only need to be the performer. An agent has to work hard to represent talent and get bookings, and they are experienced and comfortable in negotiating the best terms for a job. I believe most performers prefer to have an agent to represent them in every job.

Internet: The World Wide Web is an amazing resource for finding agencies. When surfing the Net, look under agents, look-alike agents (spell "look-alike" with and without dashes), impersonators, entertainment, booking, celebrities, party planners, event planners, and coordinators. You will find many agencies, both domestic and worldwide. You may wish to e-mail the most interesting companies a small photograph of yourself along with a short letter of introduction, and offer to send a promotional package if they are interested in learning more about you. (This is a good example of why it is a good idea to have at least one good digital photo of yourself in character, in addition to the printed photographs.)

Web site: Having your own personal website is a great way to circulate your talents all over the world. It can demonstrate your resume, photographs, live video, and audio performances. With the costs of mailing your promotional materials to each new client growing more and more expensive, having a web site that features your talents will save you time and money. You may wish to have an "agent friendly" website (see below) and I suggest having your website professionally prepared, unless you have the computer skills yourself. Also, having an e-mail account is going to be necessary for booking inquiries.

Yellow Pages: This is another valuable resource for finding agencies. Search under the same categories listed earlier for Internet searches.

Word of mouth: If you have never learned the skill of *networking*, now is the time. Networking means sharing information about yourself with everyone you meet—other performers, agents, corporate officers, entertainment planners, or any person whose knowledge of you could lead to potential bookings. It is very important to know some basic networking skills as an independent performer. Network by letting people know what you do, how long you've been doing it, any special skills or talents you have, and any important or high profile jobs you have performed. Have photographs or business cards with you in your daily life and be ready to offer them to anyone who appears interested in your work. You never know who you may meet, or where you might find yourself at the right moment. Be professional, but ready to sell your show. Remember that networking is often a give-and-take situation; so be as cordial and attentive to other people's networking efforts as you'd like them to be to yours. Be friendly and informative, but not pushy. People who remember their encounter with you as a pleasant one will be most likely to tell others about you.

Q. Can someone make a good living just being a look-alike?

The answer is, how much time are YOU willing to invest in your product - you? Putting in an eight-hour day at an office can be sitting at a computer, searching for new agents, clients, companies. You may spend days, months, and years perfecting an accent, costume, and dialogue.
What you will get out of this profession is directly related to what you put in. You cannot rely on a great look, voice, or talent in ANY entertainment field. It is what you do to promote yourself, and how often you are willing to work at what you do. Any smart businessperson knows the time it takes to devote yourself to any new business venture. If you are trying to create a way to make this a living, then I am here to tell you it can be possible (again I am living proof) but you will need to put in hours EVERY DAY in order to reap the rewards.

Author's Sample Networking idea: When I was starting out as an impersonator, I would send my creative ideas to companies about 3-4 times a week. If you have a creative networking way of thinking, you can certainly get more work for yourself. Giving people ideas can help you and the person booking you, and you just never know what job can be right around the corner for you.

Example/Idea: When Madonna's film *Who's That Girl* was about to be released in theaters, I sat and thought of ways I could incorporate myself into promotions for Madonna's movie release. (WHO'S that girl?perfect!) I wrote many letters to her record company, radio stations, and the film company that produced the film. After several letters were sent, I was finally contacted by a radio station for a great publicity stunt in correlation with the film to spot "Madonna" on the streets of L.A. The person to spot the Madonna look-alike first would be invited to the films premier. I was hired for the "Spot Madonna" contest, and after that booking, I was hired for three other jobs that were in correlation with the film release. You just never know when one booking idea will take off and turn into several bookings. Even in the case of not hearing back from someone after you send your promotional ideas, it isn't uncommon to get a call years later. It is worth the time, money, and energy to constantly submit your ideas on a regular basis.

Networking- Getting into the groove with Bea Fogleman:

Bea Fogleman has been involved in the celebrity impersonator business as the mother of a well-known Bette Midler impersonator. She is the author of several books on the entertainment industry, and has since developed a network for look-alikes, artists, agents, and show producers via the Internet. If you have Internet access and an e-mail account, make sure to get yourself listed in Bea's network. It is a great tool for talents and agents to have a constant networking system.

Bea Fogleman: "The Entertainment Network consists of over 1,500 talented people: performing celebrity impersonators, look-alikes, comedians, dancers, singers, band groups, and other performers, as well as agents, producers, and others in the industry.

Possibly, besides exposing all the talent to those who can place them on stages worldwide, one achievement was to open the door for allowing the agents to know each other and to cooperate with others in the booking of their previously "hidden" talent. A monthly newsletter, "Beg 'n Brag... News 'n Views" is placed on my website, where every person mentioned has their e-mail contact number included.

The motive is, and always has been, to acquire work for entertainers. It is my dream to see, in my lifetime, a professional industry with a Multiple Listing Service and a Guild to support it. The dream has already begun to take form.

The industry of celebrity impersonators has become vital as more and more actors take on the roles of performing artists, look-alikes, voice actors, and stand-ins for movies, films, television commercials, photo shoots, conventions, private events, production stages and more...all over the world.

What began as a small business in the early 1980s has developed into a major industry. Professional Impersonating Actors, those who make a living as artists, have learned their craft and continue to develop their act to create the best image to emulate the celebrity they are impersonating. They practice their art, study their movements and their voice, and if the star dances, their dance.
The art of impersonation has become big business, and those who wish to become part of it - and have the talent to do so - should spend some time studying some of the books that have been written about the industry, such as my books, *CopyCats, Who's Not Who* and *ShowTime*. The book that you are holding in your hands is an important addition to the library of everyone in the industry, and was written by Denise Bella Vlasis, Madonna impersonator and the author of the beautiful book, *Made You Look*. The doors to the world of the celebrity impersonator are now open for you, for those of you who have the ability and the talent and the drive to succeed."

Advice on "being seen" as a way to network:

Reggie Alcos as Tiger Woods: "Put yourself in a situation were you can be seen. I met my manager while helping out at a local summer fair. I was actually dressing up in costumes throughout the event, and the person who was in charge of the costume area thought I looked like Tiger Woods. He knew the event coordinator and introduced us. We met, he took some pics and the rest is, as they say, "history." I have been lucky enough to travel and meet some great people. Trust your gut. If you have any questions, feel free to contact me."

Reggie Alcos as Tiger Woods;
Reggie Alcos Photography

Agents and Agencies

We could not be in this business without agents, agencies, bookers, event planners, destination resource companies, party coordinators, producers, casting companies, catering companies, managers, and on. There are many different kinds of people that book look-alikes, and the majority are agents who work at some kind of entertainment company. Some are exceptional business-minded people and others are excellent performers (or were at one time) who either work for themselves or a company that specializes in entertainment. Some agents are working look-alikes, and understand this work from both the performer's point of view and the agent's. I too, know firsthand the time, patience, and hard work that goes into booking talent for an event, and with what I know, I truly believe the agents may not always get the credit they very much deserve. Most of the time their work is unseen by anyone - endless phone calls, faxes, dealing with a client who may be calling around to several agencies and putting them through the ringer to book a look-alike, sending out promotions, meeting with clients, signing contracts, and negotiating is hard work. We cannot forget about the expense just to run a successful business these days, so let us learn, right here and now, that agents work hard and deserve much more credit for what they do.

You will find that each agent has their own unique way in which they do business. As you begin to work for different companies, you will find out how they expect you to do business with them. I can say, out of experience, that the majority of agencies that book look-alikes are top quality, professional, ethical, and reputable. Of course, as in any business, you need to be aware of the very few agents who may not conduct business like the rest of the top notch companies, and you will be able to tell if someone is not treating you fairly by how they handle calling you for a booking. You can also ask other look-alikes to see if they have any bad experiences. It doesn't take a lot to do the right thing with an agent and create a warm, friendly working relationship. They just expect the standard, professional treatment, just as you do. I find many agents incredibly friendly, and I can even call many of the agents personal friends after doing business with them over the years. There are even some agents I work for that I completely trust enough to book me on a job without even quoting a price to them, as I feel that good about their honesty and integrity. There are some great people working in this industry, so get to know who they are, and find out the best ways you can best serve them and their company, and you will reap the rewards of making a new friend, and getting connected to the companies that can get you booked with work.

If you listen and understand what is important to the agent, then you cannot go wrong. Here is what some of the expert agents have to say:

Annee Pfau, Whirl Around Agency: "The number one reason I book entertainers of any kind more than once is due to one reason alone: ATTITUDE. A positive, cooperative attitude will open more doors and get you more bookings with me than any other reason. I cite the author of this book as a superstar example of this. Her attitude shines through from the moment I get her on the phone for the booking to the moment she walks out the door at the gig. Her answer is never "No," but always, "This one may be tough, but I'm going to see how I can make this work for you, Annee." Recently, we worked together on a show that was going to be a demanding situation: 5000 teenagers spread through two massive ballrooms of a hotel! Bella and her crew not only made enough time to show up punctually, but they arrived a clear 45 minutes prior to the gig. All of them arrived with huge smiles, great attitudes, and the perfect dose of professional decorum. After assuring me they were present and ready to go, they left me alone to operate the party. When showtime came, they gave a performance that had the teenagers screaming the roof off the hotel. Quite a few members of the crowd actually believed Bella was the real Madonna, and she obliged every single one of them with photos, greetings, and hugs. In short, she did more for Madonna's image than a dozen *People* magazine covers! The clearest reason any party attendee gravitates toward an entertainer is that special charisma attained only by having an inner life. If you don't know what that means, find out and then work on it. This is not a job you can merely "show up" for and expect a paycheck - at least not if you wish to do it for years on end. Practice being a kind, generous person no matter where you are and what you do, and that attitude will follow you to gigs. It sounds hokey, but the people I book constantly are the entertainers I like as people first, because that's what shows through when you're on the spot and have to deal with guests ranging from hysterical teenagers to drunk party guests. You'll get them all, and you'll have to deal with it all as a person first and an entertainer second. If you keep grounded this way, it's also easier to avoid the biggest trap I see look-a-likes fall into: believing that they are as wonderful as the stars they portray. I can share a few horror stories with you about 'comedians' who have been warned not to use profanity, but they use it anyway and then shrug their shoulders when confronted, saying they are only 'being true to the character.'

Or the 'sultry songstress' who bumped and ground through her number on the CEO's lap - with his wife sitting next to him! Or the 'screen idol' that refused to come to the gig because the limo they sent for him was the wrong color (it was the first and last time I ever sent a car for a look-a-like). Just remember that your character isn't signing your paycheck - your client is.

Above everything else, HAVE FUN WITHIN REASON. I was an entertainer before I became a planner, and the compliments I cherished the most were, "You're having so much fun up there, its contagious!" It's a full circle: the energy you put into this or anything else in life comes right back at you. Are your guests having fun? Then chances are that you are, too!"

Tom Budas, Pacific Entertainment Agency:

• Be on time, or even better, EARLY. It is far more important to the client for you to be prompt than to have extraordinary talent.

• Don't eat or drink from buffets unless you are invited to.

• Be gracious and charming to guests. (I once had a look-alike repeat a line from a movie his character was famous for: "F*** you azz****!" He said it to the CEO of the company, who almost fainted. Remember, corporate people are usually completely P.C. - politically correct. Don't take a chance.

• Don't lose yourself in your character. When the client needs to go over important information and stage cues, revert to being a "real person"/professional performer who can take direction.
I once lost a look-alike talent in the lobby of the Century Plaza because he forgot he was working for me. Know the difference between being "on" and "off."

• Don't gripe about money. One famous character is constantly asking for more money. Negotiate early and keep your communication clear and constant, whether it's a meet and greet or a performance. What you negotiate is what you get. You can't change prices in the middle of an event, unless they ask you to do something more than you were contracted to do.

• After you've introduced yourself to a prospective client, don't call too much. They know who you are and will call you when/if they need to book you. Keep in touch with clever mailing pieces announcing what you are doing that's new. You risk getting termed "Psycho Elvis" if you're too persistent.

• Remember, the more the client enjoys working with you, the more you will work for that client. Leave your personal problems, as well as traffic or parking hassles at home or in your car.

• Get overtime approval. Unless you've been requested to stay longer, when your time's up, say goodnight to your client and leave. Unauthorized overtime will not be paid.

• The ability to be hired to work at corporate events will increase as you gain a reputation as a talented performer and create an ongoing relationship with your client. It's not hard. Just use common sense!

Ruthe Moyte, Event Specialist Several Companies: "Comments for talent....Always be on time and ready to go 15-30 minutes ahead of time. This makes for easier changes if the planner has last minute requests from their client. Being reliable is an attribute that is so valuable. I always check on reliability when I am looking for new talent."

Anonymous Booking Agent: "Comment to new artists: Be punctual! if you want agents to use your act and services again and again, be there and be on time... every time.
Be flexible - the only constant in this business is change. Clients never run on schedule, but we have to be prepared to accommodate their needs and time frame. The client is our business, not just an audience."

Keith Cox and Jim Grigsby, American Convention Entertainment Services: "Hang in there - although you may not hear from a particular agent for some time, don't think they will not use you. They just haven't had the right client to book you with. Don't give up on them, and they will not give up on you."

Stan Heimowitz, Celebrity Gems Agency: "My recommendation to look-alikes and impersonators is to determine which celebrity is most marketable, and to always remain in character during the engagement. I would invest in good costuming and in good grooming. Also, it's far better to pick one or two Hollywood stars and impersonate them well than to pick several stars and do them "mediocre." Be professional. Arrive early at engagements, and be prepared to perform at the contracted time.

Joe Diamond, Joe Diamond Enterprises: "If you are a performing look-alike/sound-alike, please be prepared with readable charts and/or lead sheets that are transposed in the right key and are "taped" together prior to the rehearsal, and with enough copies for at least all of the rhythm section. Also, for mix and mingle look-alikes, please arrive at least 20 minutes prior to your start time. Do not expect to arrive at 4:00, for example, and then park and be ready at 4:00. Impossible!!"

Linda Collins, Classique Productions: "A few comments regarding talent and what they could do to help us, the agents!!!
If you move or change your phone number, e-mail, etc, LET US KNOW!!!!!! If you get several calls for the same job, quote the same price to all agents!!!! Send quality promo materials that are agent-friendly...no contact information on the tape or on the literature, but be sure you send a business card or letter so the agent knows how to reach you!!! I will tell you that when I get promo that has contact information on it, it is very time consuming for me to get it edited so that I can send it out, and many times that phone number is on the screen during the last song, which means I have to cut the entire last song and send an unfinished tape. The best idea I have seen is when a talent runs the credits at the end of their tape, and it says: "For booking information, contact the agent who sent you this tape." That is GREAT! Also, be sure the agent knows any special needs like cordless mics, barstools on stage, and other little things that might be important to make the job go more smoothly. These are just a few things that I think would make life better for us all."

Naomi, Naomi's World of Entertainment: "When receiving packets from new talent, we look for the following:
1. Hardcopy glossy 8 x 10 photos. We like to keep at least five on file because there are clients who do not have Internet access, as well as situations where we need to submit photos for press. If there are several different shots, that is even better.
2. Video of a performance, or interview with look-alike.

3. All contact information, including home address, as well as all day, evening, cell, beeper, fax, e-mail, and website info.
4. Photo (can be magazine tear-out) of the celebrity the new talent is looking to impersonate. In that way we can use the photo as guide to compare features and the guide's talent in smile, angles, hair, etc. This can help our office greatly, as sometimes we are not totally familiar with the exact look of a celebrity (could be the CEO of a company, for example) and the photos really help.
5. If the celebrity's look changes and/or the look-alike has new ideas regarding how to depict the celebrity, please communicate with us about it so that we can understand, add our input, and ultimately do a good job of representing correctly and accurately all the options available to our clients."

Carole Reed, Elizabeth Taylor Impersonator and Booking Agent: "As an Elizabeth Taylor double and also a booking agent, I can see the look-alike industry from both sides of the coin, so to speak. When I started doing impersonations as Liz, I did not have anyone to teach me anything about the industry at all. I am from Ohio and I certainly had no kind of examples of working look-alikes, so I had to learn by doing - sink or swim, so to speak.

I have learned, being an agent and a look-alike, that you as a talent should be honest to your agents. ts you work for. Yes, it is okay to work for numerous agents, but with each agent who books you for work, make sure to represent them respectfully. They have worked hard to get you that job. Do not pass out any of your business cards when working for them. I believe most look-alikes do not realize the kind of hard work and money and energy we (booking agents) spend just trying to convince a new client to use our agency. It takes years to build a database of clients, so when sending out talent for a booking, I will only hire talent I can depend on to be professional and represent me the best.

As a look-alike talent, study your character and know the correct answers to give about their lives, as people will ask you questions about your character. I do not know how many times I have had to repeat all of my eight husbands' names! (*ha-ha*)"

Angelique and Friends Entertainment
1. "**Don't be a mystery.** It's great to be a mystery to your audience, but an agent wants to know that you are a reliable, responsible person. Agents don't want to

work with people who seem to exist in cyberspace, reachable only by a pager and e-mail. And while it's great to have a stage name, if you make decent money at all with an agent, he or she will need your real name, address, and social security number. If you don't trust a certain agent with your personal information, don't use that agent; get a responsible, professional one!

2. **Be easy to reach**. Give your agent all the possible ways to reach you, and be sure to check your voicemail often. Don't be stingy and refuse to check your voicemail while you are out of town just to save a few bucks! If you develop e-mail troubles, tell your agent right away so that they don't send you messages that are lost in cyberspace.

3. **Know your pricing!** Don't waffle on pricing and try to second-guess what you might be able to get out of a job, or whether you should lower your price to snag it. That's the agent's job! No agent wants to be the middleman in an extended price negotiation between you and the client. If you are afraid that agents will lose gigs by pricing too high, or that they won't ask for enough, you should book your own gigs. If you want to receive jobs through agents, be clear about what you want to earn!

4. **Agents love it when** you have professional photos. Agents often understand when your photos aren't the best, but they *hate* it when you have professional photos and you won't part with them! Agents love to see videotape of look-alikes. Get a professional video made."

Bright Entertainment, LLC: "With look-alikes, the main selling feature, of course, is a great photo. At events, a great personality can go a looooooong way, and sometimes, make up for a person who looks only mildly like their intended persona.

As an agent, it's great to work with people who are easy to work with, who communicate quickly if they are available for the event, and people who are polished and polite, and know how to behave at events.

The truth of the look-alike business is that certain look-alikes will be "hotter" and more in demand than others.

To get a lot of look-alike work, a person can create a "telegram" - a type of 5 to 10 minute act. This is in very high demand for birthdays, at restaurants and office parties. A sort of –"buzz in-buzz out" act that requires humor. I book a lot of these, but clients are often not willing to pay as much for these types of shows."

I asked several agencies the same questions, so you can clearly see the answers are all very similar in nature. What is important to most of the agents are the same qualities: reliability, good attitude, trustworthiness, and professional presentations. I left each of the agents answers "as is" and inserted every agent that responded to my questions, so no one was left out that did not answer these questions. Even if it seems a bit redundant, the importance here is to see that what is important to each agent should determine how you make choices for your work.

Q. What does an agent look for in a look-alike talent?

Annee Chartier-Pfau, Whirl Around Entertainment: "Well, your look does matter - but more than that, do you arrive ON TIME for your gig? Are you ready to be "on," and if not, do you arrive with enough time to prepare?"

Greg Fortune, Fortune Entertainment: "Loyalty, reliability, mutual respect (same things I look for in a relationship) and a good report from my clients."

Al Lampkin Entertainment: "Well, of course they have to look like and sound like the person they are impersonating. They should also have a video so we can see how easily they work with people."

Debbie Baker, Baskow Talent: "Of course resemblance to the character is the most important thing. If the character sings, I listen for the voice quality. I also want to see that they have the "little things" down pat (the way the character turns their head or walks, etc.). Small mannerisms are important. Costumes must be authentic, in good repair, and clean."

Karla Ross, Karla Ross Productions: "Looks, costume, good energy and attitude, reliability." -

Bill, Star Celebrity Look-Alikes: "Dead ringers, or great performers. Personality is key." -

Perfect Productions Inc: "Dynamic presence, it's what carries those beyond."

Phil Chapman, Party Central: "First: Similarity to person being imitated. Second: Price." -

Lookalikes USA: "A great resemblance, able to act or learn to act (mannerisms, voice, personality) like the celebrity, outgoing personality, responsible and reliable, honesty, and willingness to learn." -

Ginger Garnitz, Bruce Garnitz Music & Entertainment: "Obviously, they have to have a close resemblance, but they also need to be able to effectively present the public persona of their celebrity and stay in character for the agreed-upon periods of time."

Q. What makes you hire a certain person more than another?

Annee Chartier-Pfau, Whirl Around Entertainment: "Attitude, attitude, attitude! If I am looking forward to seeing you, you always get my first call. I call Bella all the time just to hear her cheerful voice." -

Greg Fortune, Fortune Entertainment: "See question #1." -

Al Lampkin Entertainment: "Again, they have to have captured the essence of the person they are impersonating, plus they must be fun to talk to, cooperative, and dedicated to making sure the clients are happy." -

Debbie Baker, Baskow Talent: "Loyalty, above all else! If I can't turn my back on talent at an event without worrying about them passing out their own business card or sneaking off to smoke, then chances are I will not be using them often. I like talent to have a genuinely good attitude. Don't believe you are really the character and have that star attitude. It turns me off every time." -

Perfect Productions Inc: "Quality references." -

Karla Ross, Karla Ross Productions: "Looks, costume, good energy and attitude, reliability"-

Phil Chapman, Party Central: "Punctuality, then quality, then price."

Lookalikes USA: "Better resemblance, more acting experience, easier to work with." -

Elyse Del Francia, Celebrity Look A Likes By Elyse: "Talent and professionalism." -

Janna Joos, International Celebrity Images: "Attitude, work ethics, quality of performance, easy to work with."-

Q. What kind of promotion impresses an agent?

Annee Chartier-Pfau, Whirl Around Entertainment: "Fresh new pictures and exciting new ideas. If you can add a new twist for me, I am ready, willing, and able to go sell it to clients. I was thrilled when Bella gave a pitch for a "Moulin Rouge" show, complete with a Nicole Kidman look-alike, when that movie first broke big. Being on top of what's going on in popular culture, and adding your own unique twist to it, always impresses me."-

Greg Fortune, Fortune Entertainment: "Professional video, good pictures, and bio."-

Al Lampkin Entertainment: "Materials that show a commitment to the industry. Professional agent-friendly photos and promo."

Debbie Baker, Baskow Talent: "I require a professionally shot video from all of my look-alikes. Your photos can be great, but if the performance isn't there live, then I will have an upset client." -

Perfect Productions Inc: "Unique, and to the point."

Karla Ross, Karla Ross Productions: "Good, un-retouched photos. I once hired someone who ended up looking nothing like her highly retouched promo pic."-

Phil Chapman, Party Central: "Easy to read."-

Janna Joos, International Celebrity Images: "Packaging additional entertainment (i.e., dancers, partner, props) into your performance to enhance your character."

Elyse Del Francia, Celebrity Look A Likes By Elyse: "Agent-friendly materials. Pictures, videos and CDs. Leave space for the agent's contact information." -

Jasmine Rose, The Rose Agency: "Handing out our business cards." -

Q. Can you give advice to new talent?

Al Lampkin Entertainment: "Like any other profession, work hard, stay focused, be committed and hang in there."

Debbie Baker, Baskow Talent: "Study your character every day. Take the time and the money to make your costumes as authentic as possible. If you move, be sure to update your contact info with us. We can't hire you if we can't find you. DON'T put your personal contact info on your photos or videos. I will not send them out if my client can call you directly."

Perfect Productions Inc: "It takes an average of nine calls just to get through to most agents, so don't get discouraged."

Phil Chapman, Party Central: "Contact as many agents as you can. Let them know your preferred price, as well as your "least to leave home" price."

Lookalikes USA: "Work hard to perfect your act, respect the agent's position, and never lose site of who you are: just an actor, NOT SOMEONE FAMOUS!!! Also, never go on a TV show without being represented by an agent. Better yet, be skeptical of all TV shows wanting look-alikes without paying the talent." -

Ginger Garnitz, Bruce Garnitz Music & Entertainment: "Do your homework on your celebrity: know the back story and keep it current. 2. Invest in high-quality costumes and props, and keep them in pristine condition. 3. Realize that when you're starting out you won't command as high a fee as a more seasoned performer. 4. Know your limitations and don't overreach just to get a booking. 5. Allow adequate time between bookings to ensure you won't be late and make sure you can arrive early enough to be completely prepared and still have a few minutes to attend to personal needs before your call time. 6. Always respond to inquiries in a timely fashion."

Jeffrey L. Patterson, Patterson and Associates: "Don't skimp on the quality of your promotional material. This is the greatest investment in your career. Be ethical. Longevity in this business is built from repeat business. Take care of your clients, and they will take care of you." -

Elyse Del Francia, Celebrity Look A Likes By Elyse: "Look at yourself and be honest...do you really look like_____whoever...do you sound and act like your character? If your character is a singer/dancer...do you sing and dance exactly the same? Is this something you can really do? Then you have a chance...if you have any concerns...work on your character before getting an agent. Then be prepared and call me." -

Jasmine Rose, The Rose Agency: "Do everything as exactly as possible, learn to do your makeup so that your facial structure appears the same. (Men should use makeup for this as well.) Costumes should be exact. Little differences in facial structure, costumes, mannerisms, etc., are very noticeable. It's not enough to just look like someone, you need to transform yourself into them." -

Janna Joos, International Celebrity Images: "Aim to be the best that you can be, as there is considerable competition out there, so study, study, study the character." -

Q. Will you hire a look-alike because they belong to a look-alike guild?

Elyse Del Francia, Celebrity Look A Likes By Elyse: "No. It makes no difference if the performer belongs to a group or not"-

Al Lampkin Entertainment: "No." -

Debbie Baker, Baskow Talent: "Not necessarily. I develop personal relationships with all of my talent. This is how I get to know who I can count on."

Karla Ross, Karla Ross Productions: "Not really."

Phil Chapman, Party Central: "No- It wouldn't make a difference, but references do." -

Lookalikes USA: "Makes not too much difference, either way."

Robyn, Princess Productions: "No."

Jasmine Rose, The Rose Agency: "It doesn't matter to me if they are in a guild."

Janna Joos, International Celebrity Images: "No."

Jeffrey L. Patterson, Patterson and Associates: "No."

Q. What would make you never hire someone?

Annee Chartier-Pfau, Whirl Around Entertainment: "Overly offending my client by saying or doing something I've asked you not to do. We realize that sometimes, things just "happen" with party guests who may have had too much to drink or who are overly sensitive, but I'm pretty good about taking the pulse of my group and making it clear to you how they feel about things. The kiss of death is ignoring that! Additionally, I am under enough pressure at events to not have to worry about whether you will be on time, have an icky attitude, or not be prepared to work."

Greg Fortune, Fortune Entertainment: "Dishonesty and continued bad reports from clients."-

Al Lampkin Entertainment: "Giving out their own business cards at one of my jobs."

Debbie Baker, Baskow Talent: "Pulling a "no show" or last-minute cancellation. Giving my client your personal contact information." -

Stan Heimowitz, Celebrity Gems: "A performer who shows up late and doesn't keep in character. A performer who does not know how to work the room or comes unprepared, i.e., forgets to bring their CD for the event."

Karla Ross, Karla Ross Productions: "Bad attitude, being late"-

Phil Chapman, Party Central: "Less than good references, any lateness. If there's even one "no-show," NEVER." -

Lookalikes USA: "Irresponsible, bad look, too young, unethical, non-trusting, wrong personality, can't act very well."

Robyn, Princess Productions: "The one that is late or doesn't show up." -

Elyse Del Francia, Celebrity Look A Likes By Elyse: "Being unprofessional. I have had great relationships with most of our 900-plus performers...but I've had a couple people that have been intoxicated on the job, were caught handing out their own business cards while on a gig I booked, didn't stay in character during their mix and mingle, or they just aren't good enough to book again." -

Q. Thoughts you wish to say to look-alikes regarding money, attitudes, work ethics?

Annee Chartier-Pfau, Whirl Around Entertainment: "Again, watch the way the seasoned pros do it. They are still working for a reason. They think positively, always want to help make the party into an extra-special occasion, and realize that although they look like stars, they don't have to act like them."

Greg Fortune, Fortune Entertainment: "Money is not always the most important factor in jobs; prove yourself to be the things in question #1 and the work and $ will come."

Elyse Del Francia- Celebrity Look A Likes By Elyse "Attitude...well, that is an important element in ones success...either in this business or any other. If you are called for a job and are asked what amount of money you want or the agent tells you what the budget is...then that's the fee...it is none of your business how much we ask for you. Remember, we agents work very hard prior to even calling you, to get that client. We belong to associations, have memberships with talent buyers networks, advertise in print, buy Internet marketing, attend Trade Shows, send out promotion pieces, have a staff and work day and night to get to the decision makers. We agents work very hard to get bookings...I certainly don't sit around and wait for the phone to ring...I have to make it ring...and hopefully, ring off the hook! You will have to find an agent you trust who has been in the business for sometime...with a good reputation. If you see an agent that has a good work ethic and other performers respect that agent...then sign with them. Try it out. You'll know within a few bookings if you want to work with each other...then things take off from there."

Debbie Baker, Baskow Talent: "Be willing to work for a lower rate of pay when I don't have a large budget. I will be more willing to give you the larger jobs also. Never discuss what I am paying you with the client. Remember that I don't do this for free either. Be yourself when out of character. Be honest. The best way to get off of my preferred list is to cancel a job for me, say you are sick or - and have me find you working another event. Remember that this is a small business. Everyone knows everyone else, and we always find out the true story."

Stan Heimowitz, Celebrity Gems: "Do the entertaining as a hobby and do not consider the look-alike business as a full-time profession. There's only a handful of impersonators who can boast that they perform full-time and make a solid income."

Perfect Productions Inc: "This is no different from any sales call - we are the client, be on your best behavior."

Karla Ross, Karla Ross Productions: "Don't try to undercut the competition. Give a fair price to begin with." -

Phil Chapman, Party Central: "Money is always less than quality. Put on your best show with enthusiasm, then worry about $$."

Lookalikes USA: "Enjoy the money and don't complain. Where else can you go somewhere to shake hands with people and make $200 an hour easy money?" -

Ginger Garnitz, Bruce Garnitz Music & Entertainment: "You have chosen to become a professional entertainer. There is a reasonable expectation that you will give a 100% performance every time. I've covered almost everything else in my answers above." -

Q. What you would like to say about the look-alike business?

Annee Chartier-Pfau, Whirl Around Entertainment: "That it's been improving year after year, and we are thrilled. We love using look-alikes and hope to keep incorporating them into our events!"

Greg Fortune, Fortune Entertainment: "Performance Art! P.S. You deserve all the success that will come your way." -

Al Lampkin Entertainment: "Ain't this fun"?

Debbie Baker, Baskow Talent: "It is not easy! If your character is popular (Elvis, Marilyn, etc.) there is a lot of competition. And if your character is not as well known there may not be a lot of work." -

Stan Heimowitz, Celebrity Gems: "Consider the look-alike business as a fun and glamorous hobby where, if going to parties is a goal, then the look-alike business is a sure shot to meet these needs."

Perfect Productions Inc: "It has been far under utilized, and could stand a strong repackaging."

"Karla Ross, Karla Ross Productions: You guys are amazing. What in interesting business to be in."

Phil Chapman, Party Central: "I'm in love with a Lady, and her name is look-alike."

Lookalikes USA: "Very competitive business, (hey, but what isn't, right?) but if you have great talent, you can make a party a unique hit with impersonators."-

Ginger Garnitz, Bruce Garnitz Music & Entertainment: "It's a unique genre that requires the performer to subsume his/her own personality and still be entertaining, enthusiastic, and genuine. If you can accomplish this convincingly, there is a future for you as a look-alike."

Award Shows
and Conventions

Award shows seem to go hand in hand with the entertainment business - the Emmys, Oscars, Grammys, The People's Choice, and the list seems to never end, with new shows and award presentations popping up every year.

Award shows for look-alikes: There are a couple of award shows for look-alikes that take place annually, and they can be a fun way to meet people, network, and even get a little media attention.

Many corporate events take place around the time of the Oscars, Emmys, and Grammys, and many event planners like to book celebrity look-alikes at their events. Award shows are the perfect atmosphere for look-alikes, and many corporate events "spoof" these award shows by creating an Oscar-looking event, filled with many great celebrity look-alikes performing.

The Cloney awards are presented by Fil Jessee, and his award show will take place for the first time June 2002 in Las Vegas. The awards are voted by the look-alikes that belong to the network or the Look-Alike Guild. You can go to Fil's website to learn more about The Cloney awards.

The Reel Awards was the first and only show of its kind to present look-alikes with awards and offer an evening of entertainment to paying customers, the media, and the general public. Since 1992, Janna Joos has presented The Reel Awards yearly, honoring look-alikes in different categories and spotlighting new talent to the industry.
The Reel Awards are a nice introduction to someone just starting out, as each Reel Awards show brings out look-alikes of all levels. It is a great way to see look-alikes in action, meeting and greeting and performing live. The Reel Awards is not an example of the entire look-alike circuit, but it can be fun to meet new faces and see some old familiar ones as well. Janna works very hard each year on this show, and has great plans for future shows.

Janna Joos, International Celebrity Impersonators, founder of The Reel Awards: "They give pizzazz to a party or corporate function. It raises the level of excitement even for people who have been in L.A. and around celebrities for years. It's just that aura of celebrity, whether it's real or fake. (Clients) are buying into a fantasy. If (an impersonator) is something the company feels is necessary to make the evening happen the way they want it to happen, they will find the money, even if they have to cut down on the cost of the dessert."

The History of The Reel Awards

The Reel Awards™ was originally conceived back in December of 1989 between Nancy Casey (an Elizabeth Taylor look-alike), Janna Joos, and Alana Joos. They were discussing the look-alike industry and trying to figure out different ways to see the new talent that crops up every year along with acknowledging the existing look-alikes and sound-alikes currently working. The idea of an award show for this industry was born that winter day in the Entertainment Express offices.

Basically, The Reel Awards™ (scheduled annually on the Monday evening preceding The Academy Awards) is a spoof on all of the other awards shows (Golden Globe, People's Choice, Soul Train, Emmys, Grammys, Oscars, CMA, Tonys, Cleos, Soap Opera, ESPY, MTV Music Video, AMA, SAG, et al). In place of an 'Oscar', the award recipient receives 'The Can', which is a movie film reel can inscribed with their crowning achievement, to display with pride. 'The Can' is given in various categories, such as The Reel Dead Award, The Pop 'n Rock for Reel Award, Big Mouth Comedy Award, R & B Feelin' Good Award, Country's Hottest Hitter Award, OWOPCA (One World Order People's Choice Award), Humanitarian Award, Lifetime Achievement Award, and many more.

The evening of The Reel Awards™ begins with cocktails in the foyer/lobby of the Hollywood Roosevelt Hotel from 6:00 p.m. to 7:30 p.m. During this time you get to meet, mingle, take photos and stargaze with your favorite impersonators (Hollywood stars such as Charlie Chaplin and others from the 1920's and up; political figures such as George W. Bush and Bill Clinton; sports figures like Kobe or Tiger; and musicians from Hank Williams, Sr., to Britney Spears).

The show begins at 7:30 p.m. in the Blossom Room with a live band playing "Hooray for Hollywood." The night features a roster of celebrity look-alikes and sound-alikes singing, dancing, and doing comedic presentations. Interspersed between these 'live' performances are the awards, which are presented to outstanding impersonators. Honored are those who have contributed their talents to the special events industry throughout the previous year. Also recognized are those individuals who parallel the successes of some of Hollywood's most famous entertainers.

Q. What are your thoughts about look-alike award shows?

Betty Atchison as Cher: "They are very limited and subjective. Many of them try to encompass an area too large for them to handle. For example, how can a small group in Las Vegas evaluate look-alikes in Orlando or New York? It isn't possible. Even locally, how can anyone manage to see every performance and act to give an accurate evaluation? If they want to throw a party, that's great. Bring in some terrific acts for everyone to enjoy, and leave the trophies out of it!"

Lyndal Grant as Arnold Schwarzenegger: "I think it's a good excuse to meet and network; however, I feel the voting process is subjective and far too affected by a narrow group of vested interests."

Julie Sheppard as Judy Garland: "This year was my first visit to the Reel Awards and I was amazed at how many people participated. I pictured it on a much smaller scale, and I was pleasantly surprised. I was honored to open the show (as Judy Garland) and I hadn't planned on performing, as I had just had major surgery a week before. But Janna Joos is a big supporter of mine and was gracious enough to ask me to go on and "introduce myself" back into the world of look-alikes, which I had been away from for three years. My reception was more than I could have hoped for. Everyone was so complimentary, warm, and encouraging! I would definitely go again. I think this is a marvelous venue to see others and be seen. Are there any others I should know about?"

The Look-Alike Convention

The Annual Celebrity Impersonators Convention is held every year at The Imperial Palace Hotel, home of Legends In Concert, in Las Vegas. The convention is an effort to bring performers and agents together to discuss matters of our industry. Founded by veteran agent, Elyse Del Francia of Celebrity Look A Likes By Elyse in Rancho Mirage, California, this convention lines up speakers to educate us on how the law works for our industry, how to create "agent-friendly" materials to make your agent's job more effective, makeup demonstrations, photographers for new shots, and the direction of the Internet and how it benefits us all. Newcomers and veteran performers have three days to network, critique, and learn more about this crazy business of look-alikes and sound-alikes! The first year was covered by all major networks in Las Vegas and has stories still running on the Travel Channel. Contact Elyse for more information on next year's convention (her contact information can be found in the back of this book).

Finding Your Own Niche and Creating Your Own Character - More Possibilities from "Hey What a Great Idea" Guys: John, Jerry, and Forrest...

Sometimes you can create more work for yourself if you are a creative type performer, with an ability to re-create a memorable character from Hollywood history. The following performers have achieved great success on the look-alike market by putting together excellent impersonations of some very famous legends. Each of these performers has distinctively defined himself as a "specialty" look-alike. This can be a sure way to ensure booking potential every time an event planner is looking for a unique talent for a themed party.

Noland Anderson as John Travolta; Photography by Mittska

Don't Touch the Hair....Becoming JOHN

Noland Anderson as John Travolta: "The approach I've used in studying the characters I portray has been a combination of studying how the character was played by the celebrity I am impersonating, as well as thinking about how the character would think, act, walk, talk act...in real life. I also took into consideration what people remembered the character for, and how I could work that into my act.

To study the celebrity-played character (in my case John Travolta as Tony Manaro), I bought the movie (*Saturday Night Fever*) and watched and then re-watched him play the part. I taped the pertinent audio parts to a cassette and listened to him speak while I drove around town in my car. This helped with the accent as well as gave me lines to use at parties. I also videotaped the most important scenes and learned them to use as a performance. In my case, that meant learning the "Saturday Night Fever" solo dance. The more I watched the video and listened to the audio, the easier it became for me to slip into character. I also began to tape record my voice and videotape my dance to see if I looked and sounded how I thought I did. I would take notes and draw pictures of how I could do it better and I arrived at a position where I could perform and be proud of the overall performance, without letting the imperfections keep me from getting gigs - and most importantly *getting paid*.

In my study of the real-life character (Tony Manaro) I looked at how old my character was, what was his situation, how would someone like him act, talk, walk, etc.,... and which of my own real life experiences could I draw on to get me to be able to identify with him and express those same emotions with his accent, body language, movement etc. I found that if I could relate a similar experience, I could retain the flow of emotion needed to make his lines and situations believable when played by myself. Pretty deep for a guy whose bread and butter line is "would you like to take a picture with Travolta?"

Putting the whole package together required me to think about what people remembered the most about the movie and character and how I could use that in my act. I knew people would expect to see Travolta show up and perform the disco solo dance suited up in white. I combined the white suit with big hair, big attitude, a greasy Brooklyn accent, and some gum chewing for effect. I put that together with some gold chains and a pair of six-inch black jack disco boots. I also incorporated the disco "clock" pose to use as my look when taking pictures with the guests.

I will say that the most important thing I've done has been to tape record myself both visually and audibly. A good character study mixed with the proof of a video and audiotape performance to keep me on my toes has helped me through many a gig whether through last minute changes or on the spot improvements. Even with all this hard work and study, it's inevitable that I make mistakes now again, but with this training I know that I'm always at my current best."

Hey Lady...

David Wolf is an amazing comedic performer. Since stumbling into the role of Jerry Lewis a few years ago, his bookings as an actor have tripled. He is able to use his comedic skills to entertain audiences all over the world. Since his impressions of Jerry Lewis have gone over so well, David has teamed up with Dean Martin impersonator Robert S. Ensler. Now the two performers have created twice as much work, showcasing a clever, original performance of a legendary duo. Having a famous partner is a great way to double your work possibilities. When you put a creative idea like this together, you make the agent's job easier, as they can offer an "act" that is creative and interesting, and already ready to go.

Personal advice from David Wolf as Jerry Lewis:
"Try not to get discouraged when breaking into this business. Sometimes, impersonators (especially new ones) can get discouraged as we try to promote ourselves. Rejection is tough, but part of the business. This is why you need to understand that this is a business. Look at it as if you are a salesman trying to market a product, and the product happens to be YOU! Like any business, it is a numbers game. If you contact one hundred agents, you will probably end up getting work from 10-20 percent of them. Which, in the business world, is actually a high return. Once you are able to not take business decisions to heart, or feel that you are being personally rejected, then you will be able to see things as objective business decisions and become a more solid, grounded performer."

Forrest Gump on Waikiki Beach

Steve Weber, a.k.a. Forrest Gump: "In November of 1997, the Bubba Gump Shrimp Co. opened its first Hawaiian restaurant in Lahaina, on the island of Maui. They hired me to portray the character Forrest Gump that Tom Hanks created for the film *Forrest Gump*. I was hired to 'run' over to Waikiki Beach and tell everyone about this wonderful event (in character and costume). With Diamond Head in the background, I felt just slightly overdressed in my *Forrest* plaid shirt and tennis shoes, while beachgoers were in bathing suits, lounging on the beach. ***Stupid is as stupid does***. But being that Forrest is such a likeable character who makes friends easily, I was soon accompanied by a new friend, and was able to give out all of the chocolates before they melted. My new friend and I were quite happy, and this was a great job! And that's all there is to say about that."

Web Networking

Expert advice from graphic artist and web designer David Comfort:

"A website can be a valuable tool for marketing your talent. Where else can a potential employer read your bio, see your pictures, and watch your video without leaving their chair? Because the Internet is global, a viewer with computer access can reach your information almost immediately from anywhere in the world. No more waiting for your promo pack to arrive first. A website can also help you find employers that might not be found through conventional means. If a new agency doesn't yet have their ad in the phonebook, but needs a look-alike, they can just type in a search request and find you before you could find them. If used properly, a website can also serve as a way to gather and distribute information. The more you learn about and develop the potential of your site, the more you will discover opportunities for work."

Q: What kinds of elements should a look-alike website contain?

A: Like all websites, a look-alike website should follow these principles:

The three-click rule: A person viewing your site should be able to get wherever they need to within three clicks of the mouse.

Design for your customer: Who is going to see this site and why? What do I need to show them? (More on that later.)

A "guest book" form: Use this to create a database of who is viewing your site. There may be agents from all over the world.

Stay professional: Even if your site has a diverse group of viewers, make sure that all your content represents you in the best way.

Look-alikes should also focus on the type of content they have. Like a good marketing package they would send by mail, there should be plenty of pictures, a bio, and possibly a video. I would advise against posting your rates on any part of the site unless there is a password login that you can control.

Q: Should look-alikes make an "agent-friendly" page, and what is that?

A: Yes. The easier it is for your customer to get what they want from your site, the better it is for you. An "agent-friendly" page should be an easily accessed page or menu that has the critical info agents need: headshot, stat sheet (height, weight, special talents, etc.), and possibly a video link. An agent-friendly site means that your personal contact information is NOT on the site, so agents can refer clients to this page when booking or submitting you. Agents can suggest that potential clients view your bio, photos, or video and eliminating your personal information will prevent them from contacting you directly. This site will be strictly for agents to refer clients to, and not the same site where you solicit future bookings for yourself.

Q: How big should the website be?

A: At the very minimum, there should be an intro or main page, a contact page, an info page (described in the previous question), and an extended info page containing more details and necessary photos.

After those, I would recommend: a comments/guest book/mailing list page, an "about me" page, and perhaps a photo/video/sound clip gallery.

There really isn't a size limit as long as everything is easy to navigate. "Big" becomes a relative term in the Internet world. Your site may have 100 pages but it will probably never be as large as, say, amazon.com. As long as your viewers can see what they need to see easily and quickly, the sky - or perhaps your budget - is the limit.

Q: Should the look-alike answer the mail? Or should they answer as if they were a representative instead?

A: Remember that the "www" in Internet addresses stands for "World Wide Web." This means that your site is available to anyone with a computer, so be prepared to receive mail or letters from just about everyone. You may receive some less-than-professional letters and/or hate mail. Safety issues apply, as for any e-mail correspondence, and the Symantec website has excellent guidelines for that. Most sites will come with their own e-mail boxes so that you don't have to use your "home" email address.

All professional inquiries should be responded to ASAP. How that is done depends on the preferences of the look-alike. Obviously time is a factor, but an e-mail should be treated as a phone call for business purposes. Some sites have "auto responders" built into the site. These will automatically generate a pre-written response to whoever sent the form or e-mail. This is a good way to let your customer know that their e-mail has been received. It is very professional, but only a temporary reply until you actually respond to the e-mail specifically. You should check your e-mail at least once a day, and more often if your are involved in a communication with someone.

Q: How much does a web site cost?
(E-mail, Internet provider, monthly maintenance costs, etc.)

A: Websites are like most services, in that there is a range of price depending on quality and quantity. Many large portal companies like MSN offer a free page and free Web-based e-mail
(Hotmail is highly recommended http://www.hotmail.com.)
I just created one and it took me about 10 minutes:
The only catch is that you are using their address and probably must agree to allow them to use your page for advertising. Using their address means that the name of your site comes after the hosting portal's name in the URL. But hey, it's free!
On the other end of the spectrum, you can hire a designer to develop a site for you and have as many bells and whistles as are available. This includes Flash animation, downloadable music and/or videos, custom Java applets (little programs that do cool things), animated GIFs, etc. Costs for these kinds of sites can run into the thousands. Yes the thousands. Do you need all that stuff? Not really. So for the best solution at an acceptable budget I would recommend the following:

- **Own your own domain:**
(www.yourname.com). It's only about $15/year and it's more professional

- **Find a good host.:** I have several sites hosted by pageweb.com (including tributeproductions.com) and I would recommend them without reservation. They are very reasonable in cost and very reliable in service. Their costs at the time this book is written are as follows:
$50.00 setup for a basic site, plus $10.00/month to host it. This will come with e-mail, auto-responders, and up to 100MB of space. They can also help create the site if needed.

- **Assemble the materials you will need for the site** - photos, bio, music clips, etc.

- **In simple form, on blank horizontal sheets of paper, draw out what you want your site to show.** For example, show picture #1 in the top right corner with whatever caption you want under it, the bio on its own page, etc. Then you can bring all this to a website designer and really get what you want. Alternatively, you can bring your materials to the designer and allow them to use their creative talent to design it as they see fit. Designer prices vary, but you should expect to pay at least $250-$500 minimum for at least five pages of site. The more custom work or special features, the more money. Lastly, you can do this yourself if you feel up to it. Netscape has a "Composer" utility built into its Communicator software suite, which is free. I know designers who use it for their work. You should expect the process to take anywhere from 1-2 weeks or longer, depending on how much you are doing. You will need a computer to see or create your site, but you have options there as well. Most public libraries have computers available for free. Kinko's charges a small hourly fee to use theirs. There are also many "Internet cafes" with computer service available at the tables. Obviously, you will need access to the Internet for e-mail as well. Internet monthly charges vary, but let me caution against "the great deal for the no-name company." Stick with a solid one. AOL is the biggest, but it is very limiting and may prevent some people from being able to view your site; I would shy away from it. Earthlink, AT&T, PacBell/BellSouth, and Microsoft are very solid, and aren't going away anytime soon. These are all about $20/month for regular service. If you are going to do the creation yourself you might want to consider DSL or Cable modem for about $50/month. Both of these options will also come with e-mail as well as Internet access. Call around to various Internet service providers and ask as many questions as you can, so you can compare services before you select one.

Q. How do I get my web site registered?

How do people find it?

A. You can do the legwork yourself and register your site with each search engine individually, or you can hire a service. Most designers should be able to provide this service, and some hosts do, too. Pageweb has a SE Submit service that is free. If you hire a pro, expect to pay a nominal charge under $100. Some services specialize in this stuff and will recode your page for placement, etc. But they want big money, and the search engine game is really not defined. Most search engines charge for good placement these days, and unless you have really set yourself up, it can be hard for potential clients to find your site without it. The nice thing is that the look-alike field is pretty specialized so that fact alone REALLY helps narrow it down. For a reasonable alternative, I recommend Microsoft's BCentral. I have a developer's contract with them that allows me to provide SE submission service at a more reasonable cost, due to volume, but their Traffic Builder service is about $20/month. It really offers a lot for that price but it will require you to understand Internet marketing. They do explain it pretty well, though.

Q. Are you available to make my look-alike site?

A. My site's designer is! Send an e-mail to davidcomfort@hotmail.com so we can communicate with you about your needs, or visit www.sleeplessdigital.com. **"Mention this book and get a 20% discount"!**

Remember, if you are thinking of having a website made to promote your look-alike talent, consider the following:

You may want to talk to your favorite agent about possible representation for your booking inquiries from your website. You will get all kinds of inquiries from all kinds of people, and it may be a smart, safe idea to have a professional agent screen the general public for you. This way you can agree to a commission ahead of time, and then have an agent that you like and trust follow up on all your booking requests. Choose an agent you have confidence in, who checks e-mail frequently. Inquiries can come in all day long and you don't want to miss any.

When designing your website, make sure to use clean, professional photographs of yourself (use none of your actual celebrity, if possible). Make sure that your photo-

graphs will represent you in a clean, professional way. You want professional companies to inquire about your work, and not the fans of the celebrity.
Leave personal information off, unless you are okay with giving it out to absolutely anyone.

E-mail is almost a must nowadays for agents to connect with talent. Make sure to have a professional e-mail address and check it daily of possible. Especially if you have a look-alike website, you will get many inquiries that expect a quick reply. E-mail is also a wonderful vehicle for an entertainer, as it allows you to send photo files along with text files (in other words, you can send your photo and resume to an agent without having to mail it, and the agent will get it instantly).

If you get a pro like David to design your website, you will also be able to have short video clips of your singing or live performance on your website. This will allow future bookers and clients to see you in action, and they can view the clips any time, day or night. Saves lots of time and money!!!

Q. What can a performer do in between gigs?

Lois as Mariah Carey: "Constantly look for new ways to market yourself. If you use the Internet, use it as just one tool of marketing, but don't rely on just your website to draw you work. I first started my website as a way to promote myself as a look-alike performer, but I had several modeling offers arise from that site. The modeling keeps me busy, when the look-alike work slows down."

Q. What if an agency tells me they "already have my character?"

Denise Bella Vlasis: "Maybe an agent will tell you that he "already has 10 of" whoever you look like.
The very first words an agent ever said to me were, "Who do you look like, dear? Listen, if I were you, I would go out and get myself a Marilyn Monroe wig, because this "Madonna" will be famous for about fifteen minutes...besides, what can you do as a *Madonna look-alike*?" Rumor has it that this guy went out of business a year later."

What is your funniest look-alike memory as an agent AND talent?

Jeffrey Briar, agent and impersonator of several characters: "Once the real Dolly Parton was performing in the Midwest and thus could not attend her business manager's birthday party. Dolly (through her secretary) called my agency, Marvel Enterprises, and hired Shirley Hader (an extraordinary Dolly double) to go to her manager's party (from Los Angeles up to a ranch near Santa Barbara). Dolly sent a note along saying: *I'm sorry I couldn't attend your party, but I did the next best thing - I sent my look-alike*. The guests were amused, charmed, and delighted."

More Tips

› If you have been called for a job and another agent calls you for that same job, it is YOUR responsibility to let the second agent know that you have already been submitted for the job. You may come between agents, if you don't let them know you have already been called for a job, and that could damage your reputation in the business. You must have enough integrity to always go with the agent who called you first, and not force agents to compete for you.

›If you are wishing to work as a professional celebrity look-alike, make sure that you are ready to *be* a performer. Many people say they "look like" someone, and when an agent calls them asking for promotional materials, they do not have professional photographs or video ready. If you are going to make money in this field, you should have already invested some before you start notifying agents.

›If you have to back out of a job that you have already committed yourself to, have a "back-up" impersonator to whom you can refer the agent. There may be situations where you take a booking and then have an emergency come up. Always develop a relationship with at least one good, reliable, professional replacement of the celebrity you impersonate. If you can "network" with other performers, you can cover jobs for each other. This will come in handy when the times come to cover jobs you may have to cancel.

›*Know* who you are referring. Take the time to know the qualifications of the performer you are asking to replace you for a job. This person is going to be a representation of you, so make sure you have seen a resume, photographs, and video *before* you suggest them for any job.

›Keep your promotional materials updated. I've seen performers who send out photographs of themselves 10 years (or pounds) prior to their current look. Make sure you still look like your photographs.

› Be sure to agree to the job description before you agree to the job you take. Many times, what the original contract specifies for you to do and what you end up doing at the job are very different. You may wish to include in your contract that if the job you are asked to do changes from what the contracts states, then an additional fee of a specified amount will be charged.

Tapia as Mae West;
Photography by Johnnie Mejia
Tapia as Carmen Miranda;
Photography by John Corel

Personally Speaking: A Glimpse Into Living the Look-Alike Life

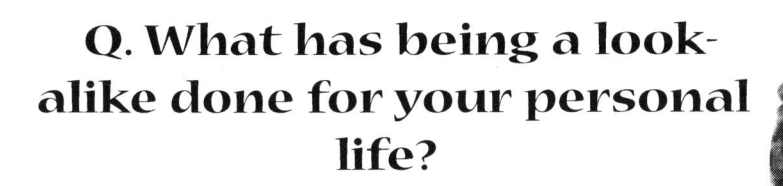

Q. What has being a look-alike done for your personal life?

Tapia Corel as Mae and Carmen: "I am married and a mother of two, and because I've worked as Mae, I have been able to retain my identity as a woman, and not gotten lost in the mother/wife role.
Advice: Be professional. While it's a lot of fun, and a lot like playing "Dress Up," people are paying you money to do a job. Never lose sight of that. Take the few extra steps or spend the extra dollars to make sure your likeness is as close as possible. This is not time for "close enough." Most of all, once you have done your homework and know your character inside and out, relax and have fun."

What about your spouse or partner?
John Corel (Tapia's hubby)
"When a spouse or partner starts to work as a look-alike, be ready for certain changes in your life. Like makeup and wigs all over the house, and having the closets filled up with costumes. It is also important to not take the look-alike work to heart. Many look-alike jobs

involve directly dealing with the public. Impersonating someone as flirtatious as Mae West is only a job, nothing more. There is no room for jealousy in any kind of entertainment work."

Q. What does your family think of your look-alike career?

J. Trusk as William Shatner: "My family gets a kick out of the situation. My whole gang is back in Minnesota, so they don't get an opportunity to see me in action. However, one of the funniest stories took place while my brother was visiting. We were having dinner at a Persian restaurant. I had just started in the business and was explaining to my brother what I was doing. I explained that I continually get told that I "look like William Shatner...Captain Kirk" all the time - almost daily. He had the same initial reaction that I had the first time I heard it:"Duh - I don't get it." No sooner had he uttered that response when the waiter approached our table to take our order. He froze, looked at me, and said (with a very distinct Middle Eastern accent), "Did anybody ever tell you that you look just like 'T. J. Hooker'? (He had obviously been watching some old reruns.) Needless to say, it initiated a hearty round of laughs."

J. Trusk as William Shatner;
Photography by Susan Stevens

Tell me about how being a school teacher changed your life as a look-alike:

Vicki Brown as Rosie O'Donnell: "My first and foremost job has been that of a high school teacher and forensics coach. I was teaching at Cypress Creek High School in Orlando, Florida, when I began my look-alike career, which by the way started out with me playing "Betty Rubble" (Rosie as Betty) at the Universal Studios theme park. When the Flintstones movie was over and Universal shut down the Flintstones live show, I resumed to my teaching, not thinking I would ever portray Rosie again.

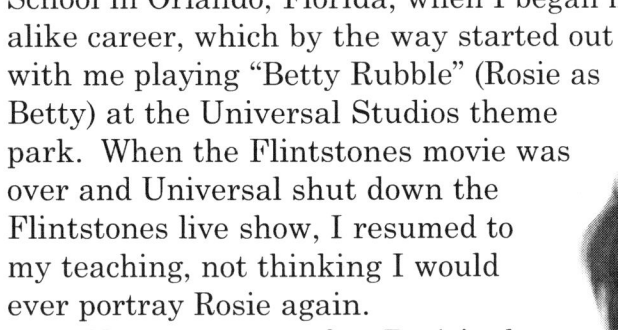

However, soon after Rosie's show hit the air, she announced that she wanted to fill the audience with look-alikes. I was encouraged by other teachers in my department to send my stuff in. Thousands applied and only 180 were selected. I was accepted, but found out I had to pay my own way - which meant hotel, plane fare, and food. last minute flings off to New York City!! I mentioned to another teacher that

Vicki Brown as Rosie O'Donnell;
Photography by Mark Russell

I had been accepted but would have to turn it down. She would not hear of it and started a "Send Our Rosie To New York" campaign.   By the next day, several teachers had cans for change in their rooms for the kids to make donations. As I walked the halls, teachers pressed $20 bills into my hand. The athletic director gave me a fifty and told me to have a steak dinner in New York! I was overwhelmed by the generosity of my students and my co-workers. Sure enough, they raised enough to cover my hotel and plane fare!!

All of the "Rosies" lined up to be escorted in. People from the show walked by picking people to do certain little parts in the show. Each time they walked by, I threw out the Betty Rubble laugh and they picked the person NEXT to me! I was not selected but I realized that everyone gets their 15 minutes of fame and I had already had mine. The show was great and then she took us all to a restaurant for lunch. I waited by the door for her and when she came in I introduced myself and then asked for a picture. Rosie agreed and as I moved to get someone to take the picture, another Rosie jumped in my place!! Rosie was on the move and now I was in the back of 180 "Rosies" who were all pawing on her to get pictures and her attention. My experience of being chased through theme parks ("Une Photo!! Une Photo!! Please! Please!") and being pawed and hauled on made me staunchly refuse to treat Rosie in this fashion.

But I was stuck. My school raised the money and now I would not even have a picture to take back to show them. That's when I overheard two women speaking - "How did you get to be Rosie's assistant??" Ah-ha! I turned around to find Rosie's assistant and I waited to speak with her. I started by saying I completely understood if she could not help me. I explained the situation, and she told me to stay where I was.

These look-alikes were not nice people. When Rosie's staff was handing out autographed pictures of Rosie, one person yanked the stack out of the hand of the person handing them out and ran out of the restaurant to sell them. The look-alikes were all over Rosie, and finally her security person sat her in a booth and told everyone there would be no more pictures. Rosie was going to eat and then leave, with NO MORE PICTURES, so he wanted everyone to just get out of her face. You must understand, he was not being unreasonable - she was really getting smothered by people. Then Rosie's assistant spoke with him and I was allowed to stand near the booth and wait for her. When she finished, the assistant spoke to her about me and then Rosie came over and took pictures with me, with Rosie telling me how cool it was that the school raised the money to send me.

I blew one of the pictures up into a poster and it was on my wall for all of the years I taught at Cypress Creek High School. Soon after that memorable moment in my life, I decided to have headshots done and send them to agents - and the rest has just been "Rosie"!!

Job Checklists
and Booking Sheets

Before you leave home to go to your look-alike jobs, go through the following checklist to make sure you have everything you will need:

Directions to the event. Make sure you are absolutely certain where you're going, and eliminate any possible confusion (such as more than one hotel having the same name). If possible, have with you the phone number of the place you are working.
• The name and phone number of the **contact person** you are to meet. Make sure you have a designated place to meet him or her. Know **which room** your job will be in.
• The **agency's emergency phone** number.
• The **company name** you are working for.
• A **full tank of gas**, as well as a Thomas Guide or **city map** in your car. (www.mapquest.com comes in handy!)
• Cash for **parking**. Not every job will validate your parking. Be prepared.
• All of your **costumes**, including extra changes of costumes or wigs, and a **coat**

or something to keep you warm in case the job is outside.
- Your **music**: CDs, cassette tapes, musical instruments, microphones, and/or sheet music. Bring extra music in case an encore is requested.
- **Power bars** or energy bars. If you are not being fed at the job and will be working longer than one hour, it is a good idea to keep your energy level up with a little protein or carbohydrates in between sets.
- **Mints,** gum, a travel toothbrush and paste, mouthwash deodorant, and cologne or aftershave.
- **Extra makeup,** powder, hairspray, curling iron, or other touchup items. If it is humid or rainy at your event, you will want to touch up your hair.
- **Comfortable shoes,** for after your job or for walking to the job. Good shoes can be a relief when you're working convention jobs that last eight hours or more.
- An **iron**, in case your costumes have become wrinkled in a suitcase or travel bag.
- A **cell phone and/or pager.** When making long drives to your job, it's always a good idea to have a cell phone handy.
- **AAA** or some other auto club service. You need to have help readily available should your vehicle break down on the way to or from a job.
- **A travel makeup mirror.** You may have to get ready at the event, and many times you will have to use a regular bathroom to get ready. If you have a makeup mirror that lights up, then you can get ready anywhere.

*Note:
When someone calls you to book your act, make sure you get all the necessary information and details. I've included the following simple worksheet that will help when someone inquires about your act. It is helpful to have in hand to make notes on when an agent calls you for a job.

JANUARY BOOKING 2003
TODAY'S DATE:

EVENT NAME and LOCATION:

CONTACT PERSON:

CHECK-IN PLACE:

AGENCY:

CONTACT:

AGENT'S EMERGENCY #:

DATE OF EVENT:

DIRECTIONS:

PARKING:

Notes:

Q. What are your thoughts about this business in general?

Lyndal Grant as Arnold Schwarzenegger: "I think this business is different for everyone. I also think it's what you make it for yourself. It's like your life: if you're good, honest, and work hard for your future, your life will provide for you. There will always be forks and turns in the road, people or situations you wished you might have avoided. What defines you and your experience will be directly related to responsibility."

Alli Spots as Marilyn Monroe: "Be professional at all times. Sometimes it is hard, but you carry your own reputation plus the person's that you are impersonating. Both reputations must be preserved."

Q. Additional advice or thoughts for look-alikes?

Julie Sheppard as Judy Garland: "I only wish that I were able to work with each and every person in your fabulous book, and in return, pass on a gig to them! A BIG FAT FABULOUS GIG!!!"

Money and All
That Goes With It

Money, prices, and questions to ask your agent or client

As a look-alike, you are an **independent contractor**. The companies and agencies that you work for will issue you a Form 1099 on or before January 31st of the year following the year in which you performed for them. **You are responsible for doing your own taxes**. This means that you must save every receipt from every expense you incur as a look-alike. Include receipts for your car maintenance, gasoline, costumes, makeup, hair, back-up dancers, bands, photos and promotional materials, studios, printing, office supplies, record-keeping materials, meals or entertainment with prospective agents or employers, and equipment used in your act. Keep a notebook containing accurate records of the jobs you do, along with information about your expense accounts.

General Price Ranges

These are examples of general prices for look-alike services in the Los Angeles area in 2002. You will need to find out the average going rates for look-alikes in your area before setting your own rates. Prices will vary per performer, job, location, and year. Agents add their fees to whatever price you charge. Keep in mind that many factors can affect the fee for a certain job; the prices quoted here are average, general ranges.

Mix and Mingle/Appearance: $200.00 to $500.00 and up per hour

Remember, the type of customer you are working for may slightly affect the price you charge, but you **do not want to charge anything less than this**. You may be hired to mix and mingle, or to simply appear at an event. Sometimes your client may use you for five minutes, but even for a brief appearance it still takes you time to get into costume and makeup and drive to the event. So always book yourself for a minimum of one hour, even when the job itself will not last an hour. When you are being hired for more than one hour, you must decide how much more you wish to charge for each additional hour. Some look-alikes charge $250 each hour. Some charge $350 for the first hour and $100 to $125 for each hour after that. As a beginner, you should charge a rate that you feel comfortable with, that will allow agents to book you easily. As you gain experience and develop a reputation, you will be able to increase your rates accordingly.

Singing Telegram/Children's Party: $35.00 to $175.00 and up

This kind of job is going to have a much lower budget than a mix and mingle event because there is usually a private person or group paying rather than a large corporation hiring you. A general price for a telegram can vary depending on the client's requests and other circumstances, the location, and the agent hiring you.

Live Performing: (15 – 45 minute show- ONE performance)
$500.00 to $2,000.00 and up

This estimate is the price to charge for your part of the job only. This range does not include backup dancers, singers, or musicians. An overall show price is up to you and your crew to determine on your own. Dancers, singers, and musicians may each charge up to $250 or more. When quoting your price, keep in mind that for **special occasions, holidays, and New Year's Eve, you should charge more than your standard prices**.

Acting with a script: $500 to $6,000 and up

Acting or performing a stand-up routine will require someone with strong acting or comedic talent. These jobs can vary, from emceeing an event and hosting the evening to performing an hour-long comedy or dramatic act on stage, to filming a television commercial, show, movie, or voice-over. If your job is union-affiliated, then you will be paid according to union scale (generally ranging from $550 to $1,200; see SAG guidelines for more information). For any acting jobs, you should request the script in advance and have your lines memorized. You should also be paid for rehearsals and for the use of your own costumes.

Print work: $250.00 to $550.00 and up

Print work inquiries can vary, from a local newspaper advertisement to a major advertisement for a major corporation. You will want to ask questions before you give a quote for your services.
Ask how long the photo shoot will take and how many hours you are being booked for. A general shoot should not exceed eight hours. You should be clear about whether you are to arrive in makeup, or if they are going to provide makeup and wardrobe for you. If your photo shoot is eight hours in length or more, you should also have a meal and break (generally one hour) included in your contract.

Voice-Over: $350.00 to $550.00 and up

Voice-over is usually for film, television or radio, so you should ask for union scale. Call SAG to find out what the scale is for the type of job you are being hired for.

Many times, with each job you are submitted for, the agent may suggest a budget they are working with and may offer a set price to you. You must decide if you are comfortable with that price. Remember, it is not important how much the agent is charging the client, as long as you have negotiated a price for your services that you are comfortable with. The fees other look-alikes are receiving are also not your concern. If you still have questions about prices you should charge, ask other working look-alikes what the going rates are for the job type and area you are working. Look-alike prices vary and the above is a general idea only to help give you an estimate when quoting your own prices. There are no standard rates, but there are ranges that vary according to the details of the work.

There are several things to consider before quoting a price to an agent for a specific job.

Ask these questions when an agent calls you:

How far away is the job? If the job is more than one hour's driving time away, you should add something to your standard fee (usually $75.00 to $100.00) to cover the extra costs of mileage, gas, and time involved in getting to the job.

How many hours are you booked for? Your price depends on your hours. Set up a standard price for the first hour and every additional hour. The type of appearance or show being requested will determine your base price. Remember, agents add their percentage on top of your price, so be sure that it is clear when an agent calls you that the price you are quoting is solely for your work, and is separate from the agent's fee.

Who are you working for? A big company? A smaller private party? A single individual? Budgets vary according to the size and type of client involved.

Who is paying for parking? If your job is at a hotel or nightclub, your parking is usually validated by the client, but not in all cases. Find out if you are expected to pay. If you are, you may want to add the cost of parking to your total price.

Does the agent wish to book you and your backup crew together?
If you have your own musicians, backup dancers, singers, technical assistants, personal security guards, hair stylists, makeup artists, or sound engineers, make sure that you put together a cost for the entire group. When an agent books you and your crew together, the agency will most likely pay you with one check. You will have to create a checking account and bookkeeping system for your crew to keep track of your payments to others. Keep these records, because you will be taxed on the total price of each job. You will need to show what you paid out to other people and issue each of those people a Form 1099, if they are independent contractors, or a Form W-2 if they are your employees.

Remember, it does not pay to undercut another look-alike. Find what the going look-alike pay rates are in your area, and stay close within those standard prices. You may initially get a job because your price is cheaper than another look-alike, but you will also set a standard for your act to be considered "the cheaper version"- *cheaper* meaning *less* quality. Most quality agencies expect quality entertainment, and your prices reflect that

Show me the money!

D. Wallace as Cuba Gooding Jr.; Photography by Treneice Kendrick and Steve as Tom Cruise; Cruise Photography

What about expenses and doing taxes as a look-alike?

It is important to find an accountant with the CPA designation. The person you hire must be knowledgeable of the entertainment business and be able to guide you regarding the importance of record keeping. I strongly recommend you keep a record of your business and professional expenses. You will need to keep accurate records for the following categories:

- Accounting fees
- Attorney/legal fees
- Admission to plays, movies, and concerts
- Advertising
- Backup dancers, singers, and musicians
- Business meals and entertainment
- Business gifts
- Car expenses: mileage, gas, taxes, tolls, and maintenance
- Cell phone expenses
- Choreographer
- Classes and educational seminars
- Commissions
- Computer and computer expenses
- Costuming
- DBA (Doing business as)
- Dry cleaning costumes
- Dues for professional memberships
- Hair styling/hair cuts (professional grooming)
- Internet, web page and e-mail
- Mailing expenses
- Makeup, makeup artists
- Office supplies
- Pager
- Parking (at events, hotels, airports)

- Phonograph records, cassettes, musical charts, CDs
- Phone calls, phone bills
- Photo shoots
- P.O. box rental
- Prints and composites
- Private trainer, nutritionist, or dietician
- Promotional materials of your celebrity (videos, magazines, films)
- Publicity materials (for yourself)
- Reel (having your video reel professional made, edited, produced)
- Resume
- Stylists
- Subscriptions to industry-related publications
- Tapes
- Taxis and other local transportation
- Telephone and telephone answering service
- Travel expenses for transportation, meals, lodging, taxis, bus, and car rental
- Travel materials
- Video dubbing, tapes
- Wardrobe and wardrobe maintenance
- Wig, hairpieces, glues, beards, mustaches, etc.

If you work abroad from time to time, make sure to keep track of all your business activities and have each agency you work for provide you with the specific details of your earnings including deductions for commissions, expenses, and any taxes withheld. Special rules may apply if you are out of the United States for more than one year.

Q. When can I expect to get paid from the agency I have worked for?

It depends on the company and agent. You can expect to receive your full payment from a job you have worked either the night of the show (which is how many agencies pay), or anytime from to one to two weeks later. You will want to have a clear answer from your agent on when you should expect payment. Some companies put all talent on payroll, and this can take up to three weeks, and other companies may hand you your payment before you do the job. Again, get your answer ahead of time, so you know exactly when to expect your money.

What do you do when an agent calls for a job, but talks so fast that you agree to a job because you feel unprepared or intimidated?

Most agents that book look-alikes are very professional, and handle bookings and phone calls in a professional manner. Once in awhile you may experience a newer agent or a less than professional agency trying to fast-talk you into a job by using an impatient tone of voice or very generic details about a possible job booking or audition. What do you do? Take a deep breath and take control of the call and the direction it is going. Remember, the caller is requesting YOUR service, and not vice versa. You can take the lead by firmly saying to the agent: "WHAT is the booking? I need firm and exact details of this job. How many hours am I working, and will there be scheduled breaks if I am working longer than three hours? I need the exact location of the event, and the type of event it is, and information about who this job is for BEFORE I COMMIT TO IT." Price: If you are clear with what you want to charge, tell the agent what price you will charge for the job, or if you are feeling unsure of what you should charge for the job, you need to firmly state to the agent: "I am not near my calendar right now, so let me call you back in 15 minutes with my price and availability," and then take the time to write it out and figure out your price for the booking before you call the agent back. Once in a while an agent may say, "There is not a huge budget on this job, can you do the job for $_____?" It is up to you to use your own judgment that the price is fair, and that this agency does not say this (the low-budget job story) every time they call you for a job. As a talent, it is NOT your business to know what the agent is charging the client for the job. I often hear look-alikes complain about what the agent charged for a job, compared to what the look-alike asked for. It is your responsibility to ask for the price you want. You should feel comfortable with the agent calling, and feel comfortable to ask questions about the job or audition. I find that many of the agents (and certainly all of the best are listed in this book) are wonderful people who work very hard at what they do. They are ethical and put in time and money to book talent. Being an agent is much more challenging than most look-alikes are aware of, so they definitely do work hard for their commissions. You will learn which agencies to work for by being able to decipher the few agencies that you can't get straight answers from, from the top notch agents who consistently book professional jobs for you. Take charge of YOU. YOU are your business!

Q. Since you are a professionally trained performer who can sing, play musical instruments, act and write your own material, what kind of advice can you give to other multi-faceted performers like yourself?

Stephen Sorrentino as Elton John: "Don't underestimate the possibilities for making money in this field. Until 1997, when I began to focus on acting, comedy, and other areas of professional performing, I had earned nothing less than $200K per year as a full time look-alike and sound-alike."

Focus: Do your homework. Study, walk, talk, sing, and carry yourself like the person that you emulate. When you're "in character," be true to it as you would if you were in a play. That's the difference between a professional look-alike and someone just dressing up to look like

Stephen Sorrentino as Sir Elton John;
Photography by Glenn Jussen

someone famous.

Promo material: Don't be cheap with your craft. Good promotional material is the essence of a solid working career. This is your calling card and must do all the talking for you in every agent's office. Because I decided to go with color 8 x 10s as opposed to black and white (three times more expensive) and do a professional videotape (in a studio, staged, and lit properly with two cameras and edited with titles and great sound), I booked most of the jobs that I was submitted for. Agents and buyers alike want to go with someone who looks like they have been successful and feel comfortable paying big money for a well-promoted and established act.

In Short: My initial investment of $2500.00 has grossed me over $2 million since 1991. That's good math! By investing in my talents as an impersonator, I have had the opportunity to perform in over 18 countries and 37 states. I have appeared on talk shows and television shows, and because I am an actor first, I was cast as the voice of Elton John in the Fox sitcom "Wake up America."

YOU Look Marvelous: A look-alike should LOOK LIKE their celebrity. Costumes, wigs, and props are something to not cut corners on. You should appear and act just like the person that you are attempting to emulate. If your character is known for their attire or fashion, then so should you. Pick out good quality fabrics when recreating that certain look that is your character. Hire a costume maker or designer. When you are working at elaborate events, you should not look as if you're a "Halloween" version of the person that you are depicting. Invest in your look.
The clothes that you wear as your celebrity should look as if you borrowed them from the star's own wardrobe closet."

Money tip:

If another fellow look-alike passes a lead (possible job) on to you, or gives your phone number to an agent/client and you get a job booked from this lead, it is smart business etiquette to either call the person who gave you this lead and thank them or send them a referral fee. You can decide how much you want to send them depending on how much you are getting paid for the job. When you do smart business, you will have more people wanting to pass work your way. **Take care of people who take care of you**. I have made decisions to continue to pass on work to the look-alikes who show appreciation to me, either in a thank you note, a phone call, or money. I will continue to give work to the talent or agents that do smart business with me. It is a great way to establish a give and take with people and network for future jobs.

Traveling Abroad
As a Performer

There are some very important things to know before you travel for a job, especially overseas. If you are a performing look-alike, chances are good that you will get a call to travel internationally. Most professional look-alikes have traveled abroad. Please review the following information if you are considering an international or even out-of-state booking.

1. **Meet with the agent who is booking you.**
You should be able to sit down with the agent and discuss all the details of the job and feel comfortable with this person. You will need to have a valid passport and possibly two passport photos for your agent to get a working visa for your travels. Remember, your passport should remain in your possession at all times. You should be able to ask any question in regard to your work and the job. If the agent is in another state and it is not possible for you to meet in person, you should have the opportunity to speak over the phone as much as you need to in order to feel comfortable with this person.

Review the **contract** that the agent gives you. NEVER leave the country without a signed contract.

When dealing with an international agency, where the agent is abroad, you should investigate the agency and the legitimacy of the company before you accept any work from them. Check their resources, references, websites, clients, and years of experience.

If you are not comfortable with booking a job with an agent who is in another country, ask your favorite local agent if they would be interested in following through with the details and booking the job for you. They will take a commission of approximately 15 % after they close the deal for you. You may feel more comfortable having a professional agent represent you in a situation like this. Dealing with international work requires many details that an agent may already be aware of. The local agent can follow through to make sure you will be safe, and follow up on any issues that may arise.

2. **Ask for a deposit.**

You should be able to get this deposit at least two weeks before you leave for the job. Clarify with the agent that you will be paid in US dollars.

3. **Confirm the agent's costs**:

a. Round trip airfare. The airplane tickets and passport should be in your possession at all times.
b. At least two meals a day, and/or a per diem.
c. All transportation to and from shows and rehearsals, as well as to and from the airport.
d. Airport taxes, your hotel room, and any calls related to the booking. (Personal phone calls are usually not included.)

4. **How many shows per day are you performing?**

Your price for the job depends on how much you work. You should be paid for every day you are working, traveling, and/or rehearsing. If you are asked to do something extra such as appear on television, pose for photographs or print ads, or perform more live shows, contact your agent immediately so he can negotiate more money for you. You may want to include an "extra performance cost" clause in your contract so it is clear before you travel that extra work will incur extra pay.

5. **Know where you are going**.

Certain places have strict customs regulations. You need to know these before you travel. Do you need shots? Should you be aware of food or water hazards? What will the weather be like? Is the area safe? Contact a travel agent and confirm that the place you are going to is safe, and get information on customs regulations and any other government requirements. Will you have a chaperone or interpreter for the whole trip? Is the hotel a four- or five-star establishment? What do you need to know about diseases or medical care? Are there airport or hotel taxes, and do you need a work permit? Call your travel agent and ask as many questions as you can think of to prepare for your trip.

6. What are your costs?

As a look-alike, there are certain costs that you are responsible for, such as the music (you should have at least three copies of your show's music on tape), costumes, props, microphones, musical instruments for your act or your band, and several backup costumes and wigs. Prerecorded music should be professionally done in a studio, and you should have several costumes as well as several wigs, if you wear them. It's up to you to have your hair and your makeup prepared. Find out before your trip if there are any other costs you will be expected to cover.

As an independent performer, you should have every agent you work with mail or fax you a signed contract before performing any job. A contract protects you as the artist, and ensures that everyone involved in the booking follows through on their agreements. If an agent does not supply a contract for you, ask the agent if he or she is comfortable signing yours.

Note: A contract may not always guarantee an agreement or stop a client from canceling, even if all parties sign, but it can usually guarantee that you will be paid something for your time.

7. Phone numbers:

Bring the agent's phone numbers with you. Double check the hotel, transportation, and client's contact information before you travel. See the following sections for cell phone ideas for travel.

When I get off the plane, should I look like my character? Should I have my makeup, hair, or wardrobe looking "in character," and will the people picking me up- expect me to look like my celebrity?

An important element many look-alikes may not be clear with is the understanding of how to look when traveling. I know for many look-alikes, creating their celebrity look requires heavy makeup or specific hairstyles that may not be practical for any kind of traveling. Some look-alikes choose to travel comfortably, and prefer to get into character once they arrive at the hotel or event. Still others decide to dress similar to their celebrity or in character when meeting a client for a traveling job. You are not expected to look exactly like your celebrity until show time and you should not feel pressured to be in character until then. However, there is a very fine line between looking like yourself and looking somewhat similar to your star when you are arriving to meet a client or agent for a job. You will want to decide how you wish to present yourself, keeping in mind that many clients have a "first impression" attitude. Looking close to your celebrity with your wardrobe or hairstyle may be a good idea when meeting a client for the first time.

The following example is from Lyndal Grant, who is an absolutely great Arnold Schwarzenegger look-alike, who recently went to India on a contract. Unfortunately, this booking turned out to be a nightmare, not only financially (as he is still fighting to get paid some of the monies owed to him) but because of the shocking conditions that he encountered while there. It is an excellent warning to anyone who is offered a contract in a third world country, to make them aware of what could go wrong. What may seem like a legitimate contract may not be, as Lyndal found out.

"This story is about an ordeal in India that had been widely communicated throughout our industry of entertainers. The ordeal was concerning at least two companies in India that had been exploiting foreign national entertainers and their agencies. These companies perpetrated transgressions against entertainers by using outright deception, false contracts, contract exploitation, and assignee companies. One assignee company sought to evade retribution by deploying vague international legal suppositions. They also claimed they were being blackmailed over the issue of poverty, while paradoxically claiming to provide photographic proof of their warmth. The other company maintains a "no comment" disposition, as if a Great Wall existed between themselves and the principle issues.

Through out this ordeal, I have kept my focus on another crime that originates not just in India, but does involve these same businesses. That is the moral crime of poverty, a crime that exists merely as a function of people not caring about one another.

Within a day of my arriving in India, I had asked to be able to exchange US cash for rupees, so I could give money to the children and poor street beggars. Children would approach my car at every single intersection that my driver stopped at. My *Brilliant Entertainment Networks* staff assistants had constantly attempted to persuade me not to give away my money. Perhaps they knew something I didn't, or worse yet, they had learned to disregard the plight of others and just did not care, in a cynical matter-of-fact way.

"Those people are always there," they would say. "Of course they are," I would respond. Ironically, the average Indian person, or at least the ones I met, blame these poor lower-caste people for what they do not have. Their theme of distrust is that the beggars are only working a racket, refusing to work like everyone else. I guess the many typical 4- and 5-year-old naked children were all in on this racket of shameful work avoidance, even the babies they were holding.

The poverty alongside every street is absolutely appalling, as were the driving standards of nearly everyone on the road. Dodging cows is a nail-biting spectator event. In case you don't know, cows are sacred in India; they roam freely wherever they prefer.

My first day, I was whisked away by my driver to the first official in-store engagement, clad in Terminator motif, not knowing that I wouldn't return until 14 hours later. The event engagement for *Shoppers' Stop* was directly associated with their "*Seven Wonders of the World*" promotions. As we drove through the streets of New Delhi, I was shocked to see what looked to be the existence of people living as if it was 1000 years ago.

As I got to *Shoppers' Stop* for my first in-store engagement I was really surprised by the transformation of civilization as we entered back into what seemed to be the familiar world of western customs. As I began performing as Arnold, I wondered how bizarre it was that I would have been asked to export the Terminator to the land of Mahatma Gandhi. As the day wore on, I began to wear out. I slowly began to realize, hour by hour, that my 3-hour-per-day contract was becoming a 12- to 14-hour per day exploitation of my good faith.

Mixed duties included photo opportunities, constant press, and on-camera media interviews. Then there were the shoppers; they were approaching me as if I was actually *was* Arnold. No small wonder, since my personal in store emcee was announcing that "THE ONE, THE ONLY, ARNOLD SCHWARZENEGGER is here to visit *Shoppers' Stop*, as a representative of *America and the Seven Wonders of the World*, in store promotion!"

My personal photographer was there to capture the moment and a hefty photo fee from the throngs of shoppers who had been hoodwinked into thinking they were posing with the real Arnold. Even before the second day began, I had fully realized who and what I had gotten myself mixed up with. Even still, I thought privately, the media coverage was a real bonus - never before had I been so sought after. Six to seven times per day was the average scheduled press interviews and/or photo sessions. In those interviews, I quickly began to focus on the sights and conditions of India.

The press, of course, was very well aware of the fact that I was not Arnold, which paradoxically seemed to be used as covert permission for *Shoppers' Stop* to actually represent me as Arnold, using the press disclosures as their fallback. The press was exceptionally interested in my American perspective. I told them how shocked I was by the conditions of so many people here in India. That in comparison, it would be a disaster in the USA not to have a car. Typical American reality.

After several days in New Delhi, I was scheduled for travel to the pink city, Jaipur. Only thing was, I had now been handed train tickets instead of airline tickets. This was a breach in contract and put me at great risk in rural India. The U.S. Department of State warns citizens not to travel in rural India, as do the CIA travel advisories for that country. I was very concerned and disgusted at this point. I had already been expressing considerable anxiety over other contractual breaches.

Brilliant Entertainment Networks and *Shoppers Stop* couldn't seem to do anything honestly, except to get me to my next engagement. The people standing by the road seemed to be much more honest in accepting their horrid conditions. In contrast, being presented as a real Hollywood superstar without proper in-store disclosure to the shoppers was not at all what I had accepted. It's one thing to look like someone, but lying directly, or lying by omission is something else.

Demoralized by God's awful truth, this experience was tough for me to endure. I had become very ill with a high fever and strep throat. Even this didn't stop the show. At least the poor souls stranded with the streets as their home led an honest existence; they had no expectations of a life outside the one they already knew. You didn't need to ask them this; the absolute resolve of their existence was only thing they had to give you, and they were "big givers." What they gave me will be with me always. It was a heartbreaking sight, more so a heartbreaking memory of the truth outside America.

The lesson learned was mine, but perhaps lost if I didn't share it with others".

Word of caution: It is not uncommon for bookings coming from overseas or international businesses to hire look-alikes with the intention to "fool the public." Many look-alikes have found themselves stuck in this situation AFTER accepting a job. Companies hiring look-alike talent may not tell the agency up front that they are wishing to book a "dead-ringer" look-alike in hopes to fool the public, but will request a dead-ringer look-alike for the job.

What to do: If you ever find yourself in this situation, it can become very uncomfortable for you and in some cases dangerous. My best advice is to nip it in the bud, before anything gets out of hand.

It is always best to speak up to the people responsible for hiring you, and tell them straight out that you are not going to complete any booking if you are going to be expected to fool anyone into believing that you are the celebrity. If you can complete the job booking by clearly stating to the audiences involved that you are a hired LOOK-ALIKE talent, then you will complete the contract obligation of the job booking.

A "What In the World-" Example
Accepting job offers that seem 'normal' are not always what they seem to be:

The booking: A well-known look-alike agency in Hollywood sent me to Mexico to meet and greet as Madonna for a nightclub opening.

The truth: The booking was agreed between "agent" and "client" that the Madonna look-alike would fool the public into thinking that she was really Madonna. Look-alike (me!) had not been informed that this was the job description, and after arriving at the job in a limo with police escorts and several bodyguards, I realized something was not quite right. There were hundreds of people lined up around the block just to get a glimpse of "Madonna" and as I entered the event, the media grabbed me to stop and "say something to the cameras." They gave me scissors to cut the ribbon to open the new hip nightclub and the hundreds of onlookers applauded my every move. I was in shock and embarrassed that I was in such a situation and did not know what I should do, as the thousands of people cheered me on, snapping hundreds of photos and chanting "MADONNA!"

This was not the first time an "industry" person hired me to fool an audience, but it was the only time I kept my mouth shut in the moment. In bookings to follow, I learned to speak up AT THE JOB to the people responsible for hiring me, to tell them that I would not continue to work at the job if I were expected to fool the audiences.
When working as a look-alike, you may also find yourself at a job booking where you are expected to appear as a *real celebrity*, rather than simply a look-alike. You are booked for a job in hopes of making the people responsible for hiring you look like VIPs by having a "celebrity" at their event.
Should this happen to you, make it known that you are not willing to portray yourself as the real celebrity, so that you will not jeopardize your work and suffer the consequences.

Warning signs:

• Not getting many details of WHO THE JOB IS FOR from the agent. For example, having wishy-washy "oh, it is a job for a radio station…something or other." This is sometimes an indication that the agent is not telling you everything about the job.
• Accepting a job in a foreign country for a brief appearance
• Having an agent ask you to "look as close to the real celebrity as possible" but without any further explanation.
• Having the client ask if you can "wear dark glasses" at the event.
• Being at the event and hearing the client tell the guests you are the real celebrity as you are performing.

Travel tips from the experts:

Lissa Negrin as Cher: "Get a good moisturizer and wig box."

Gina B as Britney Spears: "Suggest to the agent who is hiring you that for any jobs with a flight that lasts 10 hours or longer, they should fly you business class."

Romeo Prince as Prince: "When traveling as a look-alike, you may wish to invest in luggage that has wheels. When you are rushing from one gate to the next, and traveling from one city to the next, you will be grateful to be able to roll your luggage rather than carry heavy suitcases full of costumes."

Denise Bella Vlasis: "It is important to know that many international hotels have different electrical outlets than we do in the US, so your blow dryer, curling iron, electric shaver, etc., may need an adapter that will fit their electrical outlets and sockets. Many travel stores carry these adapters, and they are reasonably priced."

Denise Bella Vlasis: "When traveling for a job, it is best to book your flight for the day before your job. Flights are commonly cancelled due to weather, etc., so when you travel the day before your scheduled booking, you have that buffer of an extra day, in case you need to reschedule your flight."

Tatiana Turan as Jennifer Lopez: "Always pack your toiletries, a day's worth of undergarments, and your favorite costume in a carry-on so that they are with you at all times!! One never knows when luggage could get lost, and the last thing you want to worry about is having a show the next night and no costume! Underwear and a toothbrush are easily replaced, anywhere, but a costume isn't! I also like to pack lots of dried fruits and nuts, health bars, and any other snacks that won't go bad just in case you don't like what there is to eat! Bring a face mister, like Evian for the face, or anything that'll give you that extra lift in case you have to go on right after a day of traveling!"

Lyndal Grant as Arnold Schwarzenegger: "Keep your passport safe at all times; never leave it at a front desk or with anyone you don't already know. Keep at least two photocopies on your person at all times, and give a copy to asking parties. Before you leave your homeland, rent a cell phone that has international connectivity. I would recommend a Nextel I-2000 (visit www.nextel.com for information). Also, store your passport electronically/digitally on Hotmail or another internationally available e-mail account. You can then download and print the document if needed. Always research the country you're visiting. In the US, you can research online at the US Department of State/travel advisory section. You can also download visa applications from nearly every country on this site via the Acrobat Reader software stored on that site. The CIA also provides travel advisories online at their website."

Alli Spots as Marilyn Monroe: "Wig heads and the old-time wig boxes are the BEST. Wadding wigs is "bad." Also, take the costumes as carry-ons. PERIOD."

Julie Sheppard as Judy Garland: "I have one check list for show items and another for personal ones, that I methodically go through as I prepare my suitcase. I pack two days in advance!!! If I don't, I'll have a panic attack, as I worked on tour in Europe for FIVE years and had to move every month!!! Packing became my worst nightmare. On travel day, I leave so that I can be at least an hour early, then I relax with great coffee, a menthol cigarette, and a good book. I am always well rested and carry Tylenol, decongestant, antacid, Band-Aids, and moisturizer for the commute, just in case! I also carry my own healthy snacks, and I never start a conversation with the person I'm seated next to on a flight. Besides, I get so little time all to myself (I'm a wife and mom) that I relish trips where I can close my eyes and just be! Life is way too hectic, so I try to make travel as pleasurable for me as possible!"

Vicki J. Browne as Rosie O'Donnell: "Plane schedules are never what they seem. I like to book travel so I have at least several hours between arriving in the destination city and any type of rehearsal. Always bring a great book to read! Or as they say in *The Importance of Being Earnest*, bring a journal. One should always have something sensational to read on the train! I also pack my suit in my carry-on."

Contracts:
Get It In Writing!

Having a contract for every job you book is going to be necessary. You may wish to provide your agent or client with one of your own contracts every time you are booked for work. The best option for finding a good, solid, binding agreement is to contact an entertainment attorney and have him or her design a contract that fits your needs as a performer. You can also find basic contracts at computer stores that sell computer software. You can also review the following basic standard contract and adapt it to create your own contract.

Sample Contract

THIS AGREEMENT entered into on this _____ day of _____, 200__ between _____, known as **Talent,** and _____, known as **Agent/Client.** Talent and Client do hereby agree to the following services and terms: _____ to hire services of Talent/Look-alike _____ to appear/perform as "_____".

Agent/Client agrees to pay Talent $_____ for the following job description: _____
_____.

Agent/Client agrees to pay a deposit of $_____to Talent 2 weeks prior to engagement and the remaining balance of $_____ upon completion of performance. Deposit is non-refundable.

Event: _____

Date of Engagement: _____, 200___ **Time:** _____ **Check-In:** _____

Location of Event: _____ **Check-in person:** _____

Agent/Client Emergency Number: _____

Directions:_____ **Parking:**_____

Pay:_____ **Over-time price**:_____

Additional Special Instructions :

TALENT:
AGENT/CLIENT:
Name:_____
Name:_____
Address:_____
Address:_____
Phone:_____
Phone/Fax:_____
Signature_____
Signature_____

Upon signature of both parties, this contract serves as a binding agreement to parties said above.
_____
_____.

Entertainers are independent contractors and will take responsibility for all of their own Federal, State and Local taxes. Talent has control over means of conducting their own performance, and will conduct himself/herself accordingly. Performers agree to give performance to the best of their ability. The agreement of the artist to perform is subject to proven detention by sickness, accidents, riots, epidemics, acts of GOD, or any other legitimate conditions This Agreement is to be construed under the laws of the State of _____; venue shall be _____ (your State).

Standards and Copyrights

1. **No eating or drinking** while working (most especially alcoholic beverages). If your client offers food or non-alcoholic beverages to you during a break, make sure you are discreet and out of the public's eye. While you're in costume, people will still be watching you, so you will not want to kill the illusion for them by being out of character.

2. **Leave the job when your job time is done**. Overtime should be requested in advance, so if the guests ask you to "hang out" with them after your show is over, just kindly refuse. Many agents have had bad reviews from look-alikes who decided to take the invitation to stay longer than they were booked for.

3. **Bring someone to your job** that can look after and/or protect you. In the case of going to a private home, or some place that you are unfamiliar with, you will always want protection (especially if you're a woman) in these situations. If you are not concerned about having a personal security person, it is still wise to leave information with a friend on where you are going, and hours you are working. **If you are going to a corporate event**, you may need to leave your companion in the lobby or backstage. Most agents prefer that you do not bring guests to these kinds of events.

4. **Never pass out your own business cards** or phone number. Your agent works hard to book you. Pass out cards provided by your agent. If you do not have any, simply refer interested parties to the agent or contact person who is responsible for the booking. At some time you will almost certainly be asked to give out your personal number. Don't! This will only cut off your own sources in the long run. It is simply not fair to your agent, and if the word gets out that you are undercutting someone, your job offers will begin to dwindle.

5. **Be neat,** clean, and prepared. Give yourself plenty of time to get in costume or apply any final touches while putting on your makeup and getting into character. Breath mints are always a good idea when you will be working close to people. Check your hair and makeup occasionally during the job, if possible. Eye drops can be very helpful when you are posing for photos all night long. Apply a little Vaseline to your teeth to prevent lipstick sticking to the teeth. Every special little touch you add will improve upon your impersonation. Nail polish, props, or accessories that your celebrity would use or wear also contribute to your success in creating a complete, believable character.

6. **When your job has come to an end, check with the client** or agent to be sure that everyone is happy. You should also check for a back door to leave by, because fans or people still wanting photos may bombard you. A back door is always the cleanest exit. Remember, you are a fantasy character creating a Hollywood illusion, so try to leave quickly and quietly, and with class.

7. **Never, ever fool people** by pretending or saying you are the real star. You can get yourself into trouble if you do not honor your celebrity's privacy and image. Remember, you are borrowing someone else's identity so you can work. R-e-s-p-e-c-t that. When an agent calls you for a job that may seem like you are going to be hired to fool people (into believing that you are the real star), make it very clear with the agent that you will not accept these kinds of bookings.

8. **Bring more than one** costume, CD, or cassette to each job. You never know what emergency may occur, and if something happens to an element of your act and you don't have a backup for it, then you don't have an act.

9. **Don't talk about other people**, no matter what. It is very unprofessional for a performer to whine about a job in front of a client or guests. Save any complaints for later.

10. **Don't discuss money**. It's not anyone else's business what you're getting paid. When someone asks about money, just change the subject politely.

Brian Cole as Ricky Martin: "It is always important to portray your character with dignity and respect. Impersonation can be a great job, with great opportunity. So make sure to take the time to learn about your celebrity, and portray that person with care."

Brian Cole as Ricky Martin,
Photography by Michael Carins

What About Copyright Laws?

Suzanne LaRusch as Lucille Ball;
Photography by Andy Pearlman Studios

Legalities on a copyrighted character

For many legendary celebrity icons, there are certain celebrities that have a copyright to their star image. License agencies own the rights to many images such as Marilyn Monroe, Elvis Presley, Lucille Ball, and so many more. If you are unsure about whether the celebrity you look like is owned by a licensed agency, it is best to contact the estate of the celebrity to find out. You may wish to further investigate all legal contracts with the celebrity you wish to impersonate, before you invest in impersonating them. For example: Susan LaRusch is now one of the only performers with the legal rights to impersonate the Hollywood legend "Lucy" from the "I Love Lucy" television show.

Setting NEW standards with Suzanne LaRusch....

"When I started out in the world of impersonations, I knew the Lucy Ricardo character from the television show *I Love Lucy* would be the most recognized and fun character for the public. I studied the show (to death) and read lots of books on the show and on the star herself. I knew I had a face similar to Lucille Ball's, so I figured look-wise I might have a chance at pulling off the appearance. (I'm sorry to say, sometimes it doesn't matter how great an impressionist you are?if you don't look enough like the beloved star, your audience can take you or leave you...it definitely helps to look like them!) Next, I analyzed her makeup, skin tone, lashes, hair color, hairline, curl, style, blusher, cheek shape, shape of the lips...not too big....not too small....everything. I practiced over and over again until it looked natural....not cartoon-ish (which is the worst kind of impression, in my opinion). Then came the studying of her mannerisms, comedy timing, voice inflections, signature sounds, lines, comments, and attitudes. Then, over and above that, I had to rely on and refine my personal improvisational skills. After all, MY performances would be 94% an improv situation. Lucille had detailed scripts, but Lucille never had to think, "How would Lucy Ricardo react to a room of real estate salespeople chomping on shrimp, or getting ready for their big awards ceremony?" I had to be my own comedy writer 100% of the time...except when I was duplicating her famous routines from *I Love Lucy*, which I made sure I learned to the last detail.

Once I felt comfortable that I had a good presentation and was getting great feedback, I made a video of myself and sent it to Lucille Ball's daughter, Lucie Arnaz, who runs the estate on behalf of her mother and father. I got to speak to her on the phone shortly after that, and we had a great first chat, and have maintained a relationship since. She wanted to take the time with me because she knew things such as this were going to come up now that her mother, a legend, was gone, and she wanted control to preserve her mother's image with integrity. "I don't want my mother's face to be garbaged out there," she said, and I'll never forget it. I immediately put myself in this position: What if it was MY mother - how would I feel? I would want people to be respectful, flattering, and not take advantage of MY MOM! With Lucie, I knew I was talking to a businesswoman, an actress/entertainer in her own right...but also a daughter. She KNEW the laws as they pertained to her and her brother Desi's rights for their parents, and she was more than happy to give me the rules. She approved my portrayal right away - gave me permission to perform at Universal Studios Hollywood. She also gave me permission to perform at private hosted affairs. "But conventions are a different story," she says; "I consider that an endorsement." If you're standing in a booth - say the KODAK booth - and the image of Lucy brings people into the booth, now that company ultimately has the potential to make money because of the enticement that got them there in the first place...so they need to pay the estate a licensing fee. So Lucie advised me, "Stay away from conventions, please," anything that could be construed as an unauthorized endorsement.   Even taking pictures in front of a company sign - and for gosh sakes, make sure the pictures are a gift to the guests! If they charge, again, they are making money on something they do not have permission for. Also, any situation where they are selling tickets to see Lucy's work depicted. Again, making money without permission on an image that doesn't belong to them. Then she told me that the estate was not the only place I had to get permission from. Lucy Ricardo is a copyrighted character, from a copyrighted show, with copyrighted material. *I Love Lucy* is owned by CBS. So if I was portraying Lucy Ricardo in any way, shape, or form, I would also have to get permission from them. I subsequently started all over with them, and they basically gave me the same set of rules.

This was way back in 1991, and I've honored and stuck by the rules ever since. Even to the point of being a b _ _ _ _. How many times has a party planner accused me of being "anal" and complained, "Every other look-alike/impersonator does it; why are you being so difficult?....blah....blah....blah"
My answer? "Because THIS IS THE DEAL with my celebrity's estate and the people who own *I Love Lucy!*"

So what do I have to show for it? Ten years of making a living, being able to support my beautiful daughter by myself, the respect of Lucille Ball's family and CBS, portraying the most beautiful, talented, comedienne of all time....THAT'S what I have to show for it!

Now, I realize that the situation with Lucy is certainly the exception and not the rule. Other estates of famous people may or may not care as much....maybe until someone does something blatantly nervy. Other portrayals don't have copyright considerations. I know the laws are different for portraying a living person versus a deceased person, and then there is a "parody law," which allows programs like Saturday Night Live and Mad TV to get away with murder in their impressions of celebrities. The laws vary from state to state, but in most cases, are less strict with parodies that are not meant to be taken as serious depictions.

So...maybe people exploring this field can learn from my path with respect to copyrights and images, etc. Again, just do a great representation, do your homework, be respectful, and most likely you will be fine.
Good Luck! Love, Suzanne."

Side Note on Legality from Denise Bella Vlasis: "In 1985 I had been featured in the Los Angeles Times newspaper as a look-alike Madonna who was visiting children in hospitals and making headlines as a successful double for Madonna. In the article it featured me as Madonna, speaking of the work I had been doing at the time. Not long after the article ran in the paper did I get phone calls from agencies requesting me for future jobs, but I also received a letter from ***Madonna's attorney*** asking me to explain what my work entailed. My dad immediately suggested that this letter was not to be taken lightly, and he helped me in attaining an attorney who could represent me and help me understand (from the get go!) what I was able to do legally as a celebrity look-alike. I was informed that I was to carefully guard "Madonna's name, image, and likeness" in all of my work. From this moment on I was careful to never abuse what was rightfully owned by the star (Madonna) herself. I was able to learn, very early on, the importance of respect when working as a look-alike, and more importantly - the law. **As a look-alike, it is our job to never claim to be the "real celebrity."**

Some Things To Think About

© Before working as a celebrity impersonator, you may wish to investigate and find out if an estate owns the celebrity you look like. Certain celebrities (and the 'characters' they play in films or television shows) have copyrights to their likeness, name, image, and/or sound. If an estate owns the image of a celebrity, you will need to get written permission from the Estate stating that you have permission to portray the celebrity. It is wise to research the legalities before you invest. How do you know if an estate owns your celebrity? Most memorabilia of your celebrity will have a name printed on it, and the name of the copyright company. Research and find out before you get started. Submit yourself to the estate, and send them promotional materials with a letter stating what you intend to do as the celebrity.

® Music and lyrics of well-know songs are registered with music unions like ASCAP, so before putting on bigger productions (like a Legends type show) make sure you understand whether you are to pay a royalty for the use of the remake/song you are to perform. (Contact: www.ASCAP.com.)

© If you are filming a television show, film, or print advertisement, be very sure that the director understands that you are to be presented as a "Celebrity Impersonator" in the film and in the credits. Just because you have been cast in a film or print project does not guarantee the legal protection of a possible lawsuit. Back in the early 1980's, a well-known actor/director actually sued his look-alike for an appearance in an international commercial where the look-alike was presented as the *actor* and not an *impersonator* of the actor. The agent or director did not get sued, the look-alike did. Be sure you are not being hired to fool anyone into believing you are the real celebrity.

® For any kind of job, always present yourself as an impersonator. Use *your name* on all of your promotional photos, autographs, etc.

© Make good, well thought out decisions on jobs you select, products you endorse, and words you speak in public (as your celebrity). Think about how you would want someone to impersonate *you*. Again, respect the image you are borrowing.

® If someone asks for an autograph, *never* sign the star's name unless it is in quotes followed by your name. Or use a stage name. Present yourself as a double, stand-in, look-alike, and/or impersonator at all times.

If there are questions you have about copyright laws, it is best to ask an expert. The following article was written by William J. Briggs, II, an Attorney at Law who has dealt with "celebrity images."

HOW MUCH IS A CELEBRITY NAME WORTH?

By William J. Briggs, II, Attorney at Law

The question of how much a celebrity name is worth often arises in false endorsement cases. While the issue also arises in cases involving causes of action for Right of Publicity, (the inherent right of every individual to control commercial use of his or her own identity), this article limits itself to the valuation of a name under a Lanham Act § 43(a) false endorsement claim.

Celebrities and athletes are often sought after to endorse products and services. What would Nike be without Michael Jordan? Ford Motors has built an advertising campaign around Lindsey Wagner, the former Bionic Woman. Jerry Seinfeld and Tiger Woods are both pitchmen for American Express. Yet, in the rush to have celebrities and athletes sponsor and endorse their products, some companies either intentionally or inadvertently use the names, likenesses, or images of celebrities and athletes without their permission and consent.

In the past twenty years, celebrities and athletes have filed a number of cases involving false endorsement claims under the Lanham Act. That Act provides:

A false endorsement claim based on the unauthorized use of a celebrity's identity is a type of false association claim, for the alleged misuse of a trademark, i.e., a symbol or device such a visual likeness, vocal imitation or other uniquely distinguishing characteristic, which is likely to confuse consumers as to plaintiffs' sponsorship or approval of the product . . . . a celebrity whose endorsement of a product is implied through the invitation of a distinctive attribute of the celebrity's identity, has standing to sue for false endorsement under § 43(a) of the Lanham Act.

Woody Allen has brought at least two such claims. In one case, Woody Allen sued National Video for using a Woody Allen look-alike in an ad campaign to promote a nationally franchised video rental chain. In another case, Woody Allen sued Men's World Outlet for using a clarinet-playing look-alike who appeared in an ad campaign for a discount clothier. "The Fat Boys," a three-person rap-performing group, sued Miller Brewing Company for using look-alikes in a television commercial after they refused to participate in the commercial. Vanna White sued Samsung Electronics for its use of a robot character that was deliberately patterned after her. And Tom Waits sued Frito-Lay for its use of a sound-alike performer in an advertisement for Doritos chips. As one can imagine, most of these cases resulted in equitable relief, an injunction prohibiting further use of the celebrity's or athlete's name, likeness, or image. What about a monetary award? How much is the name, likeness, and image of a celebrity worth?

Section 35(a) of the Lanham Act provides, in pertinent part, that:

[T]he plaintiff shall be entitled . . . to recover (1) defendant's profits, (2) any damages sustained by the plaintiff, and (3) the costs of the action. The court shall assess such profits or cause the same to be assessed under its direction. In assessing profits the plaintiff shall be required to prove defendant's sales only; defendant must prove all elements of cost or deduction claimed. In assessing damages the court may enter judgment, according to the circumstances of the case, for any sum above the amount found as actual damages, not exceeding three times such amount. If the court shall find that the amount of recovery based on profits is either inadequate or excessive the court may in its discretion enter judgment for such sum, as the court shall find to be just, according to the circumstances of the case. Such sum in either of the above circumstances shall constitute compensation and not a penalty. The court in exceptional cases may award reasonable attorney fees to the prevailing party.

What damages does a celebrity or athlete sustain when someone wrongfully uses his or her name, likeness, or image? This author believes that a celebrity or athlete should be allowed to measure their damages by the profits they lost as a result of a defendant's infringement. In other words, the celebrity or athlete should be able to recover the reasonable compensation and royalty they would normally have received had they approved the use of their name, likeness, or image.

In a Fifth Circuit case, the appellate court affirmed an award where a professional sports league proved trademark infringement by a defendant who made emblems copying the insignia of league teams after having been denied a license. The court held that the damages could be measured by the license fees plaintiff would have received had they approved the use of their trademark. Boston Professional Hockey Ass'n v. Dallas Cap & Emblem Mfg., Inc., 597 F.2d 71 (5th Cir. 1979). See also National Bank of Commerce v. Shaklee Corp., 503 F.Supp. 533 (W.D. Tex. 1980) ($75,000 awarded as value of celebrity author's endorsement).

In a case that involved the largest award of a reasonable royalty as damages for trademark infringement, the Seventh Circuit affirmed a base award of nearly $10.5 million against Quaker Oats Co. Sands, Taylor & Wood v. Quaker Oats Co., 34 F.3d 1340 (7th Cir. 1994). In that case, the plaintiff was a small company that owned the THIRST-AID mark for beverages and food. It won an infringement suit against Quaker Oats for its use of the slogan "GATORADE IS THIRST-AID." The Seventh Circuit permitted judicial enhancement (an increase) of a reasonable royalty award to ensure that the infringer would bear the uncertainty of compensation, and ensure deterrence so that payment of a royalty was not viewed simply as a cost of doing business as an infringer.

Thus, in the case of a celebrity or athlete who typically earns their living through the use of their talents, and in some cases, their ability to successfully endorse products and services, they should be permitted to recover a reasonable royalty in addition to recovery of the defendant's profits, and injunctive relief. The worth of the celebrity's or athlete's name, likeness, or image is therefore the reasonable market rate they could obtain had they consented to and permitted the commercial use of their name, likeness, or image for the endorsement or sponsorship of a product or service.

William Briggs, II is a business litigator with an emphasis on Entertainment Law. He is associated with the law firm of Richman, Lawrence, Mann, Chizever & Phillips, located in Beverly Hills, CA.

Q. Have there been jobs you have refused to do?

Theresa Barnwell as Hillary Clinton: "Yes, one television show wanted me to be the "stripping Hillary." I turned them down. The producers called me back one week later and told me they would change the script. They did, and I took the job. I did a silly dance instead. It looked more like *The Swim* and we called it *The Whitewater*."

Cherise as Britney Spears: "I was hired to perform at a children's party, and the client wanted me to strip down to a bikini during my show. I declined."

Denise Bella Vlasis: "Oh, yes! Mainly insulting situations as Madonna. I have turned down too many job offers to count, where directors wanted me to portray an unflattering image as Madonna. Choosing to turn down jobs like posing for Playboy, or film roles where Madonna's image was exploited (no matter how great the pay was) was a personal choice for me - to try to honor Madonna through my career choices."

Cherise as Britney Spears;
Photography by Alex Cohen

Moving On

In the look-alike world, there is no time limit or age limit for any performer. This means that, as the entertainer, it is your responsibility to know when it may be time to move on or try something new. How do you know when it may be time to retire your character? There are many indications that should come up for you to let you know when it is time to move on, and ultimately you will *feel* when it is time by people's reactions to you, and how much work you are getting requested for. Moving on may not be an easy thing to do, as many performers have had 10, 15, even 20 years of excitement and success working as an impersonator. Having to let go of the elements this work brings to one's life can make the choice to move on even harder.

The Positives of Wanting to Keep Working:

You find your life filled with this amazing, unpredictable quality of being on movie sets, starring in films, making commercials, mingling with high-profile people and celebrities, getting paid well for what is (sometimes) fairly easy work.

People instantly recognize you everywhere you go. Whether from the work you have done as a look-alike, or because you look like someone famous. You get lots of extra attention everywhere you go?invitations, adoration, concert tickets, limo rides, free stuff, and lots of feelings that SEEM LIKE/FEEL LIKE something special.

Your life may have gone from struggling at endless auditions to an instant gig (double the pay). You may walk right into a major project and get the job easily, because of your look. Now you're working with notable directors, photographers, crew, and you feel like a superstar!

You're retired, and what a great way to make extra income.

You have the ability to travel, meet new people, and try new things.

With one slight change to your look (hair style, costume, facial expression) suddenly the world notices you and adores you (and you're not even the person who worked so hard to be famous).

Sure beats working 9 to 5!!!

> One may ask why anyone would want to move on and not work further as a look-alike. For some people, having a "more normal" life is necessary; others may become tired and wish to try something new; and still others may not know how or when to let go and move on.

The Challenges:

After many years of success as a look-alike, you find that you have aged completely differently than your celebrity. Your weight, hair, and/or skin tones have gradually become dramatically different than those of your celebrity.

Your celebrity died at a young age, and you are well beyond the age at which they died.

Your celebrity may have become controversial in our world. This has directly affected your work and inquiries for your services have suffered.

The scrutiny, criticism, competition, and nitpicking of people may make you want to quit.

You have become so attached to your celebrity and the elements of this work, that you don't know how to let go.

> Believe it or not, the psychological effects of working as a look-alike become more apparent the longer you work in this field.
> In the case of the look-alike, many times the look-alike talent will experience the same celebrity elements, praise, attention, perks, and instant notoriety, but without the years of experience and work of their celebrity. This may cause real confusion for anyone.

When a person has to deal with the constant attention of people "ooh-ing and ahh-ing" at them everywhere they go, it can become almost like an addiction for a look-alike talent. When the look-alike's life style goes from ordinary to having perfect strangers treating them as though they were a celebrity, then this is when the head trips and attachments can begin.

The look-alike realizes they are not the real celebrity; however, because of how they are being treated by so many people, they naturally want to cling tighter to the very thing that brings them this feeling of being famous. This is how a performer can become confused and forget about their original talents and love of performing, and become sidetracked and attracted to the idea of trying to live as a famous person. What happens now is that the look-alike talent needs to *feel like the celebrity*, in order to feel accomplished as a talent instead of remembering their special and unique gifts and qualities. Now the look-alike talent wants to be more like their celebrity and may lose track of who THEY are.

I have seen this happen over and over, and I too once believed it was because of Madonna that people liked what I did for a living. Sure, many people respond to a superstar like Madonna, and they want to know more about me because of my life "as her," but ultimately, it is my own uniqueness and love for what I do, that makes people respond to me in my life. I wish someone could have explained this to me when I believed otherwise. After many years, it is easy for me to detach any false ideas or illusions of feeling obligated to be more like Madonna. There is a strange feeling of obligation as an impersonator, as most people clearly expect you to "be" your celebrity. There is a very fine line between "being exact for people" and being "separate and not too much" like your celebrity. When a person is TOO much like their celebrity, audiences may make the judgment of the talent "having no identity of their own."

My advice: Be accurate and exact when you are **hired and working** to be "on," and it should be as simple as that. **Leave the show, the impersonation, and the exact accuracy and performance for the stage**, and don't lose sight of the difference between YOU and YOUR ACT. Spending outside quality time with other interests will help you to not lose touch with who you are.

Strive to remain detached from any ideas of being famous, living like your celebrity, believing or reading your own press, or thinking you are your resume. As harsh as this may sound, it can save you years of feelings of inadequacy, insecurity, or inability as a performer. Once you begin to see yourself with your own individual qualities, even as you work as another image, then you will always remember that what makes you special is YOU, and when the time comes for you to move on, you can do it more easily, since you are not living your life believing you are an image (especially when that image belongs to another person).

Making the Transition

Making your transition to move forward and on with your life can be easier for performers who have learned to become detached from the hoopla of this business and make more room for expansion in their lives. I would hope all of us would desire to have personal growth in our lives, and try new ideas and new experiences with an open mind.

A job possibility for the person who wishes to continue in the entertainment business:
You may want to continue with what you know and love by working as an agent or personal manager and/or help discover new talent. Who better than someone who has worked in the business to help provide services for new look-alikes who need the guidance? You may wish to work for a local agency or management company, or think about developing a company of your own. Talk to some of your favorite agents to see how they got their start, and see if this is a possibility for you. You may also wish to personally manage other celebrity look-alikes that are seeking management.

Trying another character may seem like a strange idea to someone who has worked as one celebrity for several years, but it just may be the very key to new success and new work opportunities for you. Many talented look-alikes have also discovered more talents within themselves by trying a new character. Again, if you can detach yourself from having to "be" your celebrity, then your mind may be more open for considering something new.

Go back to school, take a class, and network. If you're not quite sure what you would like to do for work, and you know it is not agent, manager, or entertainment work, then taking a class may help you see what else is out there to spark your interest. A good idea to help in your research is to sit down with a pencil and paper and write a list of 20 things you LOVE to do or have always wanted to do. Your list should have no limits to it, and no excuses ("Oh I can't do this...") and only include listings that answer this question: "If you could do anything in the world, what would that be?" Just write the list, and then you can come back to it later, and think about the elements you are seeking from each thing listed. From there, you can begin to get clear with where your heart really is, and begin to bring those elements into your life, one way or another. NOTHING is impossible!

In Closing

In closing, my hopes are that you now have a better understanding of how to begin working as a celebrity look-alike. I hope to have shed some light on the entertainment business in general and given you an honest idea of what agents expect from any professional performer.

There are many books on the market describing how to break into acting, modeling, or the music industry, but none describe the steps one needs to take to find work as a look-alike.

In all of my look-alike experiences throughout the years, I have encountered many talented performers asking questions about this business, and having to figure it out through trials and tribulations along the way. I, too, have learned (sometimes the hard way) how to try to make the best decisions in learning about the look-alike world. I hope I have been clear and covered every question you may have about this business. But if I have missed something that is important to you, feel free to contact me and I will gladly oblige you with any further explanation.

Becoming a star...

Entertainment can be a fickle business, and most people have a romantic notion of what it is like to live the life of a celebrity. How many times have we all heard someone say, "I just want to be famous!" Many young performers dream of what

it would be like to have instant notoriety, and very few understand that entertainment is a *business*. Business can be very shrewd.
Hollywood has idealized a concept that *being recognized by the public* is a grand and glamorous style of life.

After my personal experiences of working as a personal assistant for a very high profile celebrity, the truth should be told, and a more honest point of view of fame includes the elements that the public may never see firsthand. The sacrifice of your privacy is now a decision you must live by, and your home, family, and past will be available in full view for people to talk about, scrutinize, or judge. Suddenly, your life as you know it is no longer your own, and because you are a public figure, many people feel you owe them an explanation for your lifestyle, your personal decisions, your weight gain or loss, or even a change of hair color. I bring this up because as a look-alike, you may experience these less-than-glamorous repercussions of fame without being famous, since you aren't the real celebrity. Be prepared to experience small doses of what real celebrities experience on a daily basis. Working as a celebrity look-alike, you can certainly get the feeling of fame and all that goes with it (the good, bad, and ugly). You may find that living as a celebrity for an hour or two may give you a better understanding of fame, without making the sacrifice of your life.

I encourage look-alikes to understand the sacrifices celebrities make in order to become public icons, so that when they begin their impersonation of a star, they have a deeper respect for the image they are *borrowing*.

In becoming a professional look-alike I encourage you also to have fun, be adventurous, and allow your creativity to unleash and unfold. As you begin to discover more about who you are and what you can accomplish (with total belief in yourself), you will discover life opportunities and experiences that will change and enrich your life forever.

My personal advice: When venturing into this business, avoid the "No, I don't think so" people, and surround yourself with "Go for it!" friends. You will need this kind of encouragement in show business and your life in general.

I encourage you to say "Yes!" to your dreams, and "Go for it" with conviction!
If you find yourself doubting your abilities, just remember the following.

The girl who wrote this book:

Failed typing, writing, and English in high school, but wrote a book anyway
Has no real singing abilities, but became the most sought after Madonna double
Does not look the most like Madonna, yet has experienced the most success as "Madonna"

Had many people along her journey tell her "no," but never ever believed them
Just learned how to use a computer in 1999, and wrote a book anyway

What does this mean to you?

Believe in who you are. Keep your thoughts pure and positive. Don't ever believe you can't do something.
Go for it! Take a chance…risk…believe and dream. Be courageous… adventurous…ridiculous. Don't forget to laugh, dance, and love. Follow your heart. Be a smart businessperson, and get a contract every time.

Everyone deserves the right to follow his or her heart, go on an adventure, and try something new - so why not go for it??

As one of our generation's greatest teachers once sang:

"Everybody is a star."
- Madonna

Reference

Look-alike Contact and Booking Information:

Alli Spots as **Marilyn Monroe**
Phone: 818-388-2355
E-mail: allispotts@aol.com

Amber J as **Bette Midler**
Phone: 310-770-4577
E-mail: AmberJL@aol.com
Web: www.outtacontroltopfilms.com

Anne Kissel as **Roseanne**
Phone: 203-926-1334
Pager: 203-371-3508
E-mail: Anne4Lafs@aol.com

Annette Pizza as **several children's specialty characters**
Phone: 818-258-1551
E-mail: nettiepizzo@hotmail.com

Arlen Pantel as **Bruce Springsteen**
Phone: 714-969-4481
Pager/cell: 213-925-5665
E-mail: boss@entertainmentforhire.com
Web: www.entertainmentforhire.com

Audrey Cassel as **Cher**
Phone: 201-363-1666

Barbara Hyde as **Mimi**
E-mail: mimi_lookalike@hotmail.com
Web: www.geocities.com/mimi_impersonator

Beau as Moby
Phone: 818-513-2389
Web: www.tributeproductions.com

Betty Atchison as **Cher, Shania Twain,** and **Ernestine**
Phone: 407-342-1155
E-mail: cheriffic@aol.com
Web: www.cheriffic.com

Bill Burnham as **Chuck Norris** (Walker, Texas Ranger)
Phone: 413-594-8214
E-mail: bill-norris@webtv.net
Web: www.community.webtv.net/bill-norris/ChuckNorrisWTRlook

Bill Hair as **Donald Trump**
E-mail: JET512@aol.com

Bill Peterson as **Rodney Dangerfield**
Phone: 781-749-6882
E-mail: BBRODNEY@AOL.COM
Web: WWW.COMEDY.COM/BBRODNEY

Bill Piper as **George Clooney**
Phone: 440-835-3355
E-mail: billpiper@aol.com

Bobby Brooks as: **Jackie Wilson, Stevie Wonder, Marvin Gaye**, and **Johnny Mathis**
Contact: RL Brooks Entertainment, Inc., Manager David MacArthur
Phone: Office: 702-889-0352
Cell: 808-372-2071
E-mail: ImagineDM@cs.com

Brandy Lynn as **Trisha Yearwood**
Phone: 615-867-1187 or 615 554-7427
Email: brandylynn2769@aol.com

Brent Mendenhall as **George W. Bush**
Contact: Patrick Rick Counterfeit Bill Productions
Phone: 800-580-0731
Web: www.gwbushimpersonator.com

Brenda Miller as **Bette Midler**
Phone: 702-822 (BETTE) 2388
E-mail: brendaamiller@aol.com

Brendan Paul as **Elvis**
Phone: 702-450-9548
Fax: 702-450-9549

Brian Cole as **Ricky Martin**
Phone: 407-291-EDGE (3343)
Cell: 407-234-5690
Fax: 407-295-EDGE
E-mail: brian@edgefactory.com
Web: www.ilooklikericky.com

Bronni Bakke as **Britney Spears**, **Marilyn Monroe**, and **Olivia Newton John**
Phone: 818-719-5587
Fax: 818-753-3772

Carole Reed as **Elizabeth Taylor**
Phone: 949-951-4377
E-mail: creed4liz@earthlink.net
Web: www.carolereedentertainment.com

Casey Ferguson as **Willie Nelson**
Phone: 304-328-5859
E-mail: cas_wil@yahoocom

Cherise as **Britney Spears**
Phone: 310-863-3230
E-mail: Britneydouble@hotmail.com

Charlene Rose as **Dolly Parton**
Web: www.LookalikesByChar.com

Cheri Serna as **Xena Warrior Princess**
E-mail: Xena0810@aol.com

Christopher Dennis as **Christopher Reeve(Superman)**
Phone: 323-969-9782

Curtis Cowan as **Elvis**
Phone: 604-322-1393
E-mail: ccowan@cableregina.com
Web: www.cableregina.com/users/ccowan

D.Wallace as **Cuba Gooding, Jr.**
E-mail: dwallace@platinumtechnical.com
Phone: 954-804-2157 or 954-252-8271

Daniel T. Healy as **George Bush**
Phone: 909-795-3797

David Brighton as **David Bowie** and **George Harrison**
Phone: 661-251-0049
Pager/cell: 661-645-4406
E-mail: BowieLive@aol.com
Web: www.DavidBowieTribute.com

David Day as **John F. Kennedy, Jr.**
Phone: 858-583-1835
E-mail: hijfkjr@yahoo.com

David Wolf as **Jerry Lewis**
Phone: 805-480-9326
Fax: 805-480-9536
E-mail: Heyyylady@aol.com
Web: www.MARTINandLEWIS.com

Dawn Berhens as **Marilyn Monroe**, **Anna Nicole Smith**, **Mae West** and **Hotlips** (Loretta Swit's character on M*A*S*H)
Web: www.dawnn1.cjb.net

Dean Crownover as **Elvis Presley** and **Forrest Gump**
Phone: 404-403-9090
E-mail: dean-o@mindspring.com

Dee Dee Hansen as **Joan Rivers**
Phone: 714-538-9442
E-mail: joanclone@aol.com

Denise Bella Vlasis as **Madonna**
Phone: 818-513-2389
E-mail: Madonnadouble@hotmail.com
Web: www.tributeproductions.com

Dian Kelly as **Aretha Franklin**
Phone: 407-578-5595
Cell: 407-375-2722
E-mail: songbird149@juno.com or respectdian@hotmail.com
Web: www.diankelly.hothomepages.com

Dl as **Bono (U2)**
Phone: 818-513-2389
Web: www.tributeproductions.com

Duane Chaffee as **Ace Ventura**
Phone: 818-513-2389
Web: www.tributeproductions.com

Eileen Finney as **Joan Rivers**
Phone: 310-854 –1920
Pager: 310-960-4992
Web: www.clonedbyjoan.com

Elaine Chez as **Marilyn Monroe, Sandy** (Olivia Newton-John's character from *Grease*), **Young Peggy Lee, Jean Harlow, Deborah Harry,** and **Gwen Steffani**
Phone: 718-956-7298
Fax: 718-956-6402
Web: www.lookalike-stars.com

Elizabeth Shafer as **Marilyn Monroe**
Phone: 310-545-3050
E-mail: Carolizbth@aol.com

Ermal Walden Williamson as **Gary Cooper** and **John Wayne**
Phone: 949-645-9477
Cell: 949-275-0626
Fax: 949-645-9850
E-mail: ermal@earthlink.net or ermal@attbi.com
Web: www.ermal.com

Gail Williams as **Dolly Parton**
Phone: 800-963-5348

Garrick Sissons as **Garth Brooks**
Phone: 416-543-9219
Email: garrick@garrick.org
Web: www.garrick.garrick.org

Gary Smith as **Robert Redford**
Contact: SUNSHINE PRODUCTIONS
Phone: 818-842-7713

George Thomas as **Elvis Presley** and **John Travolta**
Phone: 818-418-2161

Gilbert Gauthier as **Frank Sinatra**
E-mail: GILBERTGAUTHIER7@aol.com
Phone: 310-890-9605

Gina Badone as **Britney Spears**
Phone: 818-513-2389
Web: www.tributeproductions.com

Gisele as **Tina Turner**, **Diana Ross,** and **Donna Summer**
Phone: 818-727-9249 or 888-986-7196

Gray Sabatini as **Jackie Onassis**
Phone: 818-763-674
E-mail: grayl2001@adelphia.net

Gregg" Letterhead" Chelew as **David Letterman**
Phone: 800-377-2252
Cell: 714-381-9855
E-mail: G chelew@aol.com
Web: gregletterhead.com

Greg Austin as **Tim McGraw** and **Travis Tritt**
Phone: 615-867-1187 or 615-554-5059
Email: austin4232@aol.com

Harmony Deen as **Britney Spears**
Phone: 703-622-6194
E-mail: snghrmny@aol.com

Harmik as **Tom Jones**
Phone: 702-220-5426
E-mail: harmik@sprintmail.com

Heather Chaney as **Marilyn Monroe** and **Britney Spears**
Phone: 407-895-4334
Cell: 407-963-0968
E-mail: glamour2c@aol.com
Web: www.members.aol.com/glamour2c/marilyn.html

Herme Chua as **Tiger Woods**
Phone: 909-520-9452
E-mail: tigerwoodsdouble@aol.com
Web: www.tigerwoodsdouble.com

Irby Gascon as **Elvis Presley** and **Ricky Martin**
Phone: 818-513-2389
E-mail: Tributeproductions@earthlink.net
Web: www.tributeproductions.com

Ironic, an **Alanis Morissette Tribute**
Phone: 310-717-4739
E-mail: AlanisTribute@aol.com
Web: www.alanistribute.com

J. Trusk as **Captain Kirk** (William Shatner)
Phone: 800-414-7253
E-mail: kirk@jtrusk.com
Web: www.jtrusk.com

Jade Roberts as **Sylvester Stallone**
Phone: 214-521-6301 or 972-307-1818
E-mail: jadesjym@juno.com

James "De" Maxwell as **Garth Brooks**
Phone: 330-945-4150 or 216-486-9200

Janice Sands as **Cher**
Phone: 702-247-1537
Cell: 702-499-6412
E-mail: Janiceslv@lvcm.com

Jeffrey Briar as **Stan Laurel, Charlie Chaplin, Inspector Clouseau** (Peter Sellers), **Ludwig Van Beethoven**, and **Chico Marx**
Phone: 949-376-1939
Fax: 949-376-1939
E-mail: JoyfulB@aol.com

Jeffrey Weissman as **Charley Chaplin, Stan Laurel, Groucho Marx, Pee Wee Herman, Roberto Benigni**, and many theme characters
Phone: 323-664-9036
Pager: 310-564-3595
E-mail: fool@flash.net or jeffrey_weissman@hotmail.com

Jenelle Jones as **Ann-Margret, Blondie**, and **Belinda Carlisle**
E-mail: jenelleski@earthlink.net

Jerry Hoban as **Ed Sullivan**
Contact: Gene Siler, Artist Management
Phone: 949-367-0339
E-mail: silerg@pacbell.net
Web: www.silerandassociates.com or www.areallybigshew.com

Jimmy Craven as **Mick Jagger The Rolling Stones Tribute**
Phone: 415-292-5556 x 636
E-mail: marvelousshow@hotmail.com
Web: www.theunauthorizedrollingstones.com

Jim Malmberg as **Johnny Carson**
Phone: 602-375-3544
E-mail: Jim@carson-johnny.com
Web: www.carson-johnny.com

Joe Dimmick as **Clint Eastwood**
Phone: 760-366-2599
E-mail: joe@dimmicksdoubles.com
Web: www.dimmicksdoubles.com

John Allen as **Sean Connery (James Bond)**
Phone: 561-243-1299
Web: www.johnallen007.com

John Mueller as **Buddy Holly**
E-mail: Mueltone@aol.com

Judith Gindy as **Queen Elizabeth**
Phone: 305-666-3463 or 305-666-3470
E-mail: jgindy@jgstarlink.com
Website: www.queentoo.hollywood.com/

Julie Sheppard as **Judy Garland**
Phone: 818-845-1388
E-mail: Mrsnormanmaine@aol.com

Karen Motherway as **Marilyn Monroe**
Phone: 877-monroe2
E-mail: karen@karenasmarilyn.com
Web: www.karenasmarilyn.com

Kimberly Jones as **Nicole Kidman** (Satine from Moulin Rouge)
Phone: 407-671-4607
E-mail: JonesKidman@aol.com

Kimberly Perfetto as **Britney Spears**
Phone: 443-994-0172
E-mail: kymperfetto@hotmail.com
Web: www.angelfire.com/fm/kimberli/britney.html

Kurt Meyers as **Harrison Ford (Indiana Jones)**
Phone: 310-399-4410
E-mail: rk.kula@verizon.net

Larry Berlin as **Al Gore**
E-mail: LarryasAl@hotmail.com

Larry Bulot as **Jim Carrey (Ace Ventura)**
Phone: 909-766-5888

Larry G. Jones, **The Man of 1,002 Voices**
Phone: 702-638-9036
E-mail: larry@lasvegasacts.com
Website: www.LasVegasActs.com

Larry Rousseve as **Carlos Santana**
Phone: 310-445-1044

Larry Turner as **George Strait**
Phone: 417-359-3654
E-mail: sdesigns@cox-internet.com
Web: www.larrydturner.com

Lissa Negrin as **Cher**
Phone: 323-462-2583
E-mail: cher_n@msn.com or lissa@premeditatedproductions.com
Web: www.premeditatedproductions.com

Lois Castillo as **Mariah Carey**
E-mail: lcasmc@juno.com
Web: www.mariahlookalike.com

Loni Pryce (Usherson) as **Liza Minnelli** and **Judy Garland**
Contact: Don Usherson
Phone: 702-233-2018
E-mail: StripScoop@aol.com

Loren Michaels as **Barbara Streisand**
Phone: 213-994-8139

Louise Gallagher as **Monica Lewinsky**, **Elizabeth Taylor** and **First Lady Laura Bush**
Phone: 800-693-9895
E-mail: LSStar500@aol.com
Web: laurabushdouble.com

Lyndal Grant as **Arnold Schwarzenegger**
Phone: 650-333-0146
E-mail: lyndallgrant@hotmail.com

Marcela Galvan-Roberts as **Selena**
Phone: 214-521-6301 or 972-307-1818
E-mail: jadesjym@juno.com

Marcel Forestieri as **Jay Leno** and **Regis Philbin**
Booking Contact: Jeff Patterson, Patterson & Associates
Phone: 323-658-1440
Fax: 323-658-1405
Email: jeffp@pattersonandassociates.com
Web: www.pattersonandassociates.com

Mark W. Curran as **Elvis Presley**
Phone: 800-582-4865
Fax: 413-425-6421
E-mail: newmediadigital@hotmail.com
Web: www.worldmar.net/Route66/

Mark Shoop as **Austin Powers** (Mike Myers), **Crocodile Hunter** (Steve Irwin), **The Grinch, Dr. Ruth Westheimer, Ozzy Osbourne,** and **Inspector Clouseau** (Peter Sellers)
Represented By: Entco International 425-670-0888
Web: www.markshoopshow.com

Marty Edwards as **Kenny Rogers**
Phone: 250-769-9003
E-mail: contact@kindakenny.com
Web: www.kindakenny.com

Marv Cline as **Alan Alda** and M*A*R*V CLINE PRODUCTIONS
Phone: 714-964-5681
Fax: 714-378-6050
Voice Mail Pager: 714-407-5355
E-mail: clineandco@earthlink.net

Melody Knighton as **Marlene Dietrich** and **Joan Crawford**
Phone: 770-966-1661
Pager: 770-223-7777
Fax: 770-528-0910
E-mail: GusandErnie@aol.com
Web: www.melodyknighton.com

Mike Vitrano as **Bruce Willis**
Web: www.bruce-willis-look-alike.com

Nancy Casey as **Elizabeth Taylor**
Phone: 661-299-5998

Noland Anderson as **John Travolta**
Phone: 818-819-2778
Web: www.nolandanderson.com

"Our Way" with Frank and Friends Gary B (as **Frank Sinatra**), Lambus Dean (as **Sammy Davis, Jr.**) and Bill Whitton (as **Dean Martin**)
Contact: Major Entertainment Productions
Phone: 702-655-8728
Fax: 702-655-8729
Toll free: 800-408-8892
Web: www.theratpackers.com
E-mail: garybdj@aol.com

Philip Martin as **Paul Stanley** **(KISS TRIBUTE)**
Phone: 949-650-2793
Cell: 949-294-9239
E-mail: philipj_martin@hotmail.com

Ralph Chelli as **Clark Gable**
Web: www.clarkable.com
E-mail: rjchelli@earthlink.net

Randy Caputo as **Gene Krupa**
Phone:714-998-9242

Randy Hartwell as **Travis Tritt**
Phone: 813-662-9197
E-mail: rhartwel@tampabay.rr.com

Raquel Choyce as Silhouette of **Janet Jackson**
Phone: 702-226-1868
Fax: 702-251-0280
E-mail: silhouette2000@msn.com
Web: www.silhouettofjanetjackson.homestead.com/

Ray Anthony as **Richie Valens**
Phone: 702-860-7897

Rebecca Young as **Judy Garland** and **Patsy Cline**
Phone: 702-812-5261
E-mail: young2sing@hotmail.com
Web: www.rebeccayoung.info

Reggie Alcos as **Tiger Woods**
Phone: 714-317-4401
Email: tiger1358@hotmail.com
Web: www.thetigerdouble.com

Rich Jennerjohn as **Garth Brooks**
Phone: 775-635-5313
E-mail: rjennerjohn@hotmail.com
Web: www.geocities.com/garthj2/cmr.html

Richard Halpern as **Austin Powers** (Mike Myers)
Phone: 213-739-3377
E-mail:richalpern@earthlink.net
Web: www.mrtinpanalley.com and www.richardhalpern.info

Richard Bowen as **Crocodile Dundee** (Paul Hogan)
Phone: 858-453-8681 or 619-301-0294
E-mail: Richardjb2@aol.com or Newickc@aol.com

Rob LeMaster as **Jack Nicholson**
Phone: 414-445-0478
E-mail: almostjack@msn.com
Web: www.geocities.com/almostJack2

Robert S. Ensler as **Dean Martin**
Phone: 510-232-1551
Fax: 510-232-4846
E-mail: RobertSEnsler@aol.com
Web: www.DeanMartin.com or www.DEANandJERRY.com

Romeo Prince as **Prince**
Phone: 323-467-9289
E-mail: jahmforce@hotmail.com
Web: www.jahmforce.com

Rosalinde Tropper as **Pamela Anderson**
Phone: 714-810-7443

Rosemarie Ballard as **Carmen Miranda**
Phone: 619-482-8856
E-mail: rosemarie@rosemarieballard.com
Web: www.rosemarieballard.com

Ross D. Seymour as **Russell Crowe/The Gladiator**
Phone: 714-920-1865
E-mail: Info@IamGladiator.com
Web: www.IamGladiator.com

Russel Sadick as **Barry Manilow**
Phone: 805-984-9513
E-mail: frradioman@aol.com

Sandra Wood as **Cher**
Web: www.cherimpersonator.com

Scot Bruce as **Elvis Presley**
E-mail: Go_cat_go!@scotbruce.com
Web: www.scotbruce.com

Scott Thom as **Jack Black**
Phone: 715-256-4192
E-mail thom_scott@hotmail.com

Sharon Daniels as **Joan Rivers**
Phone: 954-989-4712
E-mail: Impreshn21@aol.com

Sherie Rae Parker as **Bette Midler** and **Janis Joplin**
Phone: 702-870-0300
E-mail: SherieandBeav@yahoo.com

Sherrill Douglas as **Patsy Cline**
Managed by: Sandy Clark Sweet Dreams Productions
Phone: 972-661-1166
Fax: 972-661-1144
E-mail: sandyclark@sherrilldouglascom
Web: www.sherrilldouglas.com

Shon Vaughn as **Whoopi Goldberg**
Phone: 818-508-7255
E-mail:VRZANOVAV@AOL.COM
Web: WWW.SHONVAUGHN.COM.

Stacey Allemeier as **Britney Spears**
Phone: 724-516-6412
E-mail: SnifflesBichon@hotmail.com
Web: www.staceyasbritney.com

Stephen Sorrentino (aka Even Stephen) as **Elton John**
Phone: ESI management 702-240-4285
E-mail: Evenelton @aol.com
Web: www.StephenSorrentino.com

Steve as **Tom Cruise**
Contact: Tribute Productions
Phone: 818-513-2389
Web: www.tributeproductions.com

Steve Kern as **John Denver**
E-mail: skern2k2@aol.com
Web: johndenvertribute.com

Steve Marshall/Daddy Cool's Entertainment
Luisa Marshall/Tiny Tina Turner (Hail to the Queen)
Contact: Steve Marshall
Phone: 604-420-1627
E-mail: daddycools@shaw.ca
Web: www.tinytina.com

Steve Murphy as **Elvis Presley**
Contact: Denese Dody/Denese Dody Mngt.
Phone: 909-983-7315
E-mail:Denesedodymngt@aol.com or Tupeloticket@aol.com

Steve Stone as **Paul McCartney**
Phone: 661-992-2464 or 661-951-1761

Steve Ostrow as **Ozmo Kramer** (Michael Richardson's character from Seinfeld)
Phone: 858-793-0633
E-mail: kramer@ozmokramer.com

Steve Weber as **Forrest Gump** (Tom Hanks)
E-mail: fgumpweber@aol.com
Phone: 408-275-1600

Sue Quinn as **several characters**
Contact: Dorothy Findlater
Phone: 888-466-9068
Fax: 323-960-0215
E-mail: staff@mirrorimagesco.com
Web: www.mirrorimagesco.com

Susan E as **Jackie Kennedy**
Phone: 661-424-0323

Susan Griffith as **Marilyn Monroe**
Phone: 310-576-3200

Suzanne La Rusch as **Lucille Ball**
Booking Contact: Jeff Patterson, Patterson & Associates
Phone: 323-658-1440
Fax: 323-658-1405
Email: jeffp@pattersonandassociates.com
Web: www.pattersonandassociates.com

Tambilina Perazzo as **Julia Roberts**
Phone: 661-837-8443
E-mail: pperazzo@bak.rr.com
Web: www.Iamprettywoman.com

Tapia Corel as **Mae West** and **Carmen Miranda**
E-mail: Tcorel@aol.com

Tatiana Turan as **Jennifer Lopez**
Phone: 818-292-5117
E-mail: tatianat@pacbell.net
Web: www.tatianaturan.com
Web: www.tatitotes.com

Tatsuro as **Jackie Chan** and **Thomas Collier** as **Chris Tucker**
Phone: 310-478-0661
Cell: 310-721-4566
E-mail: mjdance@earthlink.net
Bookings contact: Mirror Images Co. (Dot or Nicky)
Phone: 888-466-9068
Web: MIRRORIMAGESCO.COM

Teresa Barnwell as **Hillary Clinton**
E-mail: HillaryDbl@aol.com

Terri Jayne as **Jayne Mansfield**
Phone: 901-377-8609
E-mail: terrijaynemansfield@hotmail.com

The MopTops as **The Beatles**
Booking Contact: Jeff Patterson, Patterson & Associates
Phone: 323-658-1440
Fax: 323-658-1405
E-mail: jeffp@pattersonandassociates.com
Web: www.pattersonandassociates.com

Theresa Jennerjohn as **Terri Clark**
Phone: 775-635-5313
E-mail: rjennerjohn@hotmail.com
Web: www.geocities.com/garthj2/cmr.html

Todd Sullivan as **Tim McGraw**
Phone: 843-230-6461
E-mail: GONZOPP8@AOL.COM
Web: http://hometown.aol.com/gonzopp8/TIMTRIBUTE2.html

Tom Biehn as **Bill Clinton**
Phone: 714-963-7754
E-mail: Tombiehn@att.net

Tony Mosti as **Blues Brothers, Garth Brooks,** and **Billy Joel**
Phone: 702-682-5979 or 702-631-5636
Email: Tmosti@aol.com
Web: www.geocities.com/bluesisbetter

Vaughn Suponatime as **Frank Sinatra**
Phone: 818-908-1308

Vicki J. Browne as **Rosie O'Donnell**
Phone: 407-791-3555
E-mail: Beeki925@aol.com

Vince Gibbs as **Prince**
Phone: 918-622-2659
E-mail: vincentg@flash.net
Website: www.vg.midspark.net/vince/artist.html

Wanda Grawet as **Bette Davis**
Phone: 818-513-2389
Web: www.tributeproductions.com

William Peterson as **Rodney Dangerfield**
E-mail: bbrodney@attbi.com

Will Collins as **Liberace**
Phone: 702-440-9365
E-mail:COLLINSWILL@aol.com

Female Impersonation:

Chad Michaels as **Cher, Celine Dion,** and more
E-mail: ZEPHYR2899@aol.com

Viva Sex as **Madonna**
E-mail: Vivasex1@aol.com

Agencies:

Agency name: **Absolutely Everything Entertainment Services**
Phone: 818-883-3311 or 310-414-0072

Agency name: **A Classy Act, Singing & Variety Entertainment**
Contact: Chris Thompson
Address: 4642 E. Chapman Avenue, # 308, Orange, CA 92869
Phone: 714-281-2488

Agency name: **Advance Event Group, Inc.**
Address: 1015 North Halsted Street, Chicago, IL 60622
Phone: 312-751-2610
Fax: 312-751-2632
E-mail: bmeyer@advanceeventgroup.com.

Agency name: **AIA/Sirius Entertainment**
Contact: Dan Blair
Address: 13531 Clairmont Way, #8, Oregon City, OR 97045
Phone: 877-342-4956 (toll-free)

Agency name: **Al Lampkin Entertainment**
Contact: Al Lampkin
Address: 1817 W. Verdugo Avenue, Burbank, CA 91506
Phone: 818-846-4951
E-mail: info@allampkin.com
Web: www.allampkin.com

Agency name: **Alex Carrera Show Management, SRL (ITALY)**
Contact: Michela
Phone: 0039(011) 3835255
Fax: 0039 (11) 388738
Web: www.alexcarrera.com

Agency name: **All Access Events, Inc.**
Contact: Michael D. Yorkell, President
Address: 13-25 Main Street, Suite 9B, Franklin, MA 02038
Phone: 508-553-9400
Fax: 508-541-6184
E-mail: michael@allaccessevents.com
Web: www.allaccessevents.com

Agency name: **All Time Favorites**
Contact: Brian Harrell
Phone: 651-454-1124
Fax: 651-687-0403
Web: www.alltimefavorites.com

Agency name: **Almost Famous/East Coast Event Marketing**
Contact: Pam Rimer
Phone: 704-721-3300
E-mail: primer@eccmarketing.com or primer@vnet.net
Web: www.ecemarketing.com and www.almostfamous.ws

Agency name: **Always Creative**
Contact: Paul Pursel or Renee Pursel
Address: 6843 Patayan Road, Las Vegas, NV 89146
Phone: 702-307-8111
Fax: 702-307-8118
E-mail: alwayscreative@lvcm.com
Web: www.Always-Creative.com

Agency name: **Always Entertaining**
Contact: Barbara
Phone: 702-737-3232

Agency name: **American Convention Entertainment Services**
Contact: Keith Cox, Event Producer
Phone: 800-934-2237
E-mail: ACESKCOX@AOL.COM

Agency name: **Amusing Events Entertainment**
Contact: Tom LaGravinese
Phone: 480-981-4657
E-mail: Amusingevents@aol.com
Web: www.Amusingevents.com
michael@allaccessevents.com

Agency name: **Angelique & Friends Entertainment**
Contact: Angelique
Phone: 888-830-9654 or 602-735-3107
E-mail: angelique@angeliqueandfriends.com
Web: www.angeliqueandfriends.com

Agency name: **Animal Crackers Entertainment**
Contact: Marsi
Address: 23704-5 El Toro Road, #366, Lake Forest, CA 92630
Phone: 949-487-9296
Web: www.AnimalCrackersEnt.com

Agency name: **Artistic Singing Telegrams**
Contact: Gina Bacon
Address: 12056 Mt. Vernon Avenue, #158, Grand Terrace, CA 92313
Phone: 909-799-9764
E-mail: baconbit@gte.net
Web: www.excitestores.com/stores/sing

Agency name: **Attaboy! Entertainment**
Contact: Ric or Ina Grove
Phone: 717-749-7733
E-mail: attaboy@sacho.com
Web: www.www.sacho.com

Agency name: **A Unique Presentation**
Contact: Shelly Balloon
Phone: 310-202-8787
E-mail: auniquepresentation@yahoo.com
Web: www.auniquepresentation.com

Agency name: **Background Productions**
Contact: Christine Stringer
Address: 300 Carlsbad Village Drive, Suite #108A/#231 Carlsbad, CA 92008-2999
E-mail: cstringer1@home.com

Agency name: **Bartsch Trotter & Associates**
Phone: 310-822-1882
Web: www.bartschtrotter.com

Agency name: **Baskow & Associates**
Contact: Debbie Baker
Phone: 702-733-7818
E-mail: dbaker@baskow.com
Web: www.baskow.com

Agency name: **Bay Area Models**
Contact: Diana Dawn
Phone: 209-832-2100
E-mail: Diana@CelebrityLookalikes.com
Web: www.CelebrityLookalikes.com

Agency name: **Beverly Hills Celebrity Look-Alikes Management**
Contact: Al or Bobbie Silverstein
Phone: 818-347-9952

Agency name: **Bixel**
Phone: 310-854-3828

Agency name: **Bollotta Entertainment**
Address: 4443 30th Street, Suite 110, San Diego, CA 92116
Phone: 619-295-3522
Fax: 619-295-3509
E-mail: info@bollotta.com
Web: www.bollotta.com

Agency name: **Book It, Inc.**
Contact: John McConnell
Address: 1944 Florence Vista Blvd., Orlando, FL 32818
Phone: 407-522-1432
Fax: 407-532-6907
E-mail: sales@elwoodblues.com.
Web: www.elwoodblues.com

Agency name: **Bright Entertainment LLC**
Contact: Rhonda Bright
Phone: 310-390-1345
E-mail: BrightEnt@netscape.net

Agency name: **Bruce Garnitz Music & Entertainment**
Contact: Ginger or Bruce
Web: www.proeventmusic.com

Agency name: **Carbon Copies Celebrity Look-Alikes**
Address: 9801 Cross Creek Court, Dallas, TX 75243

Agency name: **Carole Reed Entertainment**
Contact: Carole Reed
Address: 23704-5 El Toro Road, RMB #525, Lake Forest, CA 92630
Phone: 949-951-4377
E-mail: creed4liz@earthlink.net
Web: www.carolereedentertainment.com

Agency name: **Celebrity Access**
Address: 801 Brooklawn Drive, Boulder, CO 80303

Agency name: **CEI**
Contact: Marc Friedman or Michelle Cassel
Phone: 949-589-5434
Address: 45 Allyssum, Rancho Santa Margarita, CA 92688
E-mail: info@custom-events.net
Web: www.custom-events.net

Agency name: **Celebrity Doubles**
Contact: Russ Terry
Address: P.O. Box 526417, Salt Lake City, UT 84152-6417
Phone: 801-484-1960
Fax: 801-484-3386
E-mail: russ@celebrity-doubles.com
Web: www.celebrity-doubles.com

Agency name: **Celebrity Gems**
Contact: Stan Heimowitz
Phone: 510-581-5964
E-mail: celebgems@aol.com
Web: www.celebritygems.com

Agency name: **Celebrity Look A Likes By Elyse**
Contact: Elyse Del Francia
Address: 70033 Mirage Cove Drive, Suite 67,
Rancho Mirage, CA 92270
Telephone: 888-771-6611 (toll free)
Fax: 760-770-1611
E-mail: elyse@gte.net
Web: www.celebrityimpersonators.com
Agent friendly: www.1celebritylookalikes.com

Agency name: **Celebrity Look and Sound- Alikes**
Contact: Mo or Rita
Address: P.O. Box 6631, Burbank, CA 91510
Phone: 818-504 9775
Web: www.celebrity-look-alikes.com

Agency name: **Charles Banfield Productions**
Address: 1270 S. Hauser Blvd., Los Angeles, CA 90019
Phone: 323-934-4445
Fax 323-934-9994
Web: www.charlesbanfield.com

Agency name: **Chez Company**
Contact: Elaine Chez
Phone: 718-956-7298
Fax: 718-956-6402
Address: P.O. Box 2242, Astoria, NY 11102
Web: www.lookalike-stars.com

Agency name: **Cindy Raft Agency, Inc.**
Contact: Cindy Raft
Phone: 702-735-7833
E-mail: BookingU@aol.com
Web: www.VegasShowbiz.com

Agency Name: **City Connection Entertainment & Productions**
Contact: Sal Kuenzler
Address: 20969 Ventura Blvd., Suite 5, Woodland Hills, CA 91364
Phone: 818-884-1600
Fax: 818-884-1681
Web: www.CityConnectionEnt.com

Agency name: **CK Entertainment, Inc.**
Contact: Carey Kleiman
Web: www.ckentertainmentinc.com

Agency name: **Classique Productions**
Contact: Linda and John Collins
Address: 7400 Bisonwood Avenue, Las Vegas, NV 89131
Phone: 702-639-6550
Email: classique@lv.rmci.net
Web: www.classique-productions.com

Agency name: **Classy Characters & Associates**
Contact: Cheri Serna, Owner & Entertainer
Phone: 626-915-8475
Cell: 626-483-3577
Web: www.classycharacters.com

Agency name: **Clowning Around**
Contact: Michael Williams
Phone: 562-925-5598
E-mail: clowningar@aol.com
Web: www.events.clowningaround.com

Agency name: **Conjure Marketing & Event Design**
Contact: Antonia Calzetti
Phone: 718-945-9426
E-mail: acalzetti@conjuredesign.com
Web: www.conjuredesign.com

Agency name: **Corporate Entertainment Options, Inc.**
Contact: Ken Turner
Address: 3708 Mueller Road, St. Charles, MO 63301

Agency name: **Cordially Invited**
Contact: Randie Pellegrini
Phone: 310-552-3245
E-mail: rwp@cordiallyinvited.com
Web: www.cordiallyinvited.com

Agency name: **Custom Events, Inc.**
Contact: Marc Friedman and Michelle Cassel
Phone: 949-589-5434
Address: 8687 Research Drive, Irvine, CA 92618
E-mail: info@custom-events.net
Web: www.custom-events.net

Agency name: **Dawn Productions**
Contact: Dawn Rocheleau or Rob Garrett
Phone: 702-656-7424
Fax: 702-648-8139
E-mail: dawn@dawnproductions.com
Web: www.dawnproductions.com

Agency name: **Dee Dee Hansen Entertainment**
Contact: Dee Dee or Jack Hansen
Phone: 714-538-9442
E-mail: joanclone@aol.com

Agency name: **Denese Dody Prod. & Mgmt. (Specializing in Elvis)**
Contact: Denese Dody
Phone: 909-983-7315
Web: www.Denesedodymngt@aol.com

Agency name: **Dimmick's Doubles**
Contact: Joe Dimmick
Address: P.O. Box 2049, Yucca Valley, CA 92286
Phone: 760-366-2599
E-mail: joe@dimmicksdoubles.com
Web: www.dimmicksdoubles.com

Agency name: **Double Take Celebrity Doubles**
Contact: Arlen Pantel
Casting Department: P.O. Box 687, Huntington Beach, CA 92648
Phone: 714-969-4491 or 714-647-1995
Fax: 509-352-5187
Casting hotline: 714-647-1995
E-mail: Casting@entertainmentforhire.com
Web: www.entertainmentforhire.com

Agency name: **Double Take Productions**
Contact: Dawnn
Address: P.O. BOX 621, Ocoee, FL 34761
Phone: 407-290-5665
E-mail: look@servos.com
Web: www.servos.com/look

Agency name: **East Coast Event Marketing**
Contact: Pam Rimer
Address: 8910 Lenox Pointe Drive, Suite E, Charlotte, NC 28273

Agency name: **Edge Factory Productions**
Contact: Brian Cole, Producer
Address: 6567 Piccadilly Lane, Orlando, FL 32835
Phone: 407-291-EDGE
Cell: 407-234-5690
Fax: 407-295-EDGE
Web: www.edgefactory.com

Agency name: **Enloe Productions**
Contact: Jeff Enloe
Phone: 818-894-3232
E-mail: Enloeprod@msn.com
Web: www.enloeproductions.com

Agency name: **Entco International, Inc**
Contact: Neil Morris, Special Events/Artist Management
Address: 7017 196th Street SW, Lynnwood, WA 98036
Phone: 425-670-0888–
Cell:) 206-786-6996
E-mail: neilm@entco.com
Web: www.entco.com

Agency name: **Entertainment Contractor**
Contact: J. Schwartz
Phone: 323-256-9613
Email: ECPARTIES@aol.com
Web: www.ecparties.com

Agency name: **Epic Entertainment**
Contact: Ray Gosselin
Address: 77622 Country Club Drive, Suite N, Palm Desert, CA 92211
Phone: 760-360-6668
E-mail: Epic1@earthlink.net
Web: www.epic1.com

Agency name: **Essence Entertainment Talent Agency**
Contact: Mike Steffens, Talent Manager
Address: 355 Bristol Street, Suite M, Costa Mesa, CA 92626
Phone: 714-979-8933
E-mail: Info@essenceentertainment.com

Agency name: **Events R Us Today Corporation**
Contact: Tania Laguerre
Phone: 443-803-8928
E-mail: laguerre@eventsrustoday.com
Web: www.eventsrustoday.com

Agency name: **Event Works, Inc.**
Contact: Michelle Messick
Address: 340 West 131st Street, Los Angeles, CA 90061
Phone: 323-321-1793
Fax: 323-321-1799
Web: www.eventworks.com

Agency name: **Extraordinary Events**
Contact: Pamela Scrape
Address: 13425 Ventura Blvd., Suite #300, Sherman Oaks, CA 91423
Phone: 818-783-6112– (ext. 12)
Fax: 818-783-8957
Web: www.extraordinaryevents.net

Agency name: **Fast Forward International Communications, Inc.**
Contact: Bill Rezey
Phone: 518-270-9122
E-mail: ffic@nycap.rr.com
Web: www.members.tripod.com/FFIC

Agency name: **Farrington Productions**
Contact: Gina Weatherman
Address: 4350-B Arville, Suite 15, Las Vegas, NV 89103
Phone: 702-362-5452 x232

Agency name: **Fil Jessee Specialty Casting**
Contact: Fil Jessee
Address: 2760 Bluebird Circle, Duluth, GA 30096
Phone: 770-813-8336
E-mail: fil@filslookalikes.com
Web: www.filslookalikes.com

Agency name: **Five Star Talent and Entertainment, Inc.**
Contact: Terri L. Fisher
Phone: 303-635-1210
Address: 2256 Country Club Loop, Westminster, CO 80234
E-mail: Terri@5StarActs.com
Web: www.5StarActs.com

Agency name: **Fortune Entertainment**
Contact: Greg Fortune
Address: 1817 W. Verdugo Avenue, Burbank, CA 91506
Phone: 818-843-0303 or 213 687-0338
Fax: 818-846-5908
E-mail: infoatinfo@efortune.com
Web: www.efortune.com

Agency name: **Fred Martinez Vegas Talent Connection**
Contact: Fred
E-mail: talentmarketing@yahoo.com

Agency name: **Funtastic Events Full Service Entertainment and Catering Company**
Contact: Danny Ayala
Address: 251 S Glenview Place, Orange, CA 92868
Phone: 714-750-2359

Agency name: **Gayle Force Entertainment, Inc.**
Contact: Steve Blanck
Phone: 626-345-9444
Fax: 626-345-9450
E-mail: steveb@gayleforce.net

Agency name: **Hall Star Speakers and Talent**
Contact: Kelly Hall
Address: 4601 Quartz Hill Road, Quartz Hill, CA 93536
Phone: 661-943-4589
Mobile: 805-338-0363
Fax: 661-943-0252
E-mail: kelly@hallstar.net
Web: www.hallstar.net

Agency name: **ICONS Incredible Creations On Stage**
Contact: Dan Gore
Address: P.O. Box 633, South Lake Tahoe, CA 96156
Phone: 530-542-2889 or 877-500-5254
E-mail: iconsprods@aol.com
Web: www.icons.nu

Agency name: **IM Entertainment**
Address: P.O. Box 184, Bridgeville, PA 15017

Agency name: **Innovative Entertainment Group**
Contact: Michael D. Yorkell
Phone: 508-553-3939
E-mail: michaely@ncounty.net
Web: www.innovativeentertainmentgroup.com

Agency name: **International Celebrity Images**
Contact: Janna Joos
Address: P.O. Box 260766, Encino, CA 91426
Phone: 818-780-4433
Fax: 818-343-9250
Look-alike awards: www.thereelawards.com
Email: Janna@internationalcelebrityimages.com
Web: www.internationalcelebrityimages.com

Agency name: **Impostor Bostonians/DJ With Class & Co.**
Contact: Ron Bartels
Phone: 781-871-1715
E-mail: lookusa@iname.com
Web: www.Lookalikes-USA.com

Agency name: **Jam Entertainment & Events**
Contact: Dennis Morrison, Judy or Wayne
Address: 2900 Bristol St. Suite E-201 Costa Mesa, CA 92626
Phone: 714-556-9505
E-mail: dennis@jamentertainment.com
Web: www.jamentertainment.com

Agency name: **Jeffrey L. Patterson, Patterson & Associates**
Address: 8271 Melrose Avenue, Suite 205, Los Angeles, CA 90046
Phone: 323-658-1440
Fax: 323-658-1405

Agency name: **Jewel of the Desert Productions**
Contact: Maya Harman
Phone: 702-456-8377
Fax 702-434-0756
E-mail: maya@jewelofthedesert.com
Web: www.jewelofthedesert.com

Agency name: **Joe Diamond Enterprises**
Contact: Joe Diamond
Address: 3633 Royal Meadow Road, Sherman Oaks, CA 91403
Phone: 818-995-7227
E-mail: forthegoodtimes@pacbell.net
Web: www.forthegoodtimes.com

Agency name: **Julie K. Rupp, Locations and Events**
Contact: Julie Rupp
Address: 2254 Smokewood Avenue, Suite D, Palm Springs, CA 92264
Phone: 760-322-0243
Fax: 760-327-5599
E-mail: events@julierupp.com
Web: www.julierupp.com

Agent name: **Karla Ross Productions**
Contact: Karla Ross
Address: 612 N. Sepulveda Blvd., Suite 11, Bel Air, CA 90049
Phone: 310-476 5100
Web: www.karlaross.com

Agency name: **Kevin Roberts Entertainment**
Contact: Kevin Roberts
Address: 241 Apopka Cove, Destin, FL 35241
E-mail: kevin@kevinroberts.com
Web: www.kevinroberts.com

Agency name: **Kristina Custer Event Producer**
Phone: 401-286-5084
Web: www.creatEvents.net

Agency name: **Kushner & Associates**
Contact: Susan Kushner, Managing Director
Address: 1104 S. Robertson Blvd., Los Angeles, CA 90035
Phone: 310-274-8819
Fax: 310-273-9535
E-mail: s.kushner@kushnerdmc.com
Web: www.kushnerdmc.com

Agency name: **LAPD (Los Angeles Party Design)**
Phone: 310-836-5273
Address: 6368 Arizona Circle, Los Angeles, CA 90045
Web: www.lapartydesigns.com

Agency name: **Lasting Impressions**
Contact: Diana Dawn, LIM Representative or Kalie Lucas
Address: 793 S. Tracy Blvd., #199, Tracy, CA 95376
Phone: 209-832-2100
E-mail: Diana@CelebrityLookalikes.com
Web: www.CelebrityLookalikes.com

Agency name: **Legends of Rock and Roll'**
Contact: Les Vogt, Producer
Address: 613 5th Avenue, Second Floor, New Westminster, B.C. V3M 1X3 Canada
Phone: 604-525-3330
Cell: 604-831-2027
Fax: 604-525-3382
E-mail: LesVogt@direct.ca
Web: www.legendsofrock-n-roll.com

Agency name: **Leonard Neil Productions**
Contact: Leonard Neil
Phone: 310-453-1137
Fax: 310-315-0089
Web: www.leonardneilproductions.com

Agency name: **Liberty City Entertainment**
Contact: Eric
Phone: 818-344-6929
E-mail: Libertycityeric@aol.com

Agency name: **Lookalikes by Char**
Contact: Char
Web: www.LookalikesByChar.com

Agency name: **Look Twice Productions**
Contact: Audrey Cassel
E-mail: AMBERCAS@AOL.COM
Web: www.LOOKTWICE.COM

Agency name: **Lookalike.com**
Contact: David Tapley
Phone: 972-255-3967
E-mail: david@lookalike.com
Web: www.lookalike.com

Agency name: **Lucky Entertainment**
Contact: Burt
Phone: 310-277-9666

Agency name: **Mirror Images Global Entertainment**
Contact: Dorothy Findlater
Address: 7095 Hollywood Blvd., #574, Hollywood, CA 90028-8903
Phone: 888-466-9068
Fax: 323-960-0215
E-mail: staff@mirrorimagesco.com
Web: www.mirrorimagesco.com

Agency name: **Mirror Images Global Entertainment**
Contact Bill Hickey, Casting Director UK
Phone: 020 8597 0410
Mobile: 0794 4564474
Web: www.mirrorimagesco.com

Agency name: **More Zap Productions**
Phone: 323-850-8665
E-mail: INFO@MOREZAP.COM
Web: WWW.MOREZAP.COM

Agency name: **Mulligan Management**
Contact: Brian Mulligan, Kate, Lou, or Kat
Address: 11167 Morrison Street, North Hollywood, CA 91601
Phone: 818-752-9474
Fax: 818-752-9477
E-mail: mulliganmgmt@lookalikes.NET
Web: www.lookalikes.NET

Agency name: **Music As You Like It**
Address: 4633 Pescadero Avenue, San Diego, CA 92107
Phone: 619-223-5732
Web: www.musicasyoulikeit.com

Agency name: **MY Entertainment WORLD Inc.**
Contact: Abbas Bagheri
Phone: 321-773-3615
Address: P.O. Box 523, Melbourne, FL 32902-0523
E-mail: mew@myentertainmentworld.com
Web: www.myentertainmentworld.com

Agency name: **Naomi's World of Entertainment, Inc.**
Contact: Naomi **Kolstein**
Address: 85C Lafayette Avenue, Suffern, NY 10901
Phone: 800-304-4911 or 845-357-8301
E-mail: info@naomisworld.com
Web: www.naomisworld.com

Agency name: **National Special Event Locations, Inc.**
Contact: Maralou Gray
Address: 11740 Wilshire Blvd., #A-2306, Los Angeles, CA 90025
Phone: 310-231-7045
E-mail: Nselinc@aol.com

Agency name: **New York's Unique Entertainment Corp**.
Contact: Bill Peterson
Address: 1919 Route 110, Suite 20, E. Farmingdale, NY 11735
Phone: 631-293-7017
Fax: 631-756-5502
E-mail: NYUNIQUE@MINDSPRING.COM
Web: WWW.NY-UNIQUE.COM

Agency name: **Omni Events Entertainment & Services**
Contact: Bill Malinsky
Phone: 818-345-8399 or 805 648-1374
Fax: 805-648-4054
Address: P.O. Box 229, Ventura, CA 93002-0229
E-mail: bmalinsky@omnievents.com
Web: www.omnievents.com

Agency name: **One Planet Agency**
Contact: David Becker
Phone: 323-822-1991
E-mail: oneplanetagency@earthlink.net
Web: www.CAmodel

Agency name: **Pacific Event Productions, Pacific Entertainment**
Contact: See below

> **San Diego:** Joanne Mera
> Address: 6989 Corte Santa Fe, San Diego, CA 92121
> E-mail: joannem@pacificevents.com
> Website: www.pacificevents.com
>
> **Orange County, Los Angeles, and Palm Springs:** Tom Budas, Sales Manager
> Address: 1404 E. Walnut Avenue, Unit A, Fullerton, CA 92831
> Phone: 714-776-9908
> Fax: 714-776-9948
> E-mail: tomb@pacificevents.com

Agency name: **Pacific Entertainment Promotions**
Contact: Chuck Cali
Phone: 408-248-7999
Fax: 408-248-7900
Web: www.pac-ent-promo.com

Agency name: **Park's People, Inc.**
Contact: Pat Park
Phone: 702-870-0555
Web: www.parkspeople.com

Agency name: **Parties by Celebrations**
Contact: Bob Gregory
Address: 939 Hauser Blvd., Los Angeles, CA 90036
Phone: 323-938-7121
Fax: 323-935-8582
E-mail: Celebrations@mediaone.net

Agency name: **Party Magic/Celebrity Look-Alikes**
Contact: Judith or Victor
Phone: 305-666-3463 or 305-666-3470
E-mail: jgindy@jgstarlink.com
Web: www.queentoo.hollywood.com/

Agency name: **Perfect Productions Inc.**
Contact: Abigail Goldberg
Phone: 310-712-1111 ext. 113
E-mail: Abigail@perfectproductions.com
Web: www.perfectproductions.com

Agency name: **Party Central** (Phil Chapman, Founder)
Phone: 925-689-9595
Fax: 925-689-9588
E-mail: phil@partycentral.com
Web: www.partycentral.com
Entertainment: www.partycentral.com
Party Supplies: www.partycentral.makesparties.com

Agency name: **Premeditated Productions, Production Company & Agency**
Contact: Lissa Negrin
Phone: 323-462-2583
Address: 5875 Carolus Drive, Los Angeles, CA 90068
E-mail: cher_n@email.msn.com
Web: www.go2clue.com

Agency name: **Princess Productions**
Contact: Robyn Tanzer
Phone: 818-907-1743
Address: P.O. Box 57413, Sherman Oaks, CA 91413
E-mail: rt57413@aol.com
Website: www.princessproductions.cc

Agency name: **Pro Entertainment**
Address: 96 Inverness Drive East, Suite B, Englewood, CO 80112

Agency name: **Quantum Productions, Inc.**
Contact: David Snider
Phone: 858-623-8115
Web: www.quantum-production.com

Agency name: **Randal K. West** (Randal West, Vice President/Creative Director)
Address: 300 N. 16th Street, Fairfield, IA 52556
Phone: 641-472-3800 ext. 113
Fax: 641-472-4553
E-mail: rwest@hawthornedirect.com

Agency name: **Reel to the Real Productions**
Phone: 44208-4498558 (UK)
E-mail: toplookalikes@hotmail.com
Web: www.toplookalikes.co.uk

Agency name: **RNRH Entertainment- Las Vegas**
Contact: Rob Garrett
Phone: 702-648-8351
Cell: 702-338-8152
Fax: 702-648-8139
Address: 1989 Catalpa, Las Vegas, NV 89108
E-mail: info@rnrheaven.net
Web: www.rnrheaven.net or www.vegasimpersonators.com

Agency name: **Ron Rubin Events**
Contact: Ron Rubin
Address: 4924 Balboa Blvd., Suite 491, Encino, CA 91316
Phone: 310-348-6670
E-mail: Ronrubin@earthlink.net
Web: www.ronrubinevents.com

Agency name: **Ross Associates Talent Management**
Contact: Mark Anthony, President
Address: 1817 Glean Avenue, 2nd floor, Bronx, NY 10472

Agency name: **San Francisco Booking Agency**
Contact: Brian Wachhorst
Address: 745 Lexington Way, Burlingame, CA 94010
Phone: 650-548-0450
Fax: 650-558-0449
E-mail: brian@sfbooking.com
Web: www.sfbooking.com

Agency name: **Siler & Associates Entertainment Productions, Inc.**
Contact: Gene Siler
Phone: 949-367-0339
E-mail: silerg@pacbell.net
Web: www.areallybigshew.com and www.silerandassociates.com

Agency name: **Sim Production Company**
Contact: Sharon Ellis
Address: 1637 E. 87th Street, PMB 177, Chicago, IL 60617
Phone: 773-374-9298
Cell: 773-350-8812
Pager: 312-556-4819
Fax: 773-374-7510
Web: www.simproduction.com

Agency name: **StarCopy** (Belgium)
Contact: Julien Van Schevensteen
Phone: (32) 3 457.30.26
Fax: (32) 3 700.53.80
Web: http://home-2.worldonline.be/~vda09113/index.htm

Agency name: **Star Celebrity Look-Alikes**
Phone: 818-370-7070
Address: 15720 Ventura Blvd., #608, Encino, CA 91436
E-mail: Clookalikes.com

Agency name: **Sunshine Productions**
Contact: Suzanne La Rusch
Phone: 818-842-7713

Agency name: **T. Skorman Productions**
Phone: 407-895-3000 ext. 220
Fax: 407-895-1422
Address: 3660 Maguire Blvd., Suite 250, Orlando, Florida 32803
E-mail: Lee@talentagency.com
Web: www.talentagency.com

Agency name: **Tapley Entertainment and Celebrity Lookalikes**
Contact: David Tapley
Phone: 972-255-3967
E-mail: david@lookalike.com
Web: www.lookalike.com

Agency name: **Terry Thompson Productions**
Contact: Terry Thompson
Phone: 314-963-1200
E-mail: Thompspro@earthlink.net

Agency name: **The Amazing Imposters**
Contact: Richard Goldberg
Address: 354 Lockheed Avenue, Marietta, GA 30060
Phone: 770-723-7220
E-mail: imposterrg@aol.com
Web: www.amazingimposters.com

Agency name: **The Booking House, Inc.**
Contact: Roger Lapointe
Address: 2484 Spruce Needle Drive, Mississauga, Ontario, Canada L5L 1M6
E-mail: roger@bookinghouse.com
Web: www.bookinghouse.com

Agency name: **The Event Group**
Address: B6 Currie Barracks202, 25009 Dieppe Avenue SW, Calgary, Alberta T3E 7J9
Web: www.the-eventgroup.com

Agency name: **The Mars Talent Agency-South**
Address: P.O. Box 1569, Jupiter, FL 33468
Phone: 561-748-3448
Web: www.marstalent.com

Agency name: **The Protocol Group**
Address: 10732 Riverside Drive, Suite 219, North Hollywood, CA 91602-2313
Phone: 818-509-2526
Fax: 818-774-2526
E-mail: tpgadmagic@aol.com
Web: promoadmagic.com

Agency name: **The Rose Agency**
Contact: Jasmine Rose
Phone: 818-430-ROSE (7673)
Address: 2215 N. Beachwood Drive, Suite #101, Hollywood Hills, CA 90068
E-mail: jasminerose@juno.com
Web: www.rosemodels.com

Agency name: **The Wrightlook** (UK)
Contact: Bill Hickey
Phone: +44 020 8590 1723
E-mail: wrightlook@toalise.co.uk
Web: www.go.to/modelsuk

Agency name: **Tribute Productions Talent Providers**
Phone: 818-513-2389
Web: www.tributeproductions.com

Agency name: **Undercover Productions, Inc.**
Contact: Julie Grayson
Address: 7976 Timber Horn Court, Las Vegas, NV 89147
Phone: 702-227-0197
E-mail: Julieundercover@aol.com
Web: www.UndercoverProductions.com

Agency name: **Upstage Events**
Contact: Larry Friel
Address: 3315 E. Russell Road, Suite H-221, Las Vegas, NV 89119
Phone: 702-214-5481
E-mail: info@lasvegaslookalikes.com
Web: www.impersonatorshows.com

Agency name: **Unique Entertainment, New York's Entertainment Corp.**
Contact: Bill Peterson, Producer
Address: 1919 Route 110, Suite 20, E. Farmingdale, NY 11735
Phone: 631-293-7017
Web: www.ny-unique.com

Agency name: **Victoria's Destination Services, Inc.**
Contact: Victoria Papageorge
Address: 2690 Chandler Avenue, Suite 2, Las Vegas, NV 89120
Phone: 702-794-2492 ext. 102
Fax: 702-794-3451
Web: www.vdsproductionsinc.com or www.victoriasdmc.com

Agency name: **VunCannon Music DJ & Entertainment**
Contact: Terry VunCannon
Address: P.O. Box 366, Randleman, NC 27317
Phone: 336-495-5656
E-mail: tvuncannon@triad.rr.com
Web: www.home.triad.rr.com/vmusic

Agency name: **Washington Talent Agency**
Address: 14670 Rothgeb Drive, Rockville, MD 20850
Phone: 301-762-1800
E-mail: info@washingtontalent.com
Web: www.washingtontalent.com

Agency name: **Whirl-a-Round**
Contact: Barbara Sloate or Annie
Address: 2900 Bristol Street, Suite J-108, Costa Mesa, CA 92626
Phone: 714-751-3555
E-mail: wirlrnd@exo.com
Web: www.whirlaround.com

Agency name: **West End Productions** (Singapore)
Contact: Charlie Tan
Phone: 65-3460789
Web: www.westend.com.sg

Photographer Credits:

Anne Kissel as Roseanne
Devon Cass Photography (Devoncass.com)

Annette Pizza as Gwen Steffani:
Johnny G Photography (818) 694-5803

Barbara Hyde as Mimi Bobeck:
Sharon Hyde Photography Lavenderladie@hotmail.com

Betty Atchison as Cher:
Michael Cairns Entertainment Photography (407) 839-3965
www.michaelcairns.com

Brenda Miller as Bette Midler:
Brenda Miller Photography

Brent Mendenhall as George W. Bush:
Chris Barrett Photography (417) 667-6899 or barrett1@aicon.net

Brian Cole as Ricky Martin:
Michael Cairns Entertainment Photography (407) 839-3965
www.michaelcairns.com

Chad Michael as Cher:
Sarah Nee Photography (858) 465-7938

Cherise as Britney Spears
Alex Cohen Photography (310) 479-4700

D. Wallace as Cuba Gooding, Jr.
Treneice Kendrick Photography

Daniel T. Healy as George Bush:
Daniel T. Healy Photography

David Brighton as David Bowie:
Lesley Bohm Photography (213) 680-1333

David Wolf as Jerry Lewis and Robert S. Ensler as Dean Martin:
Gerald M. Craden Photography (818) 361-1888

Denise Bella Vlasis as Madonna:
All photos of D. Bella as Madonna by Johnny G Photography
(818) 694-5803, E-mail: johnnygphotography@yahoo.com
Web: www.johnnygphotography.com
EXCEPT:
   Brian Kramer Photography: Live action group shots
   John Nerone Photography: Blonde Ambition
   Michael Fiala Photography: ***A League of Their Own*** **shot**
   Glamour shots Photography: Hands on face
   David Comfort Photography: Vintage Madonna shot

Ermal as John Wayne:
Phillip Ritchie Photography (919) 642-3274

Gary Smith as Robert Redford
Robert Peters Photography (323) 356-4555 RJP4555@aol.com)

Irby Gascon as Elvis:
Brian Kramer Photography

Joe Dimmick as Clint Eastwood:
Joe Dimmick Photography

J. Trusk as Captain Kirk:
Susan Stevens Photography (866) 547-5325

Jade Roberts as Rambo:
Constance Ashley Photography (214) 747-2501
www.photographerstexas.com

Jeffrey Weissman as Charlie Chaplin
Chuck Smith Photography

Kimberly Jones as Nicole Kidman"
Michael Cairns Entertainment Photography (407) 839-3965
www.michaelcairns.com

Kurt Meyers as Indiana Jones:
Rick Bultay Photography

Lissa Negrin as Cher:
Sonia Keshishian Photography (310) 927-3490 Soniakesh@aol.com

Lyndal Grant as Arnold Schwarzenegger:
Rochelle Richards Photography

Louise Gallagher as Elizabeth Taylor:
Seth Mayer Photography (619) 702-5007, Seth@mayerstudios.com,
www.sethmayer.com

Marv Cline as Alan Alda:
Carol Morris Photography (310) 822-2412, ccalder@cse.eng.lmu.edu

Mike Vitrano as Bruce Willis:
Mike Vitrano Photography

Noland Anderson as John Travolta:
Mitshka Anderson Photography

Our Way with Frank and Friends?Gary B as Frank Sinatra, Lambus Dean as Sammy Davis, Jr., and Bill Whitton as Dean Martin:
Major Entertainment Productions and Photography (702) 655-8728

Ralph Chelli as Clark Gable:
Marty Getz Photography

Reggie Alcos as Tiger Woods
Reggie Alcos Photography (714) 317-4401

Richard Halpern as Austin Powers:
Mark David Studner Photography (818) 376-1941, markstudnerphoto@earthlink.net, www.markstudner.com

Robert Lemaster as Jack Nicholson:
Express Self Service Portraits Bill Solo and Ivan Doe Photography (414) 384-4535

Rosalinde as Pam Anderson:
Vincent B Nixon Photography (909) 984 6912, Vincent@webtv.net, Vinnieb4@hotmail.com

Ross D. Seymour as Russell Crowe/The Gladiator
Seymour Photography

Sandra Wood as Cher:
Sandra Wood Photography

Scot Bruce as Elvis:
Jack McDonald Photography

Stephen Sorrentino as Elton John:
Glenn Jussen Photography (212) 268-1340

Steve Ostrow as Ozmo Kramer:
Barbara Bancroft Photography (760) 744-7632, rur2go@earthlink.net

Sue Quinn as Several Characters:
Sandra Quinn Photography

Susan Griffith as Marilyn Monroe:
Susan Griffith Photography

Suzanne LaRusch as Lucille Ball:
Andy Pearlman Studios © Andy Pearlman 2001 (310) 306-9449,
Web: www.apstudio.com

Tapia Corel as Mae West:
Johnnie Mejia Photography
Carmen Miranda
John Corel Photography

Tatiana Turan as Jennifer Lopez:
Johnny G Photography (818) 694-5803

Vicki Brown as Rosie O'Donnell:
Mark Russell Photography (407) 616-3913

William Peterson as Rodney Dangerfield:
George M. Loring Studio (781) 749-0819 Foto@gis.net

Resources

Note: Most of the resources listed here are located in the Los Angeles area, with the exception of some companies that provide service through the Internet. If you need help finding similar companies or reps in your area, please feel free to contact me. I will gladly help!

ASCAP: American Society of Composers, Authors and Publishers
Web: www.ascap.com

Choreography
Heidi Anderson Jarrett, Mojo Productions
Phone: 818-207-2393

Costumes:

Sean LeBlanc, Costume Designer
RUSH ORDERS or MADE-TO-ORDER COSTUMES available
Address: 13812 Saticoy Street, Van Nuys, CA 91402
Phone: 818 508-9933
Fax: 818-508 9339

Impersonator Costume Specialist:
Design Concepts
Address: 5249 Wave Dancer Lane, Las Vegas, NV 89118
Phone/Fax: 702-367-6446
E-mail: Robertadumont@aol.com

Entertainment Law:
William J. Briggs, II
Address: 2049 Century Park East, Suite 2400, Los Angeles, CA 90067-2906
Phone: 310-556-3501
Fax: 310-556-3615
E-mail: wbriggs@lavelysinger.com
Web: www.lavelysinger.com

Hair and Makeup for film or photo shoot appearances:
Michael Dorian: michaeldorian58@yahoo.com
Sue Quinn: Eltonq@aol.com
Shyama: 818-731-4188 or Gracegirl76@aol.com

Lodging:
Cupid's Castle Bed & Breakfast
17622 Hwy. 76 P.O. Box 580
Pauma Valley, CA 92601
Phone: 760-742-3306
Fax: 760-742-0279

Look-Alike Convention:
Elyse Del Francia
Telephone: 888-771-6611 (toll free)
E-mail: elyse@gte.net
Web: www.celebrityimpersonators.com

Look-alike Network:
Bea Fogleman
Phone: 702-656-4800
E-mail: Bea@BeaFogelman.com

SAG: Screen Actors Guild:
National Headquarters
Phone: 213-954-1600
Address: 5757 Wilshire Blvd., Los Angeles, CA 90036-3600

Skin Care/Epicuren/Energy Work:
Leslie Sloane: 818-348-4545

Specialty Look-Alike Photography:

Los Angeles:
Johnny G Photography
Phone: 818-203-4741
E-mail: Johnny@johnnygphotography.com
Web: www.johnnygphotography.com

Florida:
Michael Cairns Entertainment Photography
Phone: 407-839-3965
Web: www.michaelcairns.com)

New York:
Devon Cass Photography
Web: www.Devoncass.com)

Studio/Casting/Choreography:
Carissa
Phone: 323-851-6585

The Cloney Awards and ICTGA Look-alike Guild:
Contact: Fil Jessee
Address: 2760 Bluebird Circle, Duluth, GA 30096
Phone: 770-813-8336
E-mail: fil@filslookalikes.com
Web: www.filslookalikes.com

The Reel Awards
Contact: Janna Joos
Address: P.O. Box 260766, Encino, CA 91426
Phone: 818-780-4433
Fax: 818-343-9250
Look-alike awards on the Web: www.thereelawards.com
E-mail: Janna@internationalcelebrityimages.com
Web: www.internationalcelebrityimages.com

Web site/Graphic Artist:
David Comfort
E-mail: davidcomfort@hotmail.com
Web: www.sleeplessdigital.com

Wig/Hair:
Wilshire Wigs
Address: 5241 Craner Avenue, North Hollywood, CA 91601
Phone: 818-761-9447
Toll Free: 800-927-0874
Fax: 818-761-9779
E-mail: Michael@wilshirewigs.com
Web: www.wilshirewigs.com
Wig specialty stylist: Deane Maitnour (818-760-4804)

Denise Bella Vlasis is a Foreword Magazine Book of the Year 2000 Award Finalist (Category: Career). In her new book YOU'VE GOT THE LOOK she is once again sharing with the public many industry trade secrets about how ordinary people can break into show business quickly and with little to no experience. Denise guides readers through a step-by-step process, and clearly explains how anyone can master the art of becoming a celebrity look-alike and well-rounded professional entertainer. With over 17 years of hands-on experience and training, Denise presents in fascinating detail every fact needed for anyone to become the "superstar" they have always wanted to be.

About the Author

Denise Bella Vlasis has been a performer for most of her life, starting with dance and theater classes at age nine. It was her first dance instructor who recognized Denise's natural abilities. Making sure Denise would continue her studies in dance classes, this very same teacher offered her free classes and encouraged her mother to make sure to "keep this one coming to class."

The lessons paid off. Denise continued her studies in dance and theater all the way through college and she was honored in 1981 and 1982 with scholarships in dance, theater, and choreography.

While in college, Denise was actively pursuing a performing career, landing small roles on television and in music videos. In 1983, a brand new cable music television channel (MTV) was born, and suddenly the comparisons to Madonna began. Denise's similarities to superstar Madonna began to get her instant recognition each time she walked through the doors of an audition. Denise slowly realized that that for most of her life she had been noticed by perfect strangers constantly telling her who they thought she looked like.

In 1984, Denise decided to enter a look-alike contest at a local mall. That very same day, there was a television producer in the audience looking for a Madonna look-alike for the filming of a well-known morning television program. After seeing Denise in action (among hundreds of other girls), the producer hired Denise on the spot to film the television show the very next morning. After the filming of this show, the calls started coming in from agents and show producers inquiring about Denise's Madonna act.

Rather than resist something that seemed to be destined, Denise allowed this new opportunity to unfold and take her life on a journey that her drama coaches and dance teachers could never have prepared her for.

Endless job offers began to land at Denise's feet, and the many enthusiastic requests to book her Madonna act resulted in Denise's commitment to become a professional impersonator.

Denise pursued impersonation with a focused, ambitious energy. While television and live show offers began to pour in for Denise, it would be her appearances for children and children's charities that would be an awakening for her. She quickly learned that this "star" element could be utilized to open hearts, and with respect to Madonna's image, Denise learned that she could "give back" in ways that changed her life and her focus forever. Her journey as Madonna began.

In 1986, MTV held Madonna's "Make My Video" contest. Denise entered a video of herself as Madonna, which was handpicked by Madonna as a top-10 finalist out of roughly 2000 videos entered. Her video was then selected as first runner-up and she was the *only* celebrity look-alike impersonator to be chosen from all of the entries. Denise met Madonna shortly thereafter, and was inspired to continue her career as a celebrity double. She has since worked with Madonna on a commercial for MTV and was hired as a makeup and costume stand-in for Madonna's 2001 Drowned World Tour.

Denise has appeared as Madonna on numerous prime-time television shows and networks, including *A Current Affair, AM Los Angeles, Americas Funniest Videos, American Journal, Baywatch Nights, Days of Our Lives, Dream On, Entertainment Tonight, Extra, Family Feud, Hard Copy, Jenny Jones, Live with Regis and Kathie Lee, Mike and Matty, Maury Povich, Not Necessarily the News, Putting on the Hits, Philly After Midnight, The Gossip Show, The Carol Burnett Show, The Carol & Marilyn Show, The Tonight Show with Jay Leno, To Tell the Truth, USA High, Vicky Lawrence*, the E-Channel, VH-1, MTV, HBO, MUCHMUSIC, and many more. She worked with film director John Boskovitch for a role in Sandra Bernhard's feature film *Without You I'm Nothing*, where Denise played the part of Shoshanna. She has traveled the world and been cast as a stand-in, voice-over, and featured entertainer for hundreds of national events. Her live show has even been requested and performed to rave reviews from Christina Aguilera, Seal, CEO executives, heads of corporations, and politicians. Denise is featured as Madonna in the books *A Day in the Life of Hollywood, Encyclopedia Madonnica* and *Who's Not Who*, as well as endless magazines, periodicals, and trade papers. She is considered an expert in the field of celebrity impersonation and is highly respected among her peers and within the industry.

Denise has set a standard in the world of celebrity look-alikes. A pioneer, like the superstar she emulates, she has paved the way for countless other people to discover their own talents and abilities.

What brings the most satisfaction to Denise's life is the opportunity to watch the people she has advised turn their hope into successful careers. Her sincere desire to help people is the motivating factor that led her to write this book. Denise hopes it will encourage readers to take the first step in reaching for their dreams.

ISBN 1553955506-4